Ideas Influencing
Early Childhood Education

A THEORETICAL ANALYSIS

EARLY CHILDHOOD EDUCATION SERIES

Millie Almy, Editor

Ideas Influencing
Early Childhood Education

A THEORETICAL ANALYSIS

Evelyn Weber

Foreword by Millie Almy

Teachers College, Columbia University
New York and London

Published by Teachers College Press, 1234 Amsterdam Avenue, New York, N.Y. 10027

Grateful acknowledgment is made for permission to reprint previously published material:

From *The Psychology of the Child*, by Jean Piaget and Barbel Inhelder. © 1969 by Basic Books, Inc., Publishers. Reprinted by permission of Basic Books, Inc., Routledge & Kegan Paul PLC, and Presses Universitaires de France.

Sigmund Freud Copyrights Ltd, The Institute of Psycho-Analysis, and The Hogarth Press Ltd for permission to quote from *The Standard Edition of the Complete Psychological Works of S.F.* (vol. XI), translated and edited by James Strachey. Also from *Five Lectures on Psycho-Analysis* by Sigmund Freud, translated and edited by James Strachey, by permission of W. W. Norton & Company, Inc., New York, N.Y. All rights reserved, 1977, by W. W. Norton & Company, Inc.

Library of Congress Cataloging in Publication Data

Weber, Evelyn, 1915–
   Ideas influencing early childhood education.

   Includes bibliographical references and index.
   1. Education, Preschool. I. Title.
LB1140.W42   1984   372'.21   84-8588

ISBN 0-8077-2762-8 (paperback)
ISBN 0-8077-2767-9 (cloth)

Manufactured in the United States of America

89 88 87 86 85 84   1 2 3 4 5 6

Contents

Foreword

In this book Evelyn Weber discusses the concepts and theories that have shaped the behavior, stimulated the thought, and aroused the emotions of several generations of teachers in early childhood education. Some ideas that have been influential in early childhood education, since it began about a hundred and fifty years ago, have created controversy, not only among teachers but also among parents and the general public. The acceptance of certain ideas comes slowly.

The nursery school was a relatively new idea when I began the study of early childhood education fifty years ago. At that time, however, the importance and validity of the idea became evident as the federal government established some 3,000 nursery schools to benefit unemployed teachers and the young children of other unemployed workers.

Fifty years before that, when another new idea, the kindergarten, was beginning to be accepted, the National Education Association made a move to assure its survival. It established a department of kindergarten education and began to urge that kindergartens be made part of the public school system.

About fifty years before the National Education Association began to promote the kindergarten, the idea had been formulated by Friedrich Froebel and the first kindergarten opened in Germany. In the years since then, kindergartens and nursery schools have enjoyed wider and wider acceptance. The idea that education and care can be provided to children outside their homes, and even as early as infancy, is no longer new.

Dr. Weber shows how all these once new ideas had their roots in the history, philosophy, and psychology of their times. Furthermore, as she suggests in her last chapter, each idea reflects in some measure the economics and politics of its period.

In our own troubled times, when technological innovations often seem to have created as many new problems as they have solved old ones, sceptics may question the relevance of knowledge of the past to the present. What does this book have to say to the beginning student learning to know young children? Or to the experienced teacher who struggles to maintain, often against serious opposition, his or her understanding of the ways children develop and learn and of the conditions necessary for optimum development? Is there a message for the parent seeking the best education for a precious child? Or for the policymaker who must reconcile the differing points of view of various constituencies, all with stakes in both the present and the future of young children?

It seems to me that all these people have much to learn from Dr. Weber's study of the ideas that have influenced early childhood education. For the beginning student, a perspective on the past provides a keener awareness of the multiple possibilities for the instruction and guidance of children and a firmer sense of the reasons for emphasizing some possibilities and ignoring others.

The experienced teacher, who knows how the theories of early childhood education have evolved, can evaluate current trends and the forces that are precipitating them. He or she can judge whether such trends are mere fads, represent nostalgia for old ways of doing things, or stem from important and well-integrated increments to the knowledge base of early education.

Parents and policymakers can also benefit. Parents, systematically reviewing the past, may be surprised at the diversity of ideas that have guided the education of young children. But they will also note the persistence of certain ideas and the growing body of evidence for them. For the policymaker, the past is indeed prologue. The conflicts that arise today, and will arise tomorrow, have their prototypes in controversies over values that have long and enduring histories.

The special merit of Dr. Weber's book lies in the ways she elaborates and clarifies the ideas that she presents. Through extended quotations from their writing she allows the protagonists of particular theories to speak for themselves. Excerpts from the writing of their contemporaries show how their ideas were accepted or rejected. By enabling a reader to confront the ideas as they were originally presented, Dr. Weber guards against the distortion that often results when ideas become popular.

The reader also gains familiarity with the historical settings for particular theorists and with the values and concerns that predominated in their times. Then one may consider the extent to which certain thinkers transcended their times while others appear to have been the product of their times. In this vein, it is interesting to speculate on how a thinker from one period might react to the controversies and the practical issues of another period. For example what would Froebel have to say about infant day care programs? How would Dewey respond to computers in the preschool?

I have found reading *Early Childhood Education: Evolving Theories* a thought-provoking and enjoyable experience. I am delighted to have had this opportunity to introduce the book to other readers who will, I am sure, be similarly rewarded.

MILLIE ALMY, Professor Emerita
University of California, Berkeley

Preface

In the roughly 150 years in which early childhood education has been a significant part of the educative process, the theoretical underpinnings of curricula have undergone periods of substantial upheaval. New ideas entering the educational scene were followed by periods of curriculum revision. One time of revolutionary change occurred at the turn of the century when Froebelian principles gave way to new scientific thought. Many years — in fact, almost a quarter of a century — were required for the curriculum changes to be worked out in practice and finally presented in written form. The revised curriculum, with some modifications, was to be found in most early childhood classrooms until the 1960s, when another major period of change began to take place. This time, it was not so much the early childhood specialists who questioned their theoretical base, but those who wished to include the youngest years for the building of a great society and were doubtful that existing practice supported such an achievement. A search for a base from both existing and emerging theory took place to support a revision of practice. As at the earlier period of change, strong debates ensued and time was required for new curricula to gain momentum. Many new practices were tried during the early period of change; more divergent practices were experimented with in the later upheaval for a wider spectrum of theoretical positions existed, some with contradictory fundamental premises. The ferment of the 1960s has extended through the 1970s and 1980s.

An understanding of the divergent practices existing in programs for young children rests upon a comprehension of the various theories that support them, including the bedrock beliefs upon which the theory is built. Only through such analysis can the practitioners assess the compatibility of various aspects of classroom procedure and their conformity with basic goals. At the level of practice these fundamentals are often hidden; only through careful examination can a consistent program result.

There is no current publication that has selected theoretical positions extensively influencing early childhood education and related them to the field as it has developed over the decades. This book addresses itself to that task. It is the result of many years of historical research and theoretical study and will fill a significant gap in the literature of early childhood education.

Tracing basic ideas that have appeared and penetrated programs for young children, the book begins with the earliest influences and brings them up to the present theories and their impact upon current programs. The ideas of Plato, Rousseau, and others are presented to show the nature of early concern for the young child and how these initial beliefs set the stage for later developments. From the beliefs of Froebel to the now dominant ideas of Piaget, each theory is presented in enough depth to encompass key premises and the underlying conceptions that support them. Fallacies are exposed, limitations discussed, and the incompatability of certain positions highlighted. Often the direct words of critics or supporters have been incorporated to illustrate points of view as they have developed. And links are laid to the early childhood field.

In order for the reader to gain not only a basic knowledge of a theory, but to acquire a feel for its originator and the manner of expressing new conceptions during a special historical interval, quotations are included from seminal publications. Over the years leaders in education have written articles and books for the early childhood professional; many important at their own time are now difficult reading. But key ideas, as selected and presented here, often illumine critical developments and give meaning to practices that have persisted for years.

While many existing publications deal with educational theory in general, this book is unique in its focus upon theory as it relates to early childhood education. Thus it is addressed to all professionals working with young children who wish to build a perspective on what has happened and is happening to influence daily procedures in the classroom. All leaders of programs for young children, some beginning students, and most advanced students in early childhood education desire and profit from such a perspective. Much of the material in this book has been used extensively with in-service teachers and found to be meaningful to them.

The opening of the book sets up a framework for viewing theoretical strands and the closing chapter focuses on the state of early childhood programs today. Theories are probed for the view of the child and the concept of learning inherent in them. It becomes very evident that as a field of study early childhood education has aligned itself with child psychology, taking on both strengths and weaknesses as they evolved. An overdependence upon psychological theory as the sole basis for curriculum planning may characterize early childhood curriculum to the detriment of careful philosophical analysis of goals and outcomes. Except for Dewey, the theorists influencing the curriculum have been psychologists. Thus the dilemmas of psychology become the dilemmas of early childhood education. The book reveals many questions being raised in child psychology today, resulting in a sphere of study in ferment.

With child study dilemmas unresolved, early childhood education is also embroiled in arguments over which view of the child and of learning should prevail. These views and the radically opposing types of curricula they support are made clear in this book.

It is hoped that this publication will help all readers to understand the basis for the ferment in early childhood education today, to recognize the theoretical positions of vastly differing practice, and to help them clarify their own theoretical position.

Acknowledgments

The author wishes to express appreciation to Dr. Alma Bent and Dr. Elizabeth Ann Liddle for their continuous support and encouragement during the extended period of writing this book. Dr. Liddle has contributed, also, in numerous other ways. To my typist, Jill Kosis, goes special thanks for her proficiency and care.

Grateful acknowledgment is also made to the following for permission to reprint previously published material.

Clark University Press: Arnold Gesell, "Maturation and the Patterning of Behavior," in *A Handbook of Child Psychology*, edited by C. Murchison (Worcester, Mass.: Clark University Press, 1931).

Erik H. Erikson, *A Healthy Personality for Every Child: A Digest of the Fact-Finding Report to the Midcentury White House Conference on Children and Youth*, 1951.

Kappa Delta Pi: John Dewey, *Experience and Education* (New York: Macmillan, 1946).

National Mental Health Association: Lawrence K. Frank, "The Fundamental Needs of the Child," *Mental Hygiene* 22 (July 1938).

Teachers College Record: Edna Shapiro and Barbara Biber, "The Education of Young Children: A Developmental-Interaction Approach," *Teachers College Record* 74 (September 1972).

Ideas Influencing
Early Childhood Education

A THEORETICAL ANALYSIS

1 Ideologies in Perspective

At no time in the history of early childhood education had so many diverse ideologies impinged upon educational practice as in the 1960s. Ideas, some new and some already in existence but not formerly utilized in early childhood education, flowed in as concern for the young child reached unprecedented fervor while early childhood education was being swept into the stream of programs that were part of the War on Poverty. Political change and social conflict spawned a conception of the "great society" as a national goal and embraced early childhood in its formulations. Based on premises about the effectiveness of early intervention as a means for breaking the cycle of economic deprivation, federally funded programs were extended to the young. Increased recognition of the crucial significance of the early experiences of the child resulted in programs as extensive as Head Start and, later, Follow Through. Hope for an improved future generation, it was believed, lay in environmental mediation — the idea that an environment planned carefully for a child could help him become more effective in his interactions with others and in all his transactions with the world. Implicit in this position was the search for the kind of environment that would enable a child with a meager background to function more adequately. In this social context the overwhelming concern was for the child considered to be "disadvantaged"; the critical nature of our times had brought into focus the problems of the poor.

This is not the first time that educators have turned to early childhood to bring about social reform. Through the ages, from Plato to the present time, education has been considered a means for alleviating social problems and this has consistently propelled a look at the roots of problems — at the beginnings of learning in school and in the home. The major difference in the 1960s was the emphasis placed upon environmental factors that, as we shall see, stemmed from newly recognized theoretical ideas of cognitive growth. If, as was assumed, environment plays a major role in determining intellectual growth, perhaps new environmental settings could be devised that would enhance the child's development.

1

An unprecedented diversity became a factor in program development in early childhood education which ranged from the use of a "talking type-writer" in what Omar Khayyam Moore called an "autotelic responsive environment" to the very direct instruction in academic learning through predominantly oral methods in the Bereiter-Engelmann program. Such programs raised great controversy as they seemed to deny theoretical positions built up over many decades.

FERMENT IN EARLY CHILDHOOD EDUCATION

While the sharp focus on early education dimmed in the 1970s, many distinct programs with divergent rationales still remain in action and in the literature. For example, one recent publication has a chapter on behavior analysis, another on Piagetian theory, and still another explaining "open" education, thus moving rapidly from theory to practice.[1] A 1977 publication contains seven chapters on distinct programs that the authors offer as "a sample of the numerous early childhood programs that have been developed." This sample indicates "the variety in principles and practices used by early childhood educators."[2]

Not since the decades around the turn of the century, when early childhood education was moving from a strict Froebelian program to incorporate new psychological views, had such diversity characterized basic curriculum conceptions. Between the 1920s and 1960s leaders in the field had succeeded in pulling from theory a fairly consistent position that was used to support the programs evident in nursery schools and kindergartens. It was conceived in a framework of maturational development, was concerned with the wholeness of growth, and was so infused with a respect for natural growth processes that it included a desire to protect children from the too early imposition of academic instruction for which they were considered unready.

Changes in social priorities placed new demands upon early childhood education in the 1960s. The heightened interest in alleviating the conditions of the poor propelled an examination of school learning where there existed visible differences in the level of school achievement between the children of the affluent and the children of the poor. Social reform could come only from attacking the bases for these differences in the early years, it was believed.

Educators and psychologists, many formerly uninterested in early childhood education, were drawn into the search for programs to increase the intellectual and academic performance of these children, labeled "disadvantaged." New programs required new theoretical groundings, so investigation ranged into theoretical positions not formerly considered applicable by workers with young children as well as new theoretical ideas that had recently emerged. The contributions of Jean Piaget and his constructivist theory of cognitive growth fostered a recognition of the significance of environmental encounters on developing cognition. One quest was to determine the nature of educational environments that could compensate for the deficits found in children of the poor. Because Maria Montessori had prepared her early education program for children of the slums in Rome, it became a source of ideas for some searchers. Others utilized the principles of behavioral psychology to develop systematic programs to increase specific performances and skills.

Reflecting competing theoretical positions, the concept of "program models" was projected into the early childhood field in the 1960s. "Models" were offered to directors of Head Start and Follow Through programs as alternative approaches to working with young children. Different descriptions of programs, written by those who developed the curriculum, were sent out by the Office of Education in 1968 and 1969. A few examples of recommendations by program developers will illustrate the widely varying conceptions of values to be gained and of the ways in which effective learning was considered to take place.[3] A brief look at the Tucson Early Education Model in conjunction with the University of Georgia's Intensive Learning Model will reveal sharp contrasts.

One major characteristic of the Tucson Early Education Model as described by Marie Hughes and her associates is what they term "orchestration." This refers to a functional type of learning in which skills are learned as they serve a larger purpose. They wrote:

> Almost all intellectual activities require some combination of "discrete behaviors". It is a central aspect of the Tucson Model that these skills are not taught separately, one after another. This is a significant departure from the linear quality of traditional programs in which time segments devoted to individual skills follow each other in repetitious fashion. When skills are acquired in real meaningful settings, it is possible to develop more than one skill simultaneously. A teacher organizing a small group of children in ice cream making, for example, will be teaching new words, the processes of proper order and sequence of events, new concepts, new technical and social skills.[4]

Contrast this with the description of the Intensive Learning Model located at the University of Georgia. It is described as:

> a curriculum concept emphasizing behavior analysis and a more carefully sequenced presentation of content and process matter. Each series of lessons

is finely graded by difficulty in order to assure students a high level of reinforcing success. Stress is strongly in the direction of: 1) teachers learning
to capitalize in this success by use of praise, or more tangible rewards, to
assure additional success on the child's part; 2) development of a teacher
attitude about learning process that shifts away from "what I am going to
do," to "what skill or knowledge do I want this child to come out of this
lesson possessing"; and 3) use of teacher aides as teachers, not just helpers.[5]

Supporting these two diverse recommendations are two contrasting
conceptions of the child and learning. One supports the learning of specific, teacher-designated skills in a linear procedure; the other approaches
the acquisition of skills in a broad setting as the child seeks to carry out
his own purposes.

The following descriptions of practice present the sharply differing
views of the goals of learning and of the manner of gearing the curriculum
to the individual nature of growth. One program sets the goal of early
childhood education as that of preparation for the education that is to
follow and believes it to be essential that all children be subjected to the
same instructional pattern. The second program elevates self-determination and individuality as goals and operates in a highly individualized
fashion. In writing about a University of Illinois program, Wesley Becker
and Siegfried Engelmann propose:

> The program is based on the idea that we must have the same set of educa-
> tional objectives for all children. We cannot have a large group of children
> for whom we have different objectives. . . . The objective of the Head Start
> instruction is to take the first step in acquainting the children with formal
> instruction and in starting to work in specific content areas — reading, arith-
> metic, and language. The idea is to give them a headstart in terms of those
> skills that serve as the foundation for what these children will be doing in
> school for at least ten years.[6]

While submitting to the word *model* with reluctance, the EDC Head
Start Approach values self-renewal and individuality. David E. Armington describes the approach as pragmatic and action-oriented:

> Because the curriculum content of this approach is not narrowly specified,
> individual schools and classes tend to develop their own personalities, which
> mirror the needs and interests of the children as well as the talent and styles
> of the teachers. . . . It is possible to describe certain classroom conditions,
> however, that may be regarded as surface indicators that the needs of the
> individual children are being ministered to. These may be summarized as
> follows:

1. With guidance from the teacher, the children plan their own activities, drawing from a range of relevant options.
2. The children are free, as individuals, to explore an interest deeply, and they are also free to disengage when an activity no longer seems appropriate. . . .[7]

Here again, we find contrasting conceptions of the nature of effective learning, as the vastly differing views of educational goals are illustrated.

How could the director of a Head Start or Follow Through program select from the wide range of classroom practices proposed? How can an educator today select from the many available techniques, materials, modes of organization, and means of evaluation to develop a meaningful, consistent, fruitful program for children? Only by sifting through practice for fundamental conceptions can the educational leader or practitioner understand what these suggestions represent, for each has a philosophical and psychological base. Goals, or the function of the school, rest upon a philosophically determined sense of what learnings are most significant for the learner in his social setting. Descriptions of how learning is to take place are supported by psychologically determined concepts of individual growth and learning. Psychological and philosophic understandings inform curriculum selection and building.

While these illustrations were derived from Head Start literature, the confused ferment spawned by the investigations of the 1960s still holds in a number of early childhood programs today. Divergent models have become a fixed aspect of the field of early childhood. Take, for example, the differing conception of the role of the learner in his own learning disclosed in two current curricula. In a behavior analysis program the child is manipulated by reinforcing contingencies. As Sidney Bijou explains it:

> The teacher plans and selects those materials, activities, and situations that, under most conditions, will lead to reaching the preestablished goals. . . .
>
> Maintaining learned behavior, often referred to as improving memory or retention, consists of arranging reinforcing contingencies so that learned behavior preserves its strength. Once a child is taught to remove his coat and hang it up, he should be encouraged by a pleasant remark, or a pat on the back so that he will continue this practice whenever he enters the house. The key principle underlying this aspect of applied behavioral analysis teaching strategy is to distribute reinforcement on a schedule that will keep the behavior vigorous, starting with frequent reinforcement and gradually reducing the frequency.[8]

In sharp contrast is the curriculum written by Constance Kamii and Rheta DeVries, which focuses on the child's activity and autonomy with people, objects, and ideas in a description of Piaget's theory as it can be used in early education. In this position the child's own construction of his knowledge is fundamental. They write:

> It is very important to remember that the child constructs all types of knowledge through his own activity. . . .
> From the Piagetian point of view, what the individual "reads off" from reality depends not so much on the stimulus as on the structure of previous knowledge into which the stimulus is assimilated. The more the child's knowledge is elaborated and structured, the more accurately and richly will he read facts off.[9]

In one conception the child plays an active role in his own learning both physically and intellectually; in the other the learner is subservient to reinforcements that lead him in designated directions. Contrasting philosophical and psychological beliefs undergird the two conceptions.

THEORY IN EDUCATION

Every program for children is built on a series of beliefs about many things including the nature of man, the process of learning, the nature of knowledge, the role of knowledge in life, and the relationship between society and education. Placed in a coherent relationship, basic beliefs of this nature form an educational theory — a group of general propositions used as principles to support a specific educational program. Theory may be explicit or implicit: many programs rest upon hidden assumptions, a belief or postulate taken for granted, not recognized. But the great theoreticians are those who have made their beliefs explicit: Plato, Rousseau, Froebel, Thorndike, Freud, and many more.

The personal background of each theoretician, as well as any theological impressions in his life, are reflected in his basic ideas. Political or sociological elements, or the ferment within those already established, have often been powerful in developing thought. Therefore, the ideas of creative educators must be read in the context of situational forces. For example, Friedrich Froebel's writings are understood only when the absolute idealism of his age is taken into consideration. Only the few, most dissident thinkers, such as Darwin or Freud, penetrate the philosophical stance of an age or a society and offer conceptions so novel that they lead into a new educational era.

The dominant influence in early childhood education has been consistently the discipline of child psychology. While the underlying bases of programs on the scene today are many and diverse, it is clear that curricular planners have generally turned to psychological theory for both general program commitments and specific practices.

In this century three major strands of scientific study of the child have relevance for understanding early childhood programs.[10] To view them in this way will bring a broad perspective to what seems to be great divergence. These three main categories may be designated as the study of behavior, the study of personality, and the study of cognition. Ideas conform to these three main divisions as each resulted from the seminal work of an intellectual giant, whose dynamic vision captured men's minds and stimulated extensive and productive research and study. The first major transformations stemmed from the work of Charles Darwin. The effects of his work in establishing new methodology and revolutionary basic assumptions supporting research made possible the study of behavior in the manner of both Edward Thorndike and Arnold Gesell. Sigmund Freud and Jean Piaget are the other two initiators of major new psychological directions. While the pursuits of Freud and Piaget would have been impossible without the leavening of thought that followed Darwin's era, each set in motion revolutionary strands of psychological study. For Freud, it was the study of personality, for Piaget the study of cognition.

The Study of Behavior

Darwin's radical impact upon theology has been widely discussed; equally strong was his influence upon psychology. Modern psychology can be said to have followed the publication in 1859 of Darwin's *The Origin of Species*.[11] Besides shattering Victorian complacency and contributing to the reshaping of intellectual thought, Darwin's data forced a reassessment of the means for obtaining knowledge. From a reliance upon intuitively discerning the logic of things and events, scientists turned to faith in scientific observation. As a biologist included on a trip to the South Pacific aboard a ship called the *Beagle*, this Englishman collected birds and animals that did not belong to any designated species and presented these as evidence to disprove the fixed nature of species. His unprecedented method of investigation opened intoxicating prospects for research and propelled a desire for study to be objective and scientific. It is against this background that one must see the budding field of child psychology, for it could be said that Darwin legitimized the scientific study of the child. Expanding upon Darwin's method, G. Stanley Hall urged the collection of data about child growth and recommended the utilization of this data in planning for the education of children. Hall's initial use of the scientific method as it applied to child study was extended by many psychologists who followed, until the empirical method came to be accepted as virtually the only means of attaining knowledge about child growth.

From an earlier belief that the orders of nature were immutable and that various living things had existed as such from the beginning, Darwin's concept of evolution proposed that the organic world was a dynamic order and that present forms exist as a process of evolutionary development. Hall's recapitulation theory, postulating stages of development in children, was explicitly evolutionary in character. Arnold Gesell carried on the basic premise of Hall and became an articulate spokesman for gradual change as a central concept of developmental psychology. The accumulation of data based on norms of growth grew steadily as the output of newly established child study centers throughout the country.

In a separate endeavor Edward L. Thorndike began an investigation of learning by observing changes in animal responses due to presented conditions. From this early experimentation Thorndike's famous laws of learning flowed. Based on the assumption that observation of animal behavior could help solve the problems of psychology, Thorndike's theory led the way in translating the results of animal research to children's learning. Both Darwin's scientific method and the doctrine of evolution are evident here, for without the acceptance of evolutionary theory, animal learning would not have been considered a suitable basis for establishing laws of learning. This belief asserts that "the idea of animal-child parallels has been subtly transmuted to remain one of the central postulates of child study."[12]

In the efforts to build a science of education, the scientists' use of precise measuring instruments were transferred to educational problems. The breakthrough for education originated in Alfred Binet's and Theophile Simon's application of a scale technique to the intelligence tests they devised. The scale idea was soon applied to achievement as well and put to work by American educators as they became involved in an orgy of test making that included every phase of the school curriculum. Thorndike and Charles Hubbard Judd were active promoters of the measurement movement, which they believed would bring efficiency to education. The scale concept of achievement and the normative view of growth meshed well as scientific undertakings.

Anyone conversant with the change in educational practice at the turn of the century can recognize the strong impact of behaviorism on day-to-day classroom procedure. The results of objective child study became a recognized part of education and formed the basis for teacher training at the early childhood level. The stimulus-response psychology of Thorndike, also a part of teacher training, became the basis for lesson planning and textbook construction. The vastly expanded measurement devices not only controlled the evaluation of learning but ultimately altered the curriculum itself.

The key developments in the study of behavior form the origins of today's behavioristic practices. Reinforcement theory, Skinner's modification of behaviorism, as the basis for teaching machines, operant conditioning, behavior modification, token economies, indeed, even the thrust for accountability in the schools, rests upon the study of behavior begun with enthusiasm during the early decades of this century. In subsequent chapters each development will be probed.

Dewey's Pragmatic Philosophy

Wholly apart from the study of behavior, the philosophy of John Dewey developed during the same period of time. He was influenced by William James' *Principles of Psychology*, as were Thorndike and Hall.[13] It was not so much the need for scientific, objective observation that touched Dewey, but the "conviction of the primacy of change and development over fixity."[14] Dewey's organism-environment metaphor, so prominent in his educational philosophy, he attributed to James, who in turn had built it out of Darwin's theory.[15] At Columbia University in 1909 Dewey gave a series of lectures on Darwin in which he paid tribute to the publication of *The Origin of Species* as "doubtless the greatest dissolvent in contemporary thought."[16] These apparent threads binding Dewey to the great revolution modifying intellectual thought allow us to consider Dewey's pragmatic philosophy of education as a contiguous although extremely different development. Along with others, Dewey played an important role in elaborating the evolutionary concept to a general interpretation of the development of man and his social institutions. Pragmatism holds that society is subject to change whenever better methods of thinking and acting are devised to meet the exigencies of life.

John Dewey's magnum opus, *Democracy and Education*, written in 1916, has been called "the most inclusive exposition of the philosophical basis of the progressive education movement."[17] That movement gained many followers in the United States and Great Britain. Of Dewey's strong influence Lawrence Cremin has written:

> In an era of excessive formalism Dewey wrote of bringing the school closer to life; in an age of educational inequity he talked of democratizing culture; at a time of unbridled economic individualism he called for a new socialized education that would further a spirit of social responsibility. The timeliness

of his criticism was its greatest strength, and it should be no surprise that a newly self-conscious teaching profession adopted him as its first major prophet.[18]

Contemporary writers turn to Dewey's philosophical principles as they search for an approach to working with young children that integrates emerging psychological theory, for Dewey's functional, interactive position allows for such integration. The basic purview of Dewey's philosophy seems to have important vitality today.

The Study of Personality

Sigmund Freud's work set in motion the second big strand of psychological theory to be considered. Breaking the bounds of the conventional society in which he lived, Freud shifted his attention from the study of the physiological mechanisms of neural functioning to the psychological mechanisms of behavior. The theory grew out of the investigation of patients' thoughts and feelings, as well as actions. Indeed, psychoanalysis viewed the thoughts and feelings, conscious and unconscious, of an individual as so important that any theory that focused on behavior solely was considered to be incomplete and inadequate, for this theory tended to view the individual as a purposer impelled by instinctual drives. Freudian psychologists considered each individual as a battleground of conflicting urges, frequently issuing from the blind drives of sex or aggression.

The treatment procedure to assist persons to resolve their unhappy, anxiety-ridden situations gradually evolved as Freud devised the technique that became standard for psychoanalysis. Freud's strategy, so at odds with behavioristic research, was one of clinical probing to reveal the causes and mechanisms of a patient's disturbances. The patient was instructed to report every thought and every idea that came to his mind — pleasant or repugnant, trivial or significant, logical or incoherent. Nothing was to be withheld. These clinical sessions, in which Freud listened to thousands of hours of expressions of thoughts and feelings, produced the data whereby the patient's difficulties could be alleviated therapeutically. They provided the raw data for the building of a theory. Both the methodology and the theory will be examined in chapters to follow.

Freud was the master builder of psychoanalytic theory; he laid the foundations, guided the course of its growth, and was adamant about maintaining the foundational premises of his theory. The positivistic climate that shaped the course of nineteenth-century physics and biology nurtured Freud's psychoanalytic position. At this time man was regarded essentially as a complex energy system maintaining itself by interactions with the world. Both physiological and psychological processes were conceived to have "the purposes of individual survival, propagation of the species and an ongoing evolutionary development."[19] However, as sociology and anthropology began to grow as independent disciplines in the late nineteenth century and expand rapidly in the twentieth, a number of followers of Freud moved to the consideration of the social conditioners of personality. "Gradually," wrote Calvin Hall and Gardner Lindzey, "these burgeoning social and cultural doctrines began to seep into psychology and psychoanalysis and to erode the nativistic and physicalistic foundations of the sciences."[20] Among those leaders who presented psychoanalysis with a twentieth-century look were Alfred Adler, Karen Horney, Eric Fromm, and Harry Stack Sullivan. As neo-Freudians added the culture as a source of the dynamics of behavior, emphasis on the significance of the child's social interactions in the early years increased. Erik H. Erikson, Lawrence K. Frank, and Daniel Prescott were among psychologists who stressed the social nature of mental health and wrote directly to elevate the importance of the child's early years in his home, family, and school for personality development.

Freud never granted the ego an autonomous position; although he accorded it an executive position in maintaining a healthy personality, he always considered it subservient to the wishes of the id. Some psychoanalytic theorists in contrast to Freud began to enhance the role of the ego in the formation of total personality. Heinz Hartmann took the lead in the growth of a new ego theory, sometimes referred to as "ego psychology" in which the ego was given a conflict-free sphere in fostering personality adjustment. Erik H. Erikson's writings favor a concept of ego psychology and explicate the relations of ego development and the existing culture.

Allied to this main stream of psychological thought through the emphasis on affectivity we will find such contemporary theorists as Carl Rogers and Abraham Maslow. Although believing their conception of the nature of man to be more in line with that of Jean Jacques Rousseau, these psychologists recognize their debt to Freud for cutting through the Victorian attitudes of his day and opening areas of study hitherto unresearched. Their argument holds that if the child is given moderately constructive circumstances, his self-direction will develop constructively. If the child is accepted and if his needs are not blocked by negative conditions, he will live harmoniously with himself and with others; he will become a fully functioning person. To achieve self-actualization the individual's capacity for creativity comes into play; he has trust in his own ability and is sensitively open to experience. These characteristics lead to uniqueness of personal response from which creative products and creative living emerge.

Early childhood education, perhaps more than any other level, has been influenced directly by aspects of the study of personality: affective development of young children has been a consistent and major concern.

The Study of Cognition

The third major strand of psychological thought deals wholly with cognition and views the child as a knower, a thinker. Ironically, the long neglected work of Jean Piaget on children's thinking is now crowding out other areas as a focus for research and study. In the past fifteen years studies have replicated those of Piaget, used them as a base for further projects, and sought to explicate the implications of Piaget's thinking for education.

The hallmark of Piagetian investigation, his *methode clinique* — a semi-clinical interview procedure borrowed in part from clinical psychology — places it at odds with the great urge to be completely scientific and objective which dominated the study of behavior. Piaget came from a tradition of science that differed from that held in the United States; through his early studies he had developed meticulous procedure and a questioning attitude. He was dissatisfied with the measuring instruments of Binet and Simon. In his work at the Binet Laboratory in Paris, Piaget came to the conclusion that standarized tests failed to really tap the young child's intellectual growth. The child's incorrect answers, he found, often provided the most significant information. The aim, as Piaget developed this semiclinical technique, was to follow the child's line of thinking in order to understand the reasons behind the child's responses and the manner in which these changed over time. The intent is to reveal the processes by which a child arrives at a particular understanding, for Piaget has been concerned consistently with the ontogenesis of intelligence, the transformation in the development of the structure of logical thinking. Piaget uncovers qualitative as well as quantitative changes in intellectual ability, thus revealing cognitive growth as demanding a long growth arc. A new conception of stages is put forth showing a lawful succession of relatively stable intellectual structures.

Piaget's theory is constructivist in nature. Intellectual growth is not deemed as unfolding nor merely a response to outside stimulation but is always a response of the underlying cognitive structure attained by the organism in interaction with the environment. Knowledge is always a structuring of the subject in living interaction with environmental circumstances and always constructed in part according to the determinants intrinsic to the learner's already developed structures. This gives an active role to the learner while also emphasizing the part of environment as essential for the realization of potential.

Writings about Piaget's work have followed rapidly from the recent recognition of his contributions. In a forceful analysis of past theoretical positions J. McVicker Hunt repudiates earlier maturational theory and argues that growth is a transactional process. He posits that the child's encounters with his environment are significant determiners of growth and learning.[21] Ira Gordon points to the crumbling concept of fixed intelligence held earlier and underscores the modifiability of behavior.[22] Millie Almy describes some of the environmental factors essential for significant learning.[23] These only indicate contemporary directions.

PROSPECTUS

Throughout this book as we look more deeply at each aspect of theory we will find that theoretical growth has not been a linear process. Some investigators have built upon the ideas of their predecessors; others have gone in completely different directions. Sometimes basic premises conflict; at other times theorists are dealing with such dissimilar phenomena that they have nothing to say to each other. This is obviously so in the three great strands of development, and, to add to the complexity of analysis, within each strand there exists a great deal of divergence along with strikingly creative thought. In each period of time the focus for study has sometimes been limited unduly and tied to particular research techniques, but excesses are the creative thrusts of individuals and society, the countercyclical reactions to yesterday's excesses, which help to remove the blinders of an earlier period.

Early childhood education has relied heavily upon whatever the contemporary knowledge of child development has been. This has led to overextrapolation of data; results valid for the subjects from which they were drawn have, at times, been generalized to the point where they become invalid. Each child psychologist putting forth data presents a picture of the growing child metaphorically. These metaphors should not be taken as ultimate "truth," but as a way of advancing our thinking about growth and learning. Taken within proper parameters, each one has brought enlightment. William Kessen delineates this gradual change:

> The history of child study is a history of rediscovery. With remarkable regularity, the same themes appear, are elaborated for a while, then fade. . . . Scientists, at least, remain committed to the eighteenth-century postulate of remediable ignorance and the stability of this commitment has led, slowly but steadily, to the accumulation of a body of reliable facts about children. It is our greater knowledge of the child as well as our changed attitude toward him that mark the passage of many years of study. The

history of child study is a history of rediscovery; it is also a history of modest advances toward truth.[24]

Three basic themes that Kessen finds reappearing with regularity he puts forth in the form of questions:

Is the child a creature of nurture or a creature of nature?
Is the child an active explorer or a passive receiver?
Is the behavior of the child best conceived as a bundle of elements or as a set of integrated structures?[25]

The complexity and interrelatedness of these questions have not generally been fully recognized. But positions taken on these persistent antimonies, although frequently not clarified, separate the great students of development and the attitudes toward children in succeeding periods of time. In the writings of psychologists considered in this book, the reader will do well to look for their stand on the role of genetic endowment, the influence of environment on learning, the meaning of "activity" on the part of the child, the uniqueness of persons, and the integrated nature of growth and learning.

The Past as Prologue

The wealth of ideas gaining favor in the twentieth century may seem a long enough span to consider in depth, yet they do not serve as a suitable beginning point. Contemporary theory has its roots in the past in a very real sense. In education tradition lingers long; ideas from the past intermingle with newer insights. Even a brief historical view will help to provide perspective.

The strong relationship between cultural patterns and beliefs about development can best be revealed by including the shift in thought brought about before the turn of this century. The dramatic change from the philosophy of idealism to the scientific thought of this era becomes apparent only as the nature of idealistic thought is first understood. To delineate this change the ideas of Froebel will serve well for his beliefs mirror the idealism of his time. Therefore, after a brief look at earlier educational leaders, we will begin with Froebel's theory. This will be followed by succeeding theoretical positions and finally culminate in future possibilities.

2 The Roots of Early Childhood Education

While a recorded educational program specifically designed for the early childhood years was proposed less than two hundred years ago, concern for the young child's development extends back to early Greece, Rome, and Palestine. Early childhood theory is a product of an interplay of inherited beliefs, changing conceptions of child nature, and more modern research efforts. The inheritance has been highly selective and the impact of beliefs uneven. Particularly when early childhood education is considered to include the primary school years, basic theoretical ideas are diverse and uncoordinated, sometimes drawing upon beliefs at odds with each other, but all are rooted in the streams of thought expanding across the ages.

Consider the following quotations from writers of other centuries. Except for the use of some precise words, they sound startlingly contemporary:

> . . . the beginning . . . of a young and tender thing . . . is the time at which the character is formed and the desired impressions more readily taken.
>
> If we wish anyone to be virtuous we must train him in early youth; if we wish him to make great progress in the pursuit of wisdom, we must direct his faculties towards it in infancy, when desire burns, when thought is swift, and when memory is tenacious.
>
> You have not got to teach him truths so much as to show him how to set about discovering them for himself.
>
> Idiosyncrasies of the individual are the greatest blessings of nature and must be respected to the highest degree.

Thus did Plato and Comenius presage current ideas concerning the significance of early childhood, Rousseau elevate learning how to learn over the accumulation of factual knowledge, and Pestalozzi recognize the significance of individual differences. You will find these quotations in the text that follows. You will also find sharp divergences in beliefs concerning the nature of the child and the relative impact of nature over nurture in learning.

CONTRASTING VIEWS THROUGH THE CENTURIES

The Hellenic Tradition

In ancient times Plato wrote, "You know also that the beginning is the most important part of any work, especially in the case of a young and tender thing; for that is the time at which the character is being formed and the desired impressions more readily taken."[1] He believed the child's body and habits of health were formed during the early years. In the same period of time Plato recommended that good breeding be promoted through sports, games, plays, and songs; more formal education followed at age six.

Within this conception is the recognition of education as a means of molding human character deliberately in accordance with an ideal. The true essence of education was the process of shaping man into his ideal form, considered the real and genuine human nature. It started from the ideal, not from the individual. Plato's philosophy of idealism stressed the permanent, absolute, eternal world of the spirit. He believed the ideal world to be founded on universal patterns of truth, goodness, justice, and beauty, which gave form to everyday encounters. A higher degree of existence or reality resided not in the realm of matter, considered a shadowy fleeting realm of change and instability, but in a knowledge of good as it grew within the individual.[2] Thus pure ideas, pure realities have to go beyond the empirical world into the world of pure reason.

One of the most embracing ideals of humanity was presented in Plato's system of idealism that envisions man as beautiful, virtuous, and efficient.[3] It posited fundamental ordering and unifying forces to exist in the universe that could be reflected in the mind of man and thus render him capable of realizing meanings and interrelationships within the mass of his personal impressions. The greatest of all human faculties was considered to be the capability of searching for what is "true." It involved an element of unfolding all the knowledge within the individual as he became attuned to eternal realities. Knowledge, innate in the immortal soul, was acquired by the process of reminiscence, in which the individual remembers what he knew before association with an imperfect body. True education meant the awakening of qualities asleep in the soul, an awakening turning the individual to the source of light. The shackles of sense experience only deluded the individual, for the body in seeking satisfaction was considered subject to lower appetites, feelings, and desires. In Plato's threefold scheme, the will, courage, and endurance formed the middle step and elevated man above bodily appetites and desires, but reason alone allowed the individual to look upon and contemplate eternal truth.

To instill in the younger generation the capacity for fulfilling this vision of man, a carefully planned education was proposed. The function of education was to train the nobler natural instincts of the individual to harmonize with the intellect and to keep the weak human elements in check. Early education was to temper the emotions so that more rational elements could be promoted later. Since the beginnings were extremely important, Plato emphasized the early learning of good character habits and here the standard of the ideal was significant. The young were to be subjected to lofty art of all kinds and to live in an environment of beauty, for the appreciation of beauty was believed to lead to appreciation of what is morally good in conduct and character. The connection between aesthetic taste and morality was considered so close that whatever tended to ennoble aesthetic taste elevated character; conversely, whatever tended to foster a taste for debased art tended equally to deprave a man's whole moral being.[4] Music provided important nourishment; rhythm and harmony, even at an early age, could sink gently into the depths of being and contribute in the slow process of forming man's ethos. Literature was part of the pattern of values generating a better type of man. It was highly inappropriate to be careless about the stories told to the young; Plato attacked Homer and Hesiod for portraying gods as too basely human. Poetry and music needed to be carefully controlled so that the child's soul would be shaped in conformity with highest ideals.[5] A healthy body was also deemed essential so sports, games, and designated play were encouraged, as they contributed to good breeding and courage.

Such positive beginnings formed the foundation for those who would arrive at the ultimate philosophical understandings. It was followed by a long period of educational experiences, for Plato felt that even the keenest intellect could not enter directly into the realm of the knowledge of truth. The knowledge of good grew slowly as the individual was lifted above the world of sense and climbed the height of philosophical truth. At age six gymnastics and rudiments of reading, writing, and arithmetic were added to the other educational elements already begun. In adolescence mathematics was given a dominant role for its supposed ability to stimulate thinking and awaken reason, and this elevation of mathematics as a keystone of philosophic education set the pattern of mental discipline. Only the most brilliant persons would continue to a regimen of philosophy that would take them to the ideal understanding of the good life and the perfect state.

The Greeks' epoch-making position in the history of education rests at least in part upon the direct expression and active awareness of a standard — their *paideia* or conscious ideal of culture and education. As Plato made his heroic ideal of character the philosophical ideal of his educational plan, he oriented his work toward humanism. "For humanism means education which is deliberately modelled on a certain ideal conception of human nature," writes Werner Jaeger.[6] Plato offered his own philosophical humanism as a direct challenge to an age.

The Republic was directed to solving the problem of educating leaders. It was written at a time when democracy was declining in Athens; it was a chaotic period full of factional conflict. Plato dreamed of an ideal state ruled by the wise and the just, so his educational system was designed to develop "philosopher kings." The good citizen followed the state's bidding whether it was to rule, to fight, or to work for it. In this tripartite division of society Plato cared little for the education of the great masses of people doing the work: his attention was given to the warrior and to the ruling class. Education not only prepared members of these classes to do the state's bidding, but it also served as a selective agency to determine the most able. In proposing a class-oriented education Plato "doubtless did a great service in showing that a system of education is integral with the welfare of the state, but he also doubtless did a great disservice to democracy by idealizing an anti-democratic kind of state."[7]

The effect of Plato's *Republic* was different than he envisioned: no state-dominated society came directly from it but rather a Western philosophy with strong impact emerged. Plato made clear the objectives of his educational system: wisdom, temperance, courage, and justice were to be attained as the individual rose to the understanding of philosophical truth, fixed and knowable. Plato's belief in the unchanging character of reality included heredity, which he considered a powerful force in the intellectual and moral sphere, for with a few notable exceptions, each child was expected to find his place in his parent's class. Knowledge, innate in the human mind, unfolded as the result of properly planned education. The desired virtues required that good be realized by the continual contemplation of the beautiful and harmonious from the child's earliest years. As a knowledge of "good" grew within the individual, as "good" became a reality, the slow process of shaping man's ethos took place to the benefit of the individual and the state. It all began in early childhood.

Aristotle and Plutarch also made statements on education for the early years. The strong Greek position on early education has been summarized in this way: "Among ancient peoples whose civilization was of a high order, the Greeks, perhaps, were most acutely conscious of the importance of utilizing the plastic period of infancy for implanting moral and aesthetic ideals and for developing a sound physique."[8] Quintilian, a Roman, also demonstrated an appreciation of the value of imitation in the training of the young, as he admonished parents and nurses to set good examples of language and morals for "we are by nature most tenacious of childish impressions."[9] However, the vision of early Hellenic and Roman writers was lost sight of for centuries. In the long span of time called the Middle Ages, which followed the fall of the Roman Empire, the most characteristic aspect of life was the large part played by the Christian church in all fields of endeavor. While there was not much concern for early education, the role of the church is significant as it projected a vastly different view of human nature.

The Influence of the Church

The church control of school in the medieval period rejected secular elements as the early Christian church fathers elevated faith as opposed to reason. The argument, as R. Freeman Butts explains, was that "the original sin of Adam and Eve made it necessary for all men thereafter to seek help in living the good life, but God promised for man the means of escape through the life and death of Christ. . . . The means of salvation were instituted on earth by God in the form of the universal church, which provides the holy sacraments by which man may begin his journey to salvation."[10]

In St. Augustine's theology the realm of true happiness was to be found in the future life, the "other" world of spirit, rather than in the present world of material things. Man, he believed, was placed on earth to achieve salvation and grace in the sight of God and could best realize this by turning his back on the material world, for the state, property, and family were founded in sin. The weakness of the flesh needed to be mortified. Man consists of a soul and a body, an admixture of potential good and evil with good evident in the immortal soul. Not through his own will, or even his own contemplation, could man gain salvation or good become transcendent; rather, this was dependent upon God's grace with Christ as the intermediary agent.[11] Ritualistic and sacramental routines were expected to awaken and quicken the mind toward the love of God and thus prepare the individual to gain his immortal soul. There was an Augustinian optimism that man could know the order of good but only as revealed and fixed by the church.

What did this mean for education? It projected a view of the child's nature as essentially evil, not to be trusted. The requirements were constant supervision and sometimes severe discipline in order that submission and obedience be attained. The religious doctrine of original sin made it seem natural for children to be stubborn and rebellious. Therefore, bodily punishment as a means of discipline was considered good for both the mind and soul.[12] For girls, seclusion and retirement were recommended as a life of perpetual chastity was glorified. The value of education was not for active life in a social setting, but in preparation for life beyond death through imbuing the soul with the Christian virtues of faith, hope, charity, and humility. All other physical and mental values were inferior to these.

To the church fathers of the Middle Ages education and gymnastics were worse than useless; development of the body interfered with progress toward salvation. Secular music diverted the emotions into improper channels. Everything was subordinate to Christian doctrine. What little direct learning existed was for the purpose of being able to read Latin, the universal medium of discourse among the educated few. Even this limited education was not for the young child.

That there was no plan for the education of young children is not surprising, as childhood was not considered a distinct stage of life, nor a time for effective education. The Hellenistic *paideia*, which presupposed a difference between the world of children and the world of adults, planned for an initiation or an education to help the child attain his status in society. Medieval civilization failed to perceive any distinction and therefore gave no thought to any transition period. The beginnings of change in this lack of perception of childhood came about gradually and from two different sources: one within the home, one outside the home.

Attitudes Toward Childhood

The changing concept of childhood as a distinct stage of development is depicted by Philippe Ariès in *Centuries of Childhood*. The medieval view of children was really one of negation:

> In medieval society the idea of childhood did not exist; this is not to suggest that children were neglected, forsaken or despised. The idea of childhood is not to be confused with affection for children: it corresponds to an awareness of the particular nature of childhood, that particular nature which distinguishes the child from the adult, even the young adult. In medieval society this awareness was lacking. That is why, as soon as the child could live without the constant solicitude of his mother, his nanny or his

cradle-rocker, he belonged to adult society. That adult society now strikes us as rather puerile: no doubt this is largely a matter of its mental age, but it is also due to its physical age, because it was partly made up of children and youths. Language did not give the word "child" the restricted meaning we give it today: people said "child" much as we say "lad" in everyday speech. The absence of definition extended to every sort of social activity: games, crafts, arms. There is not a single collective picture of the times in which children are not to be found, nestling singly or in pairs in the *trousse* hung round women's necks, or urinating in a corner, or playing their part in a traditional festival, or as apprentices in a workshop, or as pages serving a knight, etc.

The infant who was too fragile as yet to take part in the life of adults simply "did not count": this is the expression used by Molière, who bears witness to the survival in the seventeenth century of a very old attitude of mind.[13]

The discontinuance of this archaic attitude toward childhood is traced by Ariès as expressed in art, literature, iconography, and religion. By the sixteenth or seventeenth century the child was given a special costume to mark him out from adults — especially the male child. In literature the new attitude depicted the child's sweetness, his simplicity and drollery; he had become a source of amusement and relaxation for the adult. "Henceforth people would no longer hesitate to recognize the pleasure they got from watching children's antics and 'coddling' them."[14]

The "coddling" attitude involved critical reaction particularly among seventeenth-century moralists and pedagogues. Feelings of exasperation over the undue attention paid to children were turned to a psychological interest and moral solicitude for child growth. Writings show a concern that the fragile faculty of reason should be supported in order to promote thinking men and good Christians.

Summarizing these momentous developments in attitudes toward the young, Ariès writes:

The first concept of childhood — characterized by "coddling" — had made its appearance in the family circle, in the company of little children. The second, on the contrary, sprang from a source outside the family: churchmen or gentlemen of the robe, few in number before the sixteenth century, and a far greater number of moralists in the seventeenth century, eager to ensure disciplined, rational manners. They too had become alive to the formerly neglected phenomenon of childhood, but they were unwilling to regard children as charming toys, for they saw them as fragile creatures of God who needed to be both safeguarded and reformed. This concept in its turn passed into family life.[15]

MELIORATING VIEWS OF THE CHILD

Johann Amos Comenius

One of the churchmen who widened the aim of education beyond the religious was Johann Amos Comenius, a Moravian bishop writing essentially between 1628 and 1632. Of course, by this time Europe had undergone immense changes through a Renaissance, a revival of the classical spirit including an interest in classical learning, and a religious reformation, a series of religious revolts against an authoritarian church. One profound effect of the reformation was the growth of civil control over education and the extension of wider opportunities for education among all classes of people. As a deeply pious bishop, Comenius considered a knowledge of the Scriptures the ultimate guide, yet he insisted that education brought children into harmony with their particular cultural setting. Impressed with the possibilities of social reform through education, Comenius devised a complete system of schools reaching from the earliest stages of development to the university. Instruction was to be a step-by-step procedure carefully graded in sequence from the simple to the complex, from the known to the unknown. The method of education was learning through acquaintance with actual objects whenever possible.

Comenius set forth his educational plan in *The Great Didactic,* in which he emphasized the early years in these words:

> If piety is to take root in any man's heart, it must be engrafted while he is still young; if we wish any one to be virtuous we must train him in early youth; if we wish him to make great progress in the pursuit of wisdom, we must direct his faculties towards it in infancy, when desire burns, when thought is swift, and when memory is tenacious.[16]

In *School of Infancy* Comenius presented a handbook for mothers and nurses for the training of children under six years of age. The external senses were to be exercised as children learned to distinguish the objects that surround them, thus the seeds of knowledge would be implanted at an early age. All education should follow the natural order of the child's development; for the young this included all kinds of activity. "In a word," he wrote, "whatever children delight to play with, provided that it be not hurtful, they ought rather to be gratified than restrained from it; for inactivity is more injurious to both mind and body than anything in which they can be occupied."[17] The very things children loved to do — run, jump, pour out water, lift things up, carry things from place to place — were initial steps in "mechanics." With intuitive insight and concern Comenius outlined in detail a program for young children through play, games, rhymes, fairy tales, music, and manual activity. His *Orbus Pictus*, containing illustrations of many objects, introduced the picture book for school children. At the age of six children were expected to go to a vernacular school where they began instruction in the three R's, singing, religion, morals, and the mechanical arts.[18]

Comenius was one of the great sense realists — those who believed ideas to be innate but that they needed carefully planned experiences to unfold them. In this respect he set the pattern for a number of educators to follow, but Comenius, himself, was so far in advance of his own day that his impact upon schools was slight. The liberal tone of much that he wrote foreshadowed some of the cultural stirrings to come. Since Comenius would embrace all persons in his educational plan, he proclaimed the need for universal education.

John Locke

If Comenius was a leading exponent of education during the religious reformation, John Locke's conception of human nature was embedded in the scientific revolution. The reformation saw the rise of doubt, skepticism, and inquiry concerning basic philosophical ideas. In the scientific revolution the reliance on traditional authority diminished and faith again rested upon human reason as a source of knowledge, which, in turn, promoted the use of a controlled method of empirical investigation. The immense advances made by science were influenced by Sir Isaac Newton's position that the universe could be explained as operating naturally and according to fixed, physical laws. Locke, writing in the late seventeenth century, delineated human nature in a scientific manner. This he felt placed individual growth within the kind of universe Newton had described as developing in a lawful manner. The basic assumption of Locke's view was that human nature is not preformed at birth, but it is a result of the impact of the environment upon the unformed and pliable raw material of the human organism. The individual simply possessed a blank but sensitive tablet (*tabula rasa*) that was ready to receive impressions from the external world. Thus, ideas come from without the child, from his physical and social environment, not from a preexistent mind or soul.

In the view of one historian, "Locke's empirical conception of the role of experience in learning gave theoretical justification for sense realism in education. Insisting that ideas and knowledge come from the impingement of the external world upon the human mind in the form of sensation and perceptions, Locke opened the way for more attention in educational methods to the development of all the senses of the child, not merely through reading, but through the senses of sight, taste, smell, touch, and hearing."[19] It follows logically that Locke stressed the physical development of the body. He is well known for putting forth the great dictum: "A sound mind in a sound body is a short, but full description of a happy state in the world."[20]

In *Some Thoughts Concerning Education* Locke laid out with great care the family's responsibility for providing for their children's education. It detailed the relations of parent to child as well as the qualities to be promoted in the learner: virtue, wisdom, breeding, and learning. The class limitation of Locke's educational model soon becomes apparent for he admits at the outset that it is the class of gentlemen for whom the properly arranged program is designed. For the privileged child in danger of being spoiled by luxurious living, Locke recommended a regimen of physical toughening as well as exercises and studies that he expected would provide a mental rigor for the mind, thus tying his education plan to the doctrine of mental discipline.[21] Locke presented the image of the English countryman that eighteenth-century England was ready to accept, an image with a mixture of progress and conservatism that became a classic in educational literature.[22]

Locke was part of the age of Enlightenment, protesting against authoritarian regimes and proposing shared power and privilege. A new class was feeling its own strength derived not from birth but from wealth gained in industry and commerce. More than just a protest, Locke's *Treatise on Civil Government* presented a contract theory of political power in which the social contract presented was an agreement by which the citizens delegate authority to the government, in return for which the government would agree to protect the natural rights of all citizens.[23] These rights, according to Locke, were life, liberty, and property. Locke's doctrines of liberalism, limited as they were by natural and class considerations, presaged the more radical libertarianism of Jean Jacques Rousseau.

Jean Jacques Rousseau

In the writings of Comenius and Locke, efforts to understand the nature of man and of learning, to determine the objectives of education for the good life, and to choose proper educational experiences to attain these objectives only indicated changes to come. But Jean Jacques Rousseau, whose clarion call to *naturalism* has reverberated down the years, transformed education in a way that ultimately led followers to give increased attention to the earlier years. In *Émile*, published in 1762, Rousseau described an educational program for an imaginary pupil "in terms that were eloquent and radical enough to change the course of educational history."[24]

There was little in Rousseau's early life to prepare him to exert political or educational influence. Born poor in Geneva, Switzerland in 1712, he lost his mother at birth and was soon deserted by his father, an imaginative but unstable master watchmaker. Rousseau grew up indolent and unprincipled under the haphazard care of relatives. Apprenticed to an engraver who treated him cruelly, he soon ran away and later failed in the priesthood and in music, but the unusual talent he had for writing gained him a prize for an essay in Paris in 1749. During the remainder of his erratic life his writings poured out in a steady devotion to the downtrodden and to liberty. As a passionate rebel he was the great exponent of the Romantic impulse toward the elevation of the individual and toward social revolt.

How did it happen that this man elevated the morals of France, transformed education, inspired the Romantic movement, and had more effect upon posterity than any other writer or thinker of the eighteenth century? Will and Ariel Durant answer in *Rousseau and Revolution*: "Europe was ready for a gospel that would exalt feeling above thought. It was tired of the restraints of customs, conventions, manners and laws. It had heard enough of reason, argument and philosophy; all this riot of unmoored minds seemed to have left the world devoid of meaning, the soul empty of imagination and hope; secretly men and women were longing to believe again."[25] Rousseau asked the pertinent question, and gave form and feeling to common doubts and "after his death all Europe listened to him."[26] During his lifetime Voltaire, a Renaissance man with less radical ideas, was esteemed and Rousseau despised. Voltaire hoped that through the application of more reason and more civilized behavior society would improve; Rousseau believed that reason is futile unless grounded in harmoniously developed emotions and natural expressions.

The writings of Rousseau were reactions against the absolutist regimes of his day: absolute monarchy, closed economic systems, rigid social stratification, and religious authoritarianism. According to Irving Babbitt, Rousseau's treatises broke with two traditions, the classical and the Christian.[27] The advocation of naturalism, culminating as it did in a plea for genius and originality, formed a protest against the mechanical imitation and the affected decorum of a certain type of classicist. Rousseau preached against the distortions of French life that he felt held the upper classes in a harness of artificiality. In such aspects of life as manners, costumes, expressions of love, or dealings with children, Rousseau saw the individuality of man blunted instead of developed. The second break with tradition was the assertion of the natural goodness of man, a position diametrically opposed to the doctrine of total depravity so long held by austere Christians. Rousseau went to the opposite extreme by insisting that human nature is essentially good, and that the child is born with inherent impulses that are right. Upon these major premises Rousseau's social and educational principles stand. In *The Social Contract* Rousseau expressed his social and political philosophy by hypothesizing an ideal society where equality reigned. The extolling of the idea of equality rested upon an absolute faith in the power and the natural nobility of man. Out of this grew a belief that human nature is perfectible and can be improved constantly under designated social conditions. When joined with the impulses of social humanitarianism, this doctrine of human perfectibility became one of the great traditions that leavened the life of Europe and, especially, America.

It is in this context that Rousseau's educational gospel of the return to nature can be understood: education must allow the goodness of man to unfold. Breadth of personality is achieved by throwing off limitations — an idea quite opposed to the humanists' belief of gaining understanding and taste by taking on the form and style of others. To Rousseau the individual, whose potentialities were developed in all their uniqueness, would become the agent for reconstructing society toward a freer, more progressive sense of harmony.[28] For this reason the individual must become a thinking person: "You have not got to teach him truths so much as to show him how to set about discovering them for himself."[29]

Social and Educational Ideas of Rousseau.   In line with other educational leaders of his own and earlier periods, Rousseau conceived of education as character building. Although his generalized goal coincided with the thought of others, the means of attaining this goal deviated vastly from the common practice in elementary schools of emphasizing memorization, recitation, and severe discipline. Inner development and self-direction were hallmarks of Rousseau's plan. Reason, as the end result of education, would then be rooted in the soil of harmoniously developed emotions and instincts. If the early years of life were kept pure and wholesome, in harmony with the child's natural tendencies, immunity from vices would be secured, Rousseau contended. While in *The Social Contract* he pictured an ideal society, in *Émile* Rousseau insisted that the child be protected from the contemporary society he knew. He opened his educational tract with the statement: "God makes all things good; man meddles with them and they become evil."[30] He felt the simplicity of nature to be the environment best suited to promote purity of thought and action. Rousseau placed Émile outside of society as a means of educating him for society. The return to nature meant giving the child an opportunity to develop himself fully, before he had contact with any of society's corrupting influences.

A child had the right to happiness, which consisted of the enjoyment of liberty. Rousseau suggested that in the early years the child should be free from all unnatural restraints of swaddling, adult clothing, and excessive severity. Mothers should let children eat, run, and play as much as they wanted and to trust the child's spontaneous impulses.[31] "What is to be thought," he wrote, "of that cruel education which sacrifices the present to an uncertain future, that burdens a child with all sorts of restrictions and begins by making him miserable, in order to prepare him for some far-off happiness which he may never enjoy?"[32]

In the opinion of Rousseau, much too little attention had been paid to studying the child so that education could be adapted to his characteristic needs. Convinced that "we know nothing of childhood; and with our mistaken notions the further we advance the further we go astray,"[33] he devoted much of *Émile* to defining what he believed to be the natural characteristics of children at different age levels and went on to outline the type of education appropriate at each level. For the childhood years up to the age of twelve the education suggested was purely physical and sensory. A great change occurred between the ages of twelve and fifteen when reason and self-consciousness begin to appear; more intellectual aspects of education could then be handled. When later adolescence was reached social problems became the major aspect of attention for the natural development of sympathy and responsibility were felt to enable youth to move into the deep secrets of the universe.[34]

Education in Childhood.   In the early years a strong, healthy physical body was to be fostered, motor activities were emphasized, and firsthand contact with a variety of objects promoted. Rousseau advocated a hardening process to develop physical stamina, so the body would be prepared to serve the individual. The primary role of the senses in the acquisition of knowledge was affirmed by Rousseau as he pointed out:

> Since everything that comes into the human mind enters through the gates of sense, man's first reason is a reason of sense-experience. It is this that serves as a foundation for the reason of the intelligence; our first teachers in natural philosophy are our feet, hands, and eyes. To substitute books for these does not teach use of reason, it teaches us to use the reason of others rather than our own; it teaches us to believe much and know little.[35]

Thus did Rousseau repudiate the building of a verbal facade in the early years, in favor of direct meaningful sensory experiences.

Since the natural impulse of the child was to touch and handle everything, his natural tendencies led him to perceive the physical properties of heat, hardness, size, and shape. The senses, thus trained, became increasingly useful in counting, measuring, weighing, or comparing. With educatonal experiences actively engaging the learner, Rousseau contended that for Émile: "Work and play are all one for him, his games are his work; he knows no difference. He brings to everything the cheerfulness of interest, the charm of freedom, and he shows the bent of his own mind and the extent of his knowledge."[36] Education thus supplied a firm base of experience with objects before symbols were used; in Rousseau's opinion books had no place in education until the age of twelve.

The role of the teacher — or rather the tutor, for Rousseau described a tutorial relationship for Émile — was one of guidance rather than one of direct instruction. In a setting where the child could engage in activities of interest to him, where he could verify results empirically, his ideas might be few but they were expected to be precise. The motivating interest would build attention and perseverance in a way that compulsion and authority could not. The weight was put upon readiness for ideas, for Rousseau suggested that we ask "what a child is capable of learning at each stage."[37] The natural, spontaneous development of the child was to be the teacher's touchstone.

The educational program of early childhood was expected to produce self-acceptance and a lack of guilt that would support the adolescent when his interest in others expanded. There was to be no comparison with others, no rivalry. To know good and evil is essential, Rousseau believed, but he considered that "childhood is the sleep of reason," therefore, a real sense of morality had no possibility until early adolescence.[38] In early childhood, control came from things and natural consequences and the major emphasis was placed upon the child's natural impulses to feel and do what was good. Rousseau clearly emphasized emotional adjustment as opposed to the accumulation of information or skills. Emotional equanimity supplied the base for later educational growth; man needed the opportunity to develop himself fully and harmoniously. The key aspects of Rousseau's naturalism — freedom, growth, interest, and activity — radically departed from educational practice in the eighteenth century and profoundly affected the thought of educational leaders that followed. The cry *"retournez a la nature,"* demanding an education that allowed for the unrestrained growth of the child's natural capacities and powers, elevated nature over nurture. The child's needs and spontaneous growth processes were placed as the starting point of a developing educational conception.

Johann Heinrich Pestalozzi

Rousseau expounded his ideas on education widely, but it was left to others to put them into practice. One such educator was Johann Heinrich Pestalozzi, a German who wrote about education, but who also conducted schools and related basic ideas to practical classroom activities. Developing his educational program toward the end of the eighteenth century, Pestalozzi relied on children's natural instincts to provide the motives for learning and searched for methods that would adapt instruction to the individual child. Social reform, he believed, would be achieved by helping the individual to help himself.

Strong egalitarian commitment in education found a place in the schools organized and taught by Pestalozzi. The education Rousseau proposed in *Émile* was for the rich young boy; neither the poor nor the female sex were included in Rousseau's daring innovations. Since Pestalozzi, however, believed that society had no right to withhold from any man (or woman) the right to develop his capabilities, he devoted his life to the elevation of the lives of the poor. Pictures of classrooms with Pestalozzi as the teacher reveal him embracing the children of peasants, both boys and girls, clad in their rags. He believed in "man who is the same whether in the palace or in the hut."[39] To Pestalozzi's great credit he did not conceive of equality of education as meaning uniformity, but rather the full acknowledgement of nature as it develops diversely in different men. The inevitable differentiation among children made strong contributions to the richness of life. "Idiosyncracies of the individual," he wrote, "are the greatest blessings of nature and must be respected to the highest degree."[40]

The spirit of Rousseau is felt in the writings of Pestalozzi yet his work was not in imitation or discipleship. Pestalozzi worked out his own ideas step by step in written form and, most influentially, in practice, for he hoped to prepare his pupils for a life of independent action. Only in the elevation of every individual would the whole of society be transformed and the desperate plight of the poor be ameliorated. Man, made in the image of God, required protective attention and the child's powers needed this care in order to burgeon from within. His respect for the child's innate ideas were expressed in this way:

> All instruction of man is then only the Art of helping Nature to develop in her own way; and the Art rests essentially on the relations and the harmony between the impressions received by the child and the exact degree of his developed powers.[41]

Pestalozzi's emphasis on proceeding from the concrete to the abstract, from the particular to the general, was a way of adjusting instruction to the child's order of development.

In the practical application of his ideas Pestalozzi endeavored to find the right materials and the right methods of teaching. He believed in the possibility of discerning certain laws that could support a scientific system of teaching.[42] Sense perception firmly based his expansion of method, for he wrote: "'Every line, every measure, every word,' I said to myself, 'is a result of understanding generated from ripened sense-impressions and must be regarded as a means towards the progressive clearing up of ideas.' Also all instruction is essentially nothing but this."[43] Natural objects provided the material for clear perceptions and guarded against meaningless abstractions. Pestalozzi devised a whole series of "object lessons" to acquaint the child with the basic elements of form, language, and number and to enlist the child's natural propensities for action. In an intuitive way he tried to psychologize education, to understand how knowledge grows from confusion to clarity and precision.

Pestalozzi believed true moral and religious feelings to be embedded in the emotion of love that the child experienced within the family circle. In the relations between the mother and her baby the germs of love, trust, gratitude, and patience formed the first grounds for faith and the first principle of moral self-development. Positive experiences in early childhood tended to foster morally positive reactions. As the child grew out of dependency on the mother, the supreme art of pedagogy was to transfer the original emotions of love to mankind first and then to God.[44] The school atmosphere that best approximated the firm but loving climate of the home best promoted positive moral growth, and the warmth of relationships in the early years served as the foundation for self-development, social regeneration, and religious faith. Sympathy and compassion were, of course, employed in the management of children in Pestalozzi's schools.

Many visitors came to Pestalozzi's school in Yverdon, Switzerland, including educators and statesmen interested in new methods. Among those who observed and assessed the school in action was Friedrich Froebel, the translator of the eighteenth-century developments to the education of the young child.

ENDURING LEGACIES

The impact of Hellenic beliefs was not a transient phenomenon, although the strength of their effect varied in different historical periods. Certain fundamental premises extended into the nineteenth century: the assumption that truth is fixed and knowable; the conviction that character is achieved through imitation of acceptable behavior; and the confidence that certain areas of knowledge had disciplinary values for rational thought.

The conception of growth and development as the unfolding of innate ideas, initiated by Plato, was strongly held by the preponderance of writers about early education, including the influential Rousseau. Thus they were elevating the importance of nature over nurture with its corollary assumption of human nature as preformed at birth. Yet we have also seen the antithesis in Locke's proposal that the child was simply a blank but sensitive tablet (*tabula rasa*) ready to receive impressions or perceptions from the external world. In this position the emphasis was placed on nurture, for it was the impingement of the world upon the raw material of the human organism that constituted the educative process. Oddly, both groups thought of sense perception as a basic aspect of methodology in teaching. For Locke, ideas arose largely through experiences with the external world, through the senses of smell, taste, sight, touch, and hearing. Those who placed their faith in the process of unfolding also turned to the use of the senses as a means of optimal guidance in the unfoldment process. Pestalozzi, for example, devised a whole series of "object lessons" to provide for the fulfillment of the child's natural desire for developing the perceptive faculties.

Was human nature to be considered basically and naturally good, was it to be viewed as evil, or was it more properly to be thought of as formless and neutral in this respect? All three of these opinions have already been proposed. A fundamental tenet of the medieval church held man to be born in original sin and with a body that provided a continuing source of temptation and evil. In Rousseau's writings one finds the opposite argument that human nature, if kept unadulterated by contemporary society, was inherently good. A neutral ground was offered by John Locke, who believed the environment surrounding the individual could result in any number of possible characteristics.

Other dichotomous aspects related to the autonomy of the learner in his own learning. A more or less passive taking on of the rules of society or of fixed and eternal truths was the designated role for the learner in most of the educational plans discussed. Although the learner might have an active part in the process of reminiscence and in sense perception, the ultimate consideration was a taking on of what was considered the ideal that was to be fixed in thought. But Rousseau revolted against this procedure and would set free the natural impulses of childhood. The inherent goodness of man could best be realized by throwing off social restrictions and engaging in activities of interest.

While few of these ideas were held so simply or singly by any one person, they did form the legacy on which subsequent theorists could draw. In all these conceptions the function of education was broadly conceived as character development. The gaining of perceptions and of knowledge was to this end — the ability to lead the good life.

3 A Distinctive Program for the Young Child

Reaching as far back as Plato, elements of ideas presented by the educational leaders just discussed converge in the program Friedrich Froebel designed for the young child. Others had recognized that young children must be considered in building an educational plan leading to their ideal man; it was Froebel who concentrated on presenting a curriculum for the early years. In it is found the conception of harmonious interaction of Plato, much of the sense realism of Comenius, aspects of the naturalism of Rousseau, and a search for method in education similar to Pestalozzi. All these philosophical streams of thought, together with the absolute idealism of his time, Froebel's own tendency toward mysticism, and his intuitive understanding of the child, form the foundation for the principles of his kindergarten program.

A few infant schools of an earlier date were recorded. For the purpose of social and educational reform, a school for children under six was opened by John Frederick Oberlin, a Lutheran pastor, in Walbach, France in 1769.[1] Instruction was mingled with amusement as the two teachers shared moral songs, pictures of subjects from the Scriptures, and handicrafts with their pupils. Robert Owen, an English philanthropist, instituted a school for the children of workers in his model mills at New Lanark in 1816.[2] Children under ten, the minimum age for employment in the mill, were included with much attention given to play, singing, dancing, and nursery care for three- to five-year-olds. These schools, which predated Froebel's kindergarten, evidence a recognition of the importance of the early years and a search for activities appropriate to the young child.

THE EVOLUTION OF FROEBEL'S EDUCATIONAL IDEAS

Froebel stands as the great organizer of the ideas and much of the practice relating to early childhood education. The kindergarten had little in common with the sporadic development of infant schools; rather, its true heritage is found in the lines of liberal thought favoring the natural rights of man, individual freedom, and humanitarian and democratic ideals. Every word, every idea Froebel presented was formed in his own thought, yet the spirit of romanticism and idealism advancing new educational trends was always evident.

Froebel's early years lacked the unity and harmony he later valued. His childhood was devoid of parental affection, as his mother died before he was one year old and his father, a busy Lutheran pastor with an extensive parish, gave him little attention. The stepmother who came into the family when Froebel was four neglected him for her own children.[3] He was considered a troublesome, dreamy child given to introspection and mysticism. He spent his time wandering through the countryside as he was given no formal education. When, at the age of ten, he went to live with his mother's brother, he experienced four happy years. During this time he attended the town school. Later apprenticed to a forester in Thuringia, he learned forestry and surveying, but more important he puzzled about the unity between nature and the things of the spirit.

Such was the background of Froebel's restless search for a vocation and for a unified system of thought that would take him up to the opening of his institution for young children in Blankenburg, Germany in 1837. This search intensified as he attended Jena University and included brief experiences at two other universities in Göttingen and Berlin. Here Froebel was influenced by "absolute idealism," a dominant intellectual outlook in the first half of the nineteenth century. Under the leadership of German philosophers Kant, Schelling, and Hegel, the effort of idealism was "to build a complete system of thought that would reintegrate man and nature and God into a great unity expressed by the term 'Absolute.'"[4] Froebel deliberately linked his ideas to those of Schelling in his *Autobiography*. Reading Schelling's early writings was recommended to him by a young doctor of philosophy whose country estates he was surveying in 1803.[5] At this time he came into full contact with the vigorous philosophical stirrings of the idealists at Jena. He also developed an interest in mathematics and crystallography at Göttingen. Ideas gained in these studies Froebel incorporated into his own mode of thought, which was neither purely philosophical nor scientific but tinged with mysticism as he strove to formulate a satisfying, unifying explanation of man and the universe and an educational program supporting these ideas.

Before he arrived at his ultimate lifework of planning and carrying out an educational program for the young, Froebel tried the vocations of land surveyor, estate manager, official in a forest department, private secretary, director of an orphanage, tutor, and teacher. A time spent in the German army during the period of the Napoleonic Wars increased his longing for a free and united fatherland, for in the destructive influence of war he saw childhood imperiled. His commitment to education gradually emerged as his connections with various schools and tutorials aroused his interest in the methods of teaching. In 1805 when he started teaching at the Frankfurt Model School, he soon perceived that the method of instruction must be directed by the laws of development as well as by those of the subjects to be taught.[6] Two years later when he took over the tutelage of three boys, he was convinced that the isolation recommended by Rousseau was a mistake. He took the boys to live near Pestalozzi's school in Yverdon where he was impressed with the warmth and human kindness in the classroom, but felt a lack of unity in the work done. In his *Autobiography* Froebel wrote: "On the whole I passed a glorious time at Yverdon, elevated in tone, and critically decisive for my after life. At its close, I felt more clearly than ever the deficiency of inner unity and interdependence, as well as of outward comprehensiveness and thoroughness in the teaching there."[7] His developing thought is also evident in this excerpt: "The inner law and order embracing all things . . . now presented itself to me in such clearness that I could see nothing in nature or in life in which it was not made manifest."[8]

Early schools where Froebel put his own ideas into practice never really prospered, but by 1826 while he was directing one at Keilhau, his book *The Education of Man* was published. This book detailed his basic educational premises, which were by then well worked out. There are difficulties in gaining meaning from his verbose, repetitive presentation of ideas, yet it contains the main clues to the kind of program evident in the kindergarten. In his English translation, William N. Hailmann numbered sections in an effort to impose an organization on Froebel's rambling prose. Froebel's writing needs to be read with full recognition of its idealistic base, for otherwise misconceptions develop. The reader must take off his scientific, twentieth-century glasses to gain Froebel's intended meaning.

BASIC CONCEPTIONS

Unity in Life

Froebel opens his major writing with what he considered the basic tenet of life and of education: the all-pervasive sense of unity. He clearly establishes this fundamental proposition as the essence of education.

> In all things there lives and reigns an eternal law. To him whose mind, through disposition and faith, is filled, penetrated, and quickened with the

necessity that this can not possibly be otherwise, as well as to him whose clear, calm mental vision beholds the inner in the outer and through the outer, and sees the outer proceeding with logical necessity from the essence of the inner, this law has been and is enounced with equal clearness and distinctness in nature (the external), in the spirit (the internal), and in life which unites the two. This all-controlling law is necessarily based on an all-pervading, energetic, living, self-conscious, and hence eternal Unity. This fact, as well as the Unity itself, is again vividly recognized, either through faith or through insight, with equal clearness and comprehensiveness; therefore, a quietly observant human mind, a thoughtful, clear human intellect, has never failed, and will never fail, to recognize this Unity.

This Unity is God. All things have come from the Divine Unity, from God, and have their origin in the Divine Unity, in God alone. God is the sole source of all things. In all things there lives and reigns the Divine Unity, God. All things live and have their being in and through God. All things are only through the divine effluence that lives in them. The divine effluence that lives in each thing is the essence of each thing.

It is the destiny and life-work of all things to unfold their essence, hence their divine being, and, therefore, the Divine Unity itself — to reveal God in their external and transient being. It is the special destiny and life-work of man, as an intelligent and rational being, to become fully, vividly, and clearly conscious of his destiny and life-work; and to accomplish this, to render it (his essence) active, to reveal it in his own life with self-determination and freedom.

Education consists in leading man, as a thinking, intelligent being, growing into self-consciousness, to a pure and unsullied, conscious and free representation of the inner law of Divine Unity, and in teaching him ways and means thereto.[9]

Froebel's position on unity is a reflection of the philosophy of idealism, that major stream of thought in nineteenth-century Europe, which constituted a reaction against the scientific rationalism of the eighteenth-century Enlightenment. It tended to reinforce the religious temper rather than the scientific. Froebel's acceptance of the terms *absolute* and *Divine Unity* revealed how sincere an exponent he was of the effort to reintegrate man, nature, and God into a great conceptual unity.

Supported by his religious nature, this concept of unity pervades not only Froebel's writings but also extended to the manner in which the resulting educational program was formed and disseminated. Embedded, however, in the excerpt above are other fundamental aspects of Froebel's beliefs. He firmly aligned himself with learning as the process of unfoldment when he suggested that incipient thoughts need to be made consciously held. Indeed, for Froebel, education was unfoldment, the essence of man lifted into consciousness whereby he gained clarity concerning himself and all mankind. To explain this process of growth and learning Froebel frequently used an analogy to plant life for, to him, the child innately held the seeds of all later development.

Froebel described the child as neither a lump of wax nor a piece of clay, but as a self-active individual who clarifies his inner feelings and ideas by giving them outward manifestations. In making "the inner-outer and the outer-inner" Froebel wrestled with the connection between the child's inner experience and outer world, private reality and public truth. In these strivings the senses were important, but inner activity was primary. Active construction of an object objectified the child's incipient ideas and brought clarity to thought; what the child tried to represent, a form of creative self-expression, he began to understand. Objects, then, as the young child manipulated and handled them, served as "awakeners of his inner world" and nurtured subconscious thought. Even objects used through imitation and direction could serve this self-creative process in Froebel's view.

Self-activity is a term frequently incorporated into Froebel's writings, but it must be understood within the framework of his growing educational thought. To be self-active, the inner self needed to be engaged in doing something that was an outward form of inner tendencies as interpreted by Froebel. It by no means implied self-selection or even self-motivation. For this reason Froebel could develop a program with little self-initiation on the part of the child, yet believe many experiences entirely appropriate for the child. The guarding and vigilant protection of the tender bud was ever uppermost in Froebel's theory. He wrote: "Education in instruction and training, originally and in its first principles, should necessarily be *passive, following* (only guarding and protecting), *not prescriptive, categorical, interfering.*"[10]

Froebel's ability to perceive original ways of working with children resulted partly from his continued observation of them. His ideas, although intended for direct work with children, were not products of scientific observation but were essentially the results of his own intuition and continual introspection. In his frequent invitation, "Come, let us live with our children," Froebel implied a deeper living with them, encompassing a knowledge and appreciation of child nature, an ability to enter into the child's perceptions and interests.

Play in Learning

Froebel saw play as the perfect medium for self-activity — for the release of the child's inner powers. He was not content to accept the happy exuberance of play, but he watched for evidences that symbolized the awakening of the child's inner nature. "The romantic reverence that idealism led Froebel to have for the inner law of the child's self-development also enabled him to perceive the educational significance of children's play," summarized Brubacher.[11] In vivid and romantic language Froebel extolled the values of play for the growing child:

> *Play* is the highest phase of child development — of human development at this period; for *it is self-active representation of the inner — representation of the inner from inner necessity and impulse.*
>
> Play is the purest, most spiritual activity of man at this stage, and, at the same time, typical of human life as a whole — of the inner hidden natural life in man and all things. It gives, therefore, joy, freedom, contentment, inner and outer rest, peace with the world. It holds the sources of all that is good. A child that plays thoroughly, with self-active determination, perseveringly until physical fatigue forbids, will surely be a thorough, determined man, capable of self-sacrifice for the promotion of the welfare of himself and others. Is not the most beautiful expression of child-life at this time a playing child? — a child wholly absorbed in his play? — a child that has fallen asleep while so absorbed?
>
> As already indicated, play at this time is not trivial, it is highly serious and of deep significance. Cultivate and foster it, O mother; protect and guard it, O father! To the calm, keen vision of one who truly knows human nature, the spontaneous play of the child discloses the future inner life of the man.
>
> The plays of childhood are the germinal leaves of all later life; for the whole man is developed and shown in these, in his tenderest dispositions, in his innermost tendencies.[12]

The Humanist Tradition

If those "germinal leaves" were marred in the early years, the child would only with great difficulty grow into "strong manhood." But no such eventuality would ensue if the child from birth was "viewed in accordance with his nature, treated correctly, and given the free all-sided use of his powers."[13] Like Pestalozzi, Froebel thought of the home as the source of the sense of community he found so important for his educational program and for all later life. From the earliest play between mother and child perfect harmony should prevail; such harmony would gradually be extended in good relations with all family members and ultimately to a feeling of universal good will. To further the inner serenity and contentment as the fruits of an ideal family life, the child was to be presented with and surrounded by what is good, moral, and chaste. Story, poetry, and song were to "strengthen that which is noble in the youngest child" and make him "more receptive to the noble."[14] Froebel's benign view of original nature included tendencies especially amenable to influences for good.

Froebel thus presented the child's growth and learning as beginning in the family setting and extending in an orderly manner into school life. With insight into the importance of early education for the development of personality, he expected true discipline to be imbedded in feelings of human worth and respect for individuals. In harmonious human relations, especially parental, the child was to find the ideals of good behavior and evolve a sense of unity with his fellow man. Benevolent social relationships were expected outcomes of family and school life. Froebel definitely planned the kindergarten to be a happy group of children living in loving communion with others.

THE KINDERGARTEN CURRICULUM

Gifts and Occupations

The serious justification Froebel accorded play led him to consider play materials of highest importance. He designed objects with unique characteristics and called them "gifts," because he considered them divinely given to meet the needs of the child and for unfolding significant truths. "An object," he wrote, "must therefore be given to the child, not merely for his outward bodily activity, but rather for his inward activity, the activity of his soul, and for the development and cultivation of this activity."[15] Thus, play materials were dictated by two main purposes: (1) the importance of unfolding in the child's consciousness the inner connection and unity of all things, and (2) the need for enlisting the child's self-active impulses for this purpose. Froebel was not so much interested in the immediate knowledge to be gained by the senses, as in the symbolic knowledge he believed the object suggested. The ball, he proposed, symbolized the concepts of divine, all inclusive unity. In *The Education of Man* he wrote: "Gift in form and material is determined by the cosmic phase to be brought to the child's apprehension, and by the condition of the child's development at the period for which the gift is intended."[16] Froebel especially believed that the gifts would lead to fixed and knowable universal truths. Unity could best be comprehended by the young child through an understanding of part-whole relationships and the laws of connection and diversity. "Likeness conditions union: oppositeness conditions a contrast."[17] The gifts were planned to be the awakeners of perceptions of unity, relations, connections, and diversity. The first gift of the soft ball to be used by the mother with her baby was followed by the second gift consisting of a ball, a cube, and a cylinder. The cube represented the opposite of the ball and the cylinder a reconciliation of these opposites: the opposite to the round is the straight; the opposite to motion is rest.

Subsequent gifts consisted of cubes divided in numerous ways to extend perceptions of the law of opposites:

> opposite to unity is singleness
> opposite to singleness is manifoldness
> opposite to the whole is the divided
> opposite to the simple is the complex
> opposite to the outer is the inner.[18]

Not only were gifts designed to symbolize "cosmic truths," but their use was precisely designated to maximize the child's intended apprehension. In describing the use of the fourth gift Froebel describes first steps.

ITS USE

Before beginning his play with this gift the child must apprehend it as a symmetrical whole, complete in itself. The component cubes should be so packed in their box as to bring the divided cubes undermost; it is also essential that cubes similarly divided should be placed in a row. In conformity with this demand the bottom of the box must be occupied by one row of quartered cubes. The eighteen remaining undivided cubes fill the rest of the box.

If the cubes be thus arranged in the box and covered with the lid, it is only necessary to place the box on the table with the cover downward, then to draw out the cover and raise the box with a steady hand. When the box is withdrawn, the whole cube, with its parts well arranged, stands before the child.

This procedure is by no means intended merely to make the withdrawal of the box easy for the child, but, on the contrary, brings to him much inner profit. It is well for him to receive his playthings in an orderly manner — not to have them tossed to him as fodder is tossed to animals. It is good for the child to begin his play with the perception of a whole, a simple self-contained unit, and from this unity to develop his representations. Finally, it is essential that the playing child should receive his material so arranged that its various elements are discernible, and that by seeing them his mind may unconsciously form plans for using them. Receiving his material thus arranged, the child will use it with ever-recurrent and increasing satisfaction, and his play will produce far more abiding results than the play of one whose material lies before him like a heap of cobble-stones.[19]

The size of the blocks was by no means indifferent. Froebel prescribed: "The material for building in the beginning should consist of a number of wooden blocks, whose base is always one square inch and whose length varies from one to twelve inches."[20] If the blocks were too small, the representations would appear trivial; if too big the representations would be too large for the pupil to perceive the wholeness of the object. The third gift, for example, consisted of eight one-inch cubes forming a two-inch cube. The nature of the gifts with rather formal characteristics reflects Froebel's interest in mathematics and crystallography. These, with a series of more malleable, manipulative materials called *occupations*, formed the core of the kindergarten curriculum.

Intent on a distinctive curriculum for the young child, Froebel was an associate of Comenius, Locke, and Pestalozzi in marking the beginning of the development of educational methodology appropriate for training teachers.[21] Such training depended upon carefully elaborated and communicable methods, so Froebel's kindergarten procedures were presented in complete detail. By designing materials with a definite sequence and by supplying explicit directions for their use, Froebel provided an educational system with clear directives for the teacher. A portion of the description and directions for use of the fifth gift will illustrate the precise presentation of method. After delineating the sequence of gifts Froebel provides exact directions for constructing what he calls forms of knowledge (mathematical shapes), forms of life (objects in the child's world), and forms of beauty (artistic arrangements). In this selection the children are directed to make a life form in which all the parts of the gift are to be used.

Children of five years of age, who have gone through with similar exercises with the previous gifts, can build in common at the same time. For example:

Lay four times two whole cubes in an oblong before you; place perpendicularly upon them again four times two whole cubes. Over each two cubes lay two half cubes, so that they touch in the middle by their sharp edges; with the last two cubes, each of the two half cubes yet required is represented by two quarters. In the long hollow thus made sink four whole cubes. What have you made which now stands before each of you? "A house with an overhanging roof, four cubes high and two cubes broad."

What have each of you still left? "A whole cube and two cubes each divided into quarters."

Place the one whole cube by the right gable exactly in the middle of the wall.

Place one of the cubes, divided into quarters, in the same way, in the middle of the left gable wall.

Divide the quartered cube into two halves, and lay each of these halves in roof form on each of the two cubes so that the two small roofs shall slope in the same direction as the large roof. What have you now? "Two little outbuildings to the right and left of the house." "A large house with two little outbuildings, one on each side, each of the size of one cube, with an overhanging roof of a half cube." Can you, each of you, now build this alone? "Yes! yes!" Well, then, do it.

This play also gives great pleasure. This pleasure, as well as the principal characteristics of his product, can also be expressed by the child in song:

A house, a house, a house!
A house belongs to me.
A house, a house, a house!
Come here, come here and see!
In length it is four cubes,
In breadth it is two cubes;

In this house one has no fear.
Room, in grief and joy, is here
It is two cubes high;
A broad roof here I spy.
For smaller matters stand
Two houses at each hand.[22]

Other Aspects of the Curriculum

Songs, stories, and poetry, all used in the kindergarten program, were to present the ideal of good behavior. Froebel originally wrote *Mutter-und Kose-Lieder*[23] for the use of mothers in guiding their children into a life of harmony and unity. The volume contained verses, songs, pictures, mottoes, and finger and movement plays. The first verses, songs, and pictures centered on the mother as she played and talked with her child, helping him through imitation to understand his world and strengthen his fingers, arms, and legs. Ideal family relationships were presented in plays of "The Family" and "Happy Brothers and Sisters." Later, the medieval knight was used as an ideal of freedom and perfection; emphasis was always on the romantic and ideal. Although the commentaries were written for mothers they came to be regarded as important guides to kindergarten practice.

Movement plays and games were proposed, also, as a means for the child to mirror forth his inner life in objective form. The favored shape for the initiation of games was a circle for it symbolized wholeness — unity. In many games the perception of whole-part relationships was expected. Froebel pointed out: "Each member of the circle should have a chance to lead, for it is especially developing to a child to recognize himself on the one hand in his own independent activity, and on the other as the member of a well-ordered totality."[24] In one extensive lecture Froebel described in great detail a number of precise movement plays and games and their values.

Gardening provided an opportunity to watch the working of the "unseen Power." The ideal garden would have a small plot for each child and a common part with careful divisions for flowers and vegetables. In this manner the young child was expected to learn the essentials of the development of plants and also the relationship of the particular to the whole. The care of pets and walks in the countryside added informality to the program.

The goals of education became clear for they permeated all aspects of Froebel's metaphysically oriented plan; the process of education and the goal became one: it was to lead man to the inner law of Divine Unity. This was attained through nourishing good tendencies and learned through symbols.

ESTABLISHING THE KINDERGARTEN

The introduction of Froebel's educational ideas into the state schools of Germany was met with opposition. "The government," writes Brubacher, "was not mistaken in the idea that schools imbued with Froebel's pedagogy could not be contained within the existing social order but must necessarily revolutionize it."[25] For a time kindergartens were banned in Germany. Transplanted first to England and then to the United States, this "new education," as it was then called, gained rapid support. Many German students trained directly in Froebelian principles and methods came to America and were able to demonstrate the precise procedures. More importantly its idealistic base was in accord with the philosophy of a number of influential educational leaders including Henry Barnard, William T. Harris, Elizabeth Peabody, and Susan Blow.[26]

As early as 1854 Henry Barnard, who had visited a kindergarten in London, called attention to it in a report to the governor of Connecticut as "by far the most original, attractive, and philosophical form of infant development the world has yet seen."[27] At this time Barnard was secretary of the Connecticut Board of Education; later, as U.S. commissioner of education, he continued his support of the kindergarten as effective education for the young. He aided its popularization by providing a substantial literature for the movement in a volume he called *Kindergarten and Child Culture Papers*. In the "Prefatory Note" to this volume he reiterated his strong recommendation:

> Our hopes of a better popular education for our country and the world rest
> on the universal understanding and recognition in the family and the school,
> of the fundamental ideas of Froebel as the law of human development, and
> of the institutional method of both Pestalozzi and Froebel, as the surest pro-
> cess at once of mental discipline and valuable attainment.[28]

These beliefs in the efficacy of kindergarten education were seconded by
writers from Europe and America whose articles Barnard included in his
publication.

A contemporary of Barnard, Elizabeth Peabody, helped to spread
kindergartens through lecturing and writing. In a book published in 1877
with her sister, Mary Mann, Peabody wrote: "No greater benefit could
be conferred on our country, than the far and wide spread of Kindergartens, *as an underpinning*, so to say, of our noble public-school system,
giving adequate moral foundation, thoroughness, and practicality to the
national education."[29]

A later U.S. commissioner of education, William T. Harris, continually
expressed support for kindergartens. In a speech given in 1879 Harris
stated:

> The genius of Froebel has provided a system of discipline and instruction
> which is wonderfully adapted to this stage of the child's growth, when he
> needs the gentleness of nurture and the rational order of the school in due
> admixture.[30]

Harris in indicating the nature of kindergarten as "worthy of a place in
the common-school system" was well qualified to talk on the subject, as
earlier he had been the first superintendent of schools in the United States
to open a public school kindergarten. Susan Blow, another ardent follower of Froebel, had collaborated with Harris to incorporate this "new
education" into the public school system of St. Louis in 1873.

Frequent addresses were given in meetings of the National Education
Association in the 1870s and 1880s to explain the characteristics of Froebel's
program and its educational value.[31] In 1885 a separate department on
kindergarten instruction was established in the NEA to facilitate the
dissemination of ideas.

The expansion of the kindergarten movement in the United States coincided with a wave of humanitarian concern for the squalor of urban
slums, and this concern embraced the kindergarten as a means of starting
the young child on the right path in life. The kindergarten was a strong
force in liberalizing attitudes toward childhood and in fostering an acceptance of a loving benevolent nurture as a reasonable expectation for
all children.

While liberating the general thought about child nature, Froebel's program itself became excessively formal; what was creatively conceived became mechanical and dull. Despite the efforts of many followers to disseminate not only the methodology but the spirit of Froebel's program, in the hands of some kindergarten teachers the principles were lost in the specifics of daily practice. An exaltation of the sequence of gift use became a fetish. William Hailmann, in a speech chastising kindergarten teachers for allowing their work to become so routinized, called this attenuation of gift work "a certain one-sided, exclusive, and more or less pharisaical intellectualism that takes pride in wordy phrases and formulas."[32] Thus did Froebel's program become involved in a metamorphosis that has been the fate of many a program whose basic ideas were not thoroughly understood.

It was not the gradual transformation of Froebel's program into a dry husk of metaphysical symbolism that brought about its gradual diminution, but the rise of differing views concerning the nature of the child and the growth of contrasting psychological theories. Actually the changes to come in early childhood programs reflected in microcosm the vast revolution reshaping intellectual thought in America between the Civil War and World War I. Investigations in the physical and biological sciences, and, above all, the theory of evolution forced a reassessment of inherited beliefs. Education was inevitably caught up in the ferment; the kindergarten was not immune. Leaders in emerging psychological and social thought — G. Stanley Hall, John Dewey, Edward Thorndike — wrote directly to kindergarten teachers, first dissecting the misconceptions of Froebel and supplanting them with newer beliefs.

4 A Scientific Approach to Child Study

"In an age when all things are being tested and tried, and only those things which can prove their worth can survive, it is fortunate for the kindergarten that its advocates are bringing the spirit of the scientist into their work, testing kindergarten theory and practice," explained a leader in early childhood education in 1913.[1] This statement, made by Louise Alder at a meeting of the National Education Association, epitomized the vast change in thought about working with young children evident in the decades around the turn of the century. Imbedded in the new thought are profound modifications in the conception of the child, in beliefs about learning, and in basic principles for the formulation of an educational program leading to revised daily practice in the classroom. The new age described by Alder arrived only after the cherished beliefs of idealism were challenged by evolutionary thought, and the introspective psychology of an earlier age was replaced by objective methods for obtaining data. Moreover, Louise Alder's statement reveals an acceptance of new beliefs that, at the early childhood level, came about only after long, emotionally tinged debates, followed by a protracted period of curriculum reform.[2]

SWEEPING CHANGES IN AMERICAN THOUGHT

Looking at these radical advances across new frontiers we find them embracing the totality of life in America. They began slowly after the Civil War but accelerated toward the turn of the century. Henry Steele Commager has compared the decade of the 1890s to a great watershed of American history in which "the new America came in as on flood-tide."[3] It marked the end of an era and the beginning of a new one, not only economically and politically but intellectually and psychologically. This period saw an acceleration of the move from an agrarian society to one that became predominantly urban and industrial, experiencing profound changes in population, social institutions, economy, and technology. It was an America still in the making, a nation becoming more

46

conscious of its unique character and destiny, still permeated with optimism, with confidence in the infinite possibilities of human development.

The adjustments Americans faced, however, in this watershed period were not only to new social and technological ways of life but to challenges to their basic philosophical assumptions. Previously conforming, intellectually at least, to the religious and moral principles inherited from the seventeenth and eighteenth centuries, society was now confronted with shattering scientific and philosophical precepts. Charles Darwin's *The Origin of Species*, the culmination of a trend of thought long developing, set this ferment into motion.[4] The principles of natural selection and the transmutation of species marshalled overwhelming evidence against the belief of fixed species. Darwin's book lessened faith in a fixed and knowable truth and put in its place thoughts of change, adaptation, development, and survival. Ultimately Darwin's concept of organic evolution tended to break down the wall between the animal kingdom and man, which then opened the whole arena of animal learning as a suitable area of study for a psychologist.[5] Eminently significant was the reversal of means for obtaining knowledge from the intuitive discernment of the innermost logic of things to a faith in scientific observation. Perry Miller highlighted the impact of new methodology when he wrote: "Within a few years — or even months — after *The Origin of Species* shattered Victorian complacency, acute minds began to see that the least of its revolutionary meanings was its substantial denial of fixed species, or even its implied discrediting of Christian morality; what struck them was its unprecedented method of investigation."[6]

The ferment of new ideas made this a particularly fruitful period for science, psychology, philosophy, and education. An extraordinary succession of seminal publications appeared: G. Stanley Hall's *The Contents of Children's Minds* (1883), Edward L. Thorndike's *Animal Intelligence* (1898), John Dewey's *The School and Society* (1899). These were the leaders in psychology and philosophy whose impact was felt rapidly in early childhood education. A new kindergarten curriculum becoming well established by the mid-1920s reflected the power of new ideas to transform educational practice.

Out of the new thought and emphasis on direct observation for the collection of data came a strong desire to make psychology and education scientific. Developments took a number of forms. Child study in the observational mode was initiated by G. Stanley Hall, continued by Arnold Gesell, and extended in many centers established for this purpose in colleges and universities. Laws of learning were proposed as a result of the continuous observation of behavior by Edward L. Thorndike and others. The scientists' use of measuring techniques was applied to education in all areas of human growth and learning. Always the desire was for objectivity with the conviction that the road to improved education would be built in this way. The work of G. Stanley Hall was among the first to influence early childhood education.

THE PSYCHOLOGY OF G. STANLEY HALL

By utilizing objective, observational techniques G. Stanley Hall expected to give "a new scientific character to education."[7] Child study was at the very heart of psychology, which he believed should be considered genetically and this would have an immediate bearing on the work of the school. The "true needs" of the pupil would be revealed through direct study of the child in naturalistic settings. When he became president of Clark University in 1888, Hall provided a center for child study where he sought to awaken students to the exciting and fruitful possibilities within the field of genetic psychology.[8]

Early childhood educators — still the leaders in the kindergarten movement — were drawn to Hall's work very rapidly. First, he had criticized Froebel's principles by ridiculing the symbolic aspects and urging more attention to the child's physical health: "I would like to see organized a work of rescue to deliver the modern kindergarten from the metaphysicians, and to give it over to the philosophical hygienists, who should make it everywhere and first of all a place of health."[9] The gifts and occupations tended to overwork children and "lay too great stress on sedentary activities and the finer and late developed accessary muscles."[10] To replace the void created by tearing away Froebelian practices Hall proposed the data of child study. Kindergarten teachers needed to know the growth rate of the child, his spontaneous play and games, the development of language, powers of control, and imagination.

Hall enlisted the cooperation of four kindergarten teachers in Boston to gather information for one of his early surveys. He provided the teachers with a questionnaire as a basis for probing the children's concepts of nature, numbers, and religion. The data provided in this way formed the basis for Hall's first major contribution to receive widespread notice, "The Contents of Children's Minds."[11] The conclusion drawn from the data by Hall was mild enough: he simply proposed that with the advent of urbanization children now coming to public schools had knowledge dissimilar to those with an agrarian background. City children were unable to explain the origins of milk and butter; the school should acquaint the child with needed information. Thus did Hall proclaim early one of his major theses: the data of child development should provide the content of the curriculum.

When Clark University became the center for child study, the pioneer institution in this aspect of psychology, early childhood educators travelled to be present at summer conferences. Patty Smith Hill, Anna Bryan, Alice Putnam, and Jenny B. Merrill, searching for more fundamental knowledge about the child on which to base a new kindergarten program, attended the summer sessions in 1895 and 1896.[12] Child study seemed a realization of their hope that they could base education on the nature of the child as Froebel had recommended, only now it would rest not upon an intuitive recognition but upon scientific observation. Hall, himself, believed that Froebel would have rejoiced in the development of a child study movement.[13] Among the men and women enthusiastic about the new "science" who flocked to Clark University in the 1890s were those who would advance in an even more scientific way the studies already begun — Lewis Terman and Arnold Gesell.

In preparing for a career in psychology Hall had come under the dominant interests of the day. In 1878 he received the first American degree in psychology at Harvard, where he had the opportunity to study with William James who was applying the doctrines of evolution to the phenomena of mind.[14] He went on to work with Wilhelm Wundt and other German scientists at Leipzig. Thus Hall had direct experience with leaders working within the major strands of developing thought. Edwin Boring has noted that two main streams converged to form American psychology: one was German, including the work of Wundt; the other English, drawing from Darwin and Herbert Spencer.[15] Hall borrowed selectively and ended up proclaiming a psychological position clearly his own and designed for education in America as he found it.

"There is no question of Hall's extraordinary ability: he was an inspired speaker, an incomparable organizer, and an indefatigable author and editor," wrote Lawrence Cremin.[16] Hall's abilities at organizing and writing were more evident in his child study publications than in his systematic, scientific work. While he demonstrated a keen eye for detail and a sympathy for, and understanding of, children, he spent little time in diligently collecting observational data himself. Typically, he selected a general pattern of behavior — fear, anger, crying, laughing, types of play — and recruited a number of enthusiastic disciples to gather the evidence. The questionnaire as a technique for studying development was eminently suited to this method of observation and Hall was committed to it. More than one hundred questionnaire studies, all relating to his particular interests concerning child growth, were produced at Clark University during Hall's tenure there. One was a study of dolls as one of the chief toys of childhood.[17] From 648 returns of questionnaires sent to 800 teachers and parents his colleague, Ellis, tabulated and digested the observations. Hall examined in detail child preferences in dolls, the intensity of the relationships established, and concluded that the educational values of doll play were enormous.

Besides providing Hall with an observational method, Darwinism supplied Hall with the basis for a theory of psychic recapitulation: ontogeny, or the development of the individual, recapitulates phylogeny, the evolution of the race. As Hall explained it, the child in his development retraced the cultural evolution of mankind. The basic assumption was that the psychic life and behavior of the individual developed in a series of stages through which the race had passed. Specifically, the young child's stage of development was analogous to the hunting, the cave, and the building periods of ancient cultural evolution. The normal course of the mind, Hall explained, required living through each stage thoroughly. "Let them play their lies of fancy and imagination," he told teachers of the young. "That is play — the play of the mind."[18] He recommended a free play program in which children had contact with many materials — sand, mud, clay — that they could use freely, as well as all kinds of animate life.

The stages Hall delineated, extending through adolescence (an area of psychological investigation he eventually created), were the only supportable basis for building an educational program, in his opinion. In one of his most influential addresses to the National Education Assocation, Hall, in 1901, put forth his version of the child-centered school. After protesting that no such ideal school existed, Hall suggested certain principles of respect for the child.

> Beginning with the deep philosophy often embedded in words, "school," or "schole," means leisure, exemption from work, the perpetuation of the primeval paradise created long before the struggle for existence began. It stands for the prolongation of human infancy, and the no whit less important prolongation of adolescence. It is sacred to health, growth, and heredity, a pound of which is worth a ton of instruction. The guardians of the young should strive first of all to keep out of nature's way, and to prevent harm, and should merit the proud title of defenders of the happiness and rights of children. They should feel profoundly that childhood, as it comes fresh from the hand of God, is not corrupt, but illustrates the survival of the most consummate thing in the world; they should be convinced that there is nothing else so worthy of love, reverence, and service as the body and soul of the growing child.
>
> Practically, this means that every invasion of this leisure, the provision of a right measure of which is our first duty to youth, has a certain presumption against it, and must justify itself by conclusive reasons. Before we let

the pedagogue loose upon childhood, not only must each topic in his curriculum give an account of itself, but his inroads must be justified in the case of each child. We must overcome the fetichism of the alphabet, of the multiplication table, of grammars, of scales, and of bibliolatry, and must reflect that but a few generations ago the ancestors of all of us were illiterate; that the invention of Cadmus seemed the sowing of veritable dragon's teeth in the brain; that Charlemagne and many other great men of the world could not read or write; that scholars have argued that Cornelia, Ophelia, Beatrice, and even the blessed mother of our Lord knew nothing of letters. The knights, the élite leaders of the Middle Ages, deemed writing a mere clerk's trick beneath the attention of all those who scorned to muddle their wits with others' ideas, feeling that their own were good enough for them.[19]

General pronouncements on "health, growth and heredity" were followed by the educational reforms needed from kindergarten through the high school.

The kindergarten age is from two or three to six or seven. Here, before the ideal school can be inaugurated, we need some work of rescue from the symbolists. Now the body needs most attention, and the soul least. The child needs more mother, and less teacher; more of the educated nurse, and less of the metaphysician. We must largely eliminate, and partly reconstruct, the mother-plays, while transforming and vastly enlarging the repertory of the gifts and occupations. We must develop the ideal nursery, playgrounds, and rooms, where light, air, and water are at their best. The influences of the new hygiene have been felt least here, where they are needed most. The neglect of these basal principles suggest that we have still among us those whose practice implies a belief that any old place is good enough to hatch out beautiful souls, provided only Froebelian orthodoxy of doctrine and method is steadfastly maintained. In place of a magic mongering with them, the cubes, spheres, cylinder, and also the top, soap-bubble, doll, dances, marches, circus, and scores of other free plays and games; and in place of two or three fish, insects, animals, plants, several score must be provided, and a museum and *catalogue raisonné* of toys must be at hand. Eating bread, milk, fruit, with some simple table manners, and using paper napkins, sometimes do wonders for these human larvae. Feeding brightens the mind and saves the disposition; a full stomach opens the mouth, and good courses of lessons could be derived from the viands themselves. . . .

Teachers should study every child, not necessarily by any of the current technical methods. They should learn far more than they can teach, and in place of the shallow mannikin child of books they should see, know, and love only the real thing. After this metempsychosis, the kindergarten should be, and should become, an integral part of every school system.[20]

These recommendations, pointed directly at kindergarten teachers, were followed by other suggestions to the guardians of children in subsequent stages. During the transition period at seven or eight years of age, work and strain needed to be reduced; from eight to twelve or thirteen, child nature suggested that it was a period amenable to drill, habituation, and mechanics; in adolescence, feelings and emotions were in the ascendence. The ideal school would deal with each separate stage of development according to the demands of the precise characteristics revealed.

Evaluation of Hall's Doctrines

In one sense the doctrine of evolutionary development, which Hall espoused with such enthusiasm, was an optimistic concept. As popularly interpreted it fit well with the dominant mode of Americans who had faith in progress and in the future; evolution not only supported the idea of progress but gave it scientific standing. That everything good and great in the world sprang out of the increasingly improving depths of human nature confirmed faith and buttressed hope. All this appealed greatly to the strong spirit of romanticism with which Hall was embued in his youthful years and which led him to emphasize the feeling side of his life.[21] While Hall was part scientific psychologist, there was also a strong element of mysticism in his writings not found in the work of subsequent psychologists calling themselves scientific.

Doubts about the validity of the scheme of recapitulation appeared early, but Hall's discussions had impressed upon both psychologists and educators the idea that children progress through specific, identifiable stages. This, together with the belief that heredity was a strong determining factor, stressed a large predetermined force in human development. Actually, in Hall's conception of development, heredity was a stronger determining factor than environment. This fundamental position, more evident in the work of those who followed in child study research, did not ultimately provide a hopeful foundation for education. Indeed, Hall accepted eugenics as a long-term remedy for society. In the meantime education had a role to play in following the natural growth of the child with the school facilitating, never obstructing, the appropriate impulses and instincts of childhood.

The child study movement, once initiated, gained great impetus, thereby drawing many into the search for fundamental facts of child development by means of personal investigation. By 1893 a Child Study Department was established in the National Education Association and in 1895 reports were given from centers of study in Iowa, Minnesota, New York,

Indiana, and California. Lines of investigation included tests of sight and hearing, studies of children's drawings, and investigation to determine whether large physical development paralleled precocity; these investigations were designed to determine the physical, intellectual, and emotional characteristics evident in classroom work. The method utilized by all included observation of specific aspects of growth, careful recording and interpretation of data "by an expert," and summarization by a member of Clark University a bit later.[22]

But it was Hall's work that was referred to widely by the leaders of the kindergarten movement. His articles and speeches were constantly reprinted in contemporary journals such as the *Kindergarten Review* and the *Kindergarten Magazine*. No doubt these leaders thought less about Hall's basic premises than about his educational recommendations. Ideas directly presented to them caused them to modify practice; for example, no idea influenced them more than the pronouncement that the large fundamental muscles must be developed before the fine, accessory ones.[23] It meant, among other things, that Froebel's gifts were inappropriate for the young child who must have play materials that encouraged the use of large, fundamental muscles. Here was a problem that they could attack concretely.

While his methodology was new, Hall's emphasis on knowledge of the child as a basic factor in determining an educational program extended back to Rousseau, Pestolozzi, and Froebel, so it demanded no new recognition on the part of kindergarten leaders. It reinforced beliefs already firmly held. Hall's elevation of the importance of understanding the early years made child study a requisite for a teacher of the young. The younger the pupils, the greater the need to study them to adjust. Hall opened a discourse on kindergarten education in these words:

> The more advanced the student and the more specialized the teaching, the less pedogogy and genetic educational philosophy figure. As we go down the scale of age or of intelligence, and as the interval between the knowledge and development of the teacher on the one hand and the taught on the other increases, the proportion of method to subject matter increases.[24]

Such advice together with Hall's appreciation of the love of children he found in kindergartens cultivated strong followers.

Hall always underscored his basic theme concerning education: the curriculum should be determined by the results of child study. Schooling must be molded to fit the child, to follow "the rightness of nature." "Hall's respect for physiological development," wrote Charles Strickland and Charles Burgess, "was such that he looked to it to define the goals of the school as well as the conditions of learning."[25]

Hall appealed to all who wanted to understand and rescue the child; he was the entrepreneur and evangelist of child study. His place in the history of child psychology is secure; he initiated and raised it to a level of acceptance. His place as a scholar in the field of psychology, however, remains clouded, for fellow psychologists considered his research methods unscientific. No objective evidence could support his stance on recapitulation. However, in early childhood education Hall's influence was strong. Materials for children's use were gradually modified to conform to Hall's insistence on the priority of the large fundamental muscles for use in early childhood. More than this, he convinced kindergarten teachers that only as they learned more about the child and applied that knowledge to the curriculum could an effective program result.

ARNOLD GESELL'S AGES AND STAGES

Arnold Gesell's work belongs to the decades somewhat after the turn of the century, but his child study was grounded so clearly in some of G. Stanley Hall's fundamental beliefs that a discussion of his contributions logically follows here. As one of Hall's most influential students, Gesell obtained his Ph.D. at Clark University and then went on to earn an M.D. at Yale. At his suggestion he was given a room and some equipment for the Yale Clinic of Child Development in 1911. His work at the clinic extended over a thirty year period with his domination so complete that it was often referred to as "Gesell's clinic." His observational research work was always carefully planned, meticulously carried out, and the data accurately recorded. In data collection he incorporated a number of innovative research techniques that included use of the one-way vision screen and cinematography.[26] He and his colleagues disseminated a whole new literature of descriptive data: specialized studies of different traits and capacities of children.

The theoretical base of Gesell's work — the concept of inherent or genetic predetermination — made it, in this sense, an extension of Hall's. The more or less automatic unfoldment of behavioral organizations as a function of morphological development, Gesell called *maturation*. He used the term globally to represent the endogenous regulatory mechanisms responsible for the direction of all development and this mechanism, maturation, he considered to be fundamental and powerful. In emphasizing the innate processes of growth he wrote to parents and teachers: "The total ground plan is beyond your control. It is too complex and mysterious to be altogether entrusted to human hands. So nature takes over most of the task, and simply invites your assistance."[27] Thus strength was given to the belief of individual potential as fixed at birth.

In *A Handbook of Child Psychology*, edited by Carl Murchison, Gesell's lengthy chapter explained maturation. While he admitted it to be a somewhat imprecise term, he advanced it as "a useful aid both to experimental investigation and theoretical interpretation," as well as helpful to offset the "extravagant claims which have been made for processes of conditioning and of habit formation."[28] Here Gesell defined maturation:

> The term maturation also is equally applicable to mental and physical phenomena. Maturation is the intrinsic component of development (or of growth) which determines the primary morphogenesis and variabilities of the life-cycle. Although the word *growth* is sometimes loosely used as synonymous with maturation, the former is the more comprehensive term including all the developmental differentiations of the organism in response to external as well as internal environments.[29]

While "growth" included the constitution and conditions of the organism it also recognized factors of environment or of training and Gesell recognized this reciprocal relationship. But this recognition did not reduce his strong stand on the importance of internal factors. Here Gesell states his position:

> Accordingly there is a very reciprocal interrelationship between heredity and environment. The intimacy of this relationship may not, however, prevent us from ascribing a priority and possibly even some preponderance to heredity factors in the patterning of human behavior. Although it is a truism, it should be emphasized that no environment as such has the capacity of growth. Environmental factors support, inflect, and modify, but do not generate the progressions of development. Growth as an impulsion and as a cycle of events is uniquely a character of the living organism and neither physical nor social environment contains any architectonic arrangements even analogous to the mechanism of growth.

THE GROWTH CYCLE AND GENES

And where does this growth cycle of events have its source? We shall briefly consider some of the biological facts which underlie the development of the human embryo; because the role and the manner of maturation in the shaping of the individual are foreshadowed in the earliest genetic stages. . . .

Are these genes more than a hypothetical formula? They are realities. They are too small actually to be seen by the ultramicroscope; but by experimental methods as many as fifty have been identified in one chromosome of the fruit fly. Maps have even been drawn up showing the relative positions of such genes in the chromosome. Estimating the number of genes through the mutations produced by X-rays in thousands of flys, the total number in one cell is said to be not less than 14,380. The size of a single gene measures about one-quintillionth of a cubic centimeter, or the equivalent in volume of fifteen protein molecules.

In these myriad genes we have an ample basis for the operation of maturational processes throughout the whole life-span of the individual, including infancy. The genes should not be thought of as little eugenic packets which determine hereditary characteristics prior to birth. They should be thought of as the biochemical agencies which constantly participate in the complex physiology of both prenatal and postnatal development.[30]

With his thesis plainly stated, it remained only for Gesell to collect data revealing the effects of maturation in children. It was on the basic patterns of growth, for which maturation provided "the stabilizing and inexpungable factors," that Gesell concentrated in collecting observational data. With developmental sequences regarded as relatively invariable, age became a significant dimension. Age was the convenient line along which the orderliness of development could be readily shown. Norms of growth answered the scientist's call for qualitative precision; they also gave the educators a way of looking to a child within a group.

Through observational studies in laboratory settings Gesell and his followers charted the pattern of growth in innumerable areas of human development. These were presented as gradients of growth, "a series of stages or degrees of maturity by which a child progresses toward a higher level of behavior."[31] Growth gradients were developed to include all aspects of growth — physical, emotional, mental — as well as school skills. Some examples will exemplify Gesell's work. The exact detailed nature of each piece of research is illustrated in the normative studies of pellet prehension that revealed a lawful progression of visual-manual behavior.

The following normative synopsis covers twelve lunar-month periods beginning at eight weeks:

  8 weeks: no visual regard for pellet
12 weeks: transient regard for pellet (rarely)
16 weeks: more prolonged regard, usually delayed
20 weeks: immediate, definite regard, sometimes with increased hand-arm activity
24 weeks: approaches pellet with pronate hand; contacts pellet with little or no finger adjustment

28 weeks: approaches pellet with raking flexion of fingers, without thumb opposition; occasional delayed palmar prehension

32 weeks: approaches pellet with raking flexion but with increased thumb participation and digital prehension

36 weeks: approaches and contacts with simultaneous flexion of fingers; prehends with defined thumb and index opposition

40 weeks: approaches with all fingers extended; contacts with index finger and later prehends by drawing index finger against thumb

44 weeks: promptly prehends with index and thumb and with increased obliquity of hand attitude

48 weeks: approaches with index finger extended and lateral digits flexed; prehends with delimited plucking by index and thumb

52 weeks: approaches and plucks pincerwise with increased deftness

If the foregoing table is studied in perspective it shows that the development of eye-hand behavior in the infant does not consist so much in an increase in skill as in a progressive differentiation of the mechanical form of behavior. To be sure, there is a trend toward economy of movement; but this is not an end-result of practice but an alteration in the very pattern of response. The developmental reorganization of this pattern is outwardly a morphological phenomenon primarily correlated with changes in the inner morphology of the nervous system, and secondarily with changes in ligaments, joints, and musculature. Howsoever environment may inflect and condition the expression of the visual-motor functions, the mechanics of the behavior and the basic form of the patterns are primarily the product of maturational factors.[32]

To further explain this behavior Gesell stressed that each present growth hinged on past growth. Each new behavior grew out of the old and retained a connection with the old.

School skills were also considered to be subject to the principle of developmental readiness. Reduced to simple terms the growth gradient for reading behavior showed the following pattern.

READING BEHAVIOR

1)	15 months	Pats identified picture in book.
2)	18 months	Points to an identified picture in book.
3)	2 years	Names 3 pictures in book.
4)	3 years	Identifies 4 printed geometric forms.
5)	4 years	Recognizes salient capital letters.
6)	5–6 years	Recognizes salient printed words.[33]

For Gesell, the ages assigned to the stages in gradients represented normative trends and were subject to variations with respect to age values.

Over and over again in his writings Gesell pointed to the necessary differences in individuals. "Considerateness" was a term he used to indicate a perceptiveness that would enable a person to appreciate the differences of another. It was designated as "an alert liberalism which is sensitive to distinctive characteristics in other individuals";[34] all children were entitled to this courtesy. To understand individuality, however, the underlying processes needed to be understood; it was through norms that variations were revealed. He emphasized the individual nature of growth when he wrote: "We know that every child is an individual and that he travels at his own tailor-made schedule."[35] Yet his interest in individuality was obscured by the appeal of norms, which were popularized in a number of ways. A series of films characterizing particular ages (for example, "Terrible Twos and Trusting Threes," "Frustrating Fours and Fascinating Fives") were widely used in teacher training. Although made by an Ontario-based film producer for the National Film Board of Canada, they so epitomized the normative concept as to seem an extension of the work of the Yale clinic.

READINESS FOR LEARNING

Growth gradients had a significant usefulness for the psychologist, parent, and educator, for according to Gesell: "a) they define the developmental traits characteristic of childhood in general; b) they enable us to determine in an individual child the attained levels of maturity for these traits."[36] Used as frames of reference growth gradients could locate a child's stage of development. Educational and guidance measures could then estimate the developmental ground a child had already attained and the ground that still needed to be achieved. "Failure to interpret his maturity status," wrote Gesell, "leads to wasted effort, to harmful interference and unjust discipline."[37] Thus, the educational postulate coinciding with maturation was readiness, the belief in a most propitious time for a new experience, an optimal period in which training could be most effective. Training, before the neural mechanisms were ready, was not only futile but conducive to frustration, so adults were admonished to wait for maturation before planning specific activities.

To Gesell, his work and basic reasoning formed the legitimate basis on which educational programs should be built. In warning against a curriculum attempting to mold the child in many directions he wrote:

> Parents and teachers who think that the child is so plastic that he can be
> made over by strenuous outside pressure, have failed to grasp the true na-

ture of mind. The child may be likened to a plant, but not to clay. For clay does not grow. Clay is moulded entirely from without. A plant is moulded entirely from within through the forces of growth. . . .

Intelligent guidance begins with the concept of growth. To understand a child whether in infancy or in the school years, one must become acquainted with the gradients of growth which determine the trends and patterning of his behavior.[38]

Psychologists designate Gesell as a man out of step with his time, stating that in psychology it was a time uncongenial to the notion that the major dimensions of a child's growth were determined by automatic unfolding.[39] There were supporting trends, however. Early studies of embryology, referred to in Gesell's writings, reinforced predeterminism. So did the laws of genetics proposed at that period. The measurement movement, as we shall see, employed a scale idea built on a series of graded problems. But probably the major reason early childhood specialists turned so whole-heartedly to Gesell's normative data was its coincidence with their basic framework of thinking. The analogy of development to the growth of a plant, so familiar to early childhood educators by now, made it easy for them to think of the child's growth patterns as gradually unfolding; Gesell's work gave them the satisfaction of operating within the realm of scientific thought. They began talking in the same developmental terms and espousing the necessity of readiness for learning. It seemed obvious to them that there was an optimum period in which learning experiences would be the most effective.

Gesell addressed early childhood educators in their professional journals to reinforce their commitment to the child's early years. "The very word pre-school," he wrote in 1925, "is new. . . . We shall soon be writing it and printing it without a hyphen."[40] Gesell could write about preschool education for children from the ages of two to six, for at the time of this article nursery schools embracing the concept of nurture for very young children were gaining momentum in the United States. According to one U.S. Office of Education bulletin, nursery schools increased from 3 to 262 in the decade between 1920 and 1930.[41] Gesell lauded this downward extension of kindergarten as a dynamic conception of education in which actual practice could be "a policy of developmental supervision."[42] This he wrote in an article in *Childhood Education,* the official journal established by the organization then called the International Kindergarten Union and which later became the Association for Childhood Education International. Such a journal Gesell welcomed as a means of giving prominence to the problems and trends in the field of preschool education. Gesell wrote frequently for *Childhood Education,* describing the work of the child study clinic at Yale and the normative charting of behavior in areas of motor development, language, adaptive behavior, and personal habits.[43]

Maturation and readiness were terms permeating the literature of early childhood education in the 1930s, 1940s, and 1950s. A normative view of a five-year-old child was presented to teachers in the opening chapters of books on kindergarten education. In one chapter about the five-year-old the authors state: "Before we consider what kind of experience to provide the child of five, it may be well to review what is known of his development and his abilities."[44] They continued by describing the five-year-old's physical development, motor abilities, language, interests, emotions, social development, and imagination. Most of these statements depicted traits easily charted through observation. A picture of an "average" child was presented to the teacher so that he or she could plan a program appropriate for the children's stage of development. As late as 1959 Ilse Forest, with a long historical view of kindergarten, stressed a program supported by concepts of maturation and readiness. In addressing schoolmen with an interest in young children she reminded them that the research of Gesell and others had underscored the fact that in the achievement of any skill "the development of structure must precede the development of function."[45] Any program of readiness by necessity must relate to knowledge of child growth. "The task of child care," she summarized, "is not to mould the child behavioristically to some predetermined image, but to assist him step by step, guiding his growth."[46]

INFLUENCE OF THE NORMATIVE VIEW

Research other than that of Gesell contributed to the normative view of the child. Reports of norms on physical, motor, social, and mental growth were produced in many new centers established in various universities across the country. The Iowa Child Welfare Research Station, which opened in 1917, was followed by others such as the Child Welfare Institute at Teachers College, Columbia University (1924) and a similar institute at the University of California (1927). Thus, the interest on child development initiated in the 1890s expanded with the foremost principle a devotion to scientific research. Hundreds of children — mostly from university settings — were studied and growth curves charted. Through the 1950s the research was dominated by the assumption that growth proceeds from within.[47]

Professional advancement of the field of child development was given an added impetus during the 1920s when a foundation, The Laura Spelman Rockefeller Memorial, guided by Beardsley Ruml and Lawrence K. Frank, furnished funding for research. The establishment of the Society for Research in Child Development in 1933 helped to disseminate new findings. The collection of information was accompanied by a commitment to make it available to teachers. This was the prime purpose of the Institute for Child Study started at the University of Maryland in 1947.

Child study has continued unabated but the premises upon which Hall and Gesell built their research have come under strong attack both for the way in which data were used and for fallacies in the basic beliefs that have become evident. The manner in which Gesell's data were presented tended to deny his frequent recognition of individual differences. What was intended to present a central tendency among the children studied was equated with average or "normal" behavior, so that parents and teachers looked askance at the child who lagged behind the norm. Of course, by the very means for determining a norm some children would obtain the behavior at an earlier age, some later.

Furthermore, Gesell used in his studies the children readily available to the Yale Clinic of Child Development; these were the children of students and professors. Norms derived from this population of children were generalized to all children, evidencing a complete disregard for environmental influence. This was the blinder erected by such faith in development as inherently or genetically predetermined.[48] The belief in automatic unfolding, or maturation, led in many instances to a neglectful attitude toward certain children; in the interest of not pushing a child, of recognizing the limits set by the genes and maturational aspects, a hands-off attitude was encouraged. Although the fallacies of this point of view may seem readily evident today, it has been a pervasive influence on child study and education. Hunt estimates that for over a half century both child study investigation and educational practice have been "dominated by the assumptions of fixed intelligence and predetermined development."[49] But we shall see other theoretical positions gradually gaining force and affecting child study.

5 The Search for a Science of Education

In 1923 an exceedingly influential book about kindergarten education was published, outlining a reconstructed curriculum as the culmination of many years of study and experimentation. The introduction contained a description of the step-by-step application of new guiding ideas as they were utilized with children. In the experimentation, initiated at the Speyer School in New York City in 1905, the rigid formalism of the Froebelian kindergarten was loosened and children were given the freedom to follow some of their own purposes and to learn from each other. Patty Smith Hill, the author of the description, considered the Speyer School experiment one of the earliest attempts to apply the principles of democracy to school organization. She wrote: "Not only the teachers who participated, but the majority of those who observed consecutively, were convinced that a social organization based on wisely directed liberty was the only medium in which the habits of self-direction and social cooperation could be established. In this way the school served as a laboratory of democracy, in which the technique of democratic citizenship would be gradually acquired."[1]

Ten years later the experimentation was followed up at Horace Mann School, the laboratory school for Teachers College, Columbia University, where Patty Smith Hill, from her strategic position as head of the kindergarten-primary department, wielded a strong influence on the changing kindergarten curriculum. This was a time when such notables as John Dewey, William Kilpatrick, and Edward L. Thorndike were also members of the Teachers College faculty. We shall see that the classroom as an "embryonic community" for learning democratic social responsibility was a fundamental premise of Dewey's educational plan. But as the experimentation continued at Horace Mann School it became modified in a way that brought it closer to Thorndike's emphasis on the formation of habits and the need to measure change of behavior. The curriculum reconstruction came first from the desire to convince "conservative pedagogical minds" that the democratic social organization of the classroom was neither radical nor wasteful. Experimenters developed a record sheet for the recording of children's progress. When psychologists told them that the categories being used for observation were not sufficiently objective for measurement, they sought help in breaking down the captions into the more specific abilities and habits involved. The resultant Habit Inventory was used to gradually transform the curriculum by applying the principles of habit formation to all school experiences. In the 1923 publication, which presented a new curriculum, appropriate activities were listed in one column with a parallel column listing the desired change in thought, feeling, and conduct. "As this inventory was used," wrote Miss Hill, "the observers noted, not only the obvious improvement and acceleration of habit-formation with children, but also that the supervisors and classroom teachers began to think of all instruction in terms of desirable changes in thought, feeling, or conduct; in other words, in terms of changed behavior due to a changed nervous system."[2]

Specificity of goals, habit formation, situations to elicit appropriate behavior, connections in the nervous system: these were the terms Thorndike was using to explain learning in a behavioral context. It was a conception of learning radically different from that of Froebel. Instead of a mystical introspective view of the child, Thorndike emphasized objective data; instead of considering growth as unfolding, Thorndike viewed the child as simply a mass of "original tendencies" to be exploited for good or bad. Let us turn to these ideas, very revolutionary at that time, and see how they had developed.

EDWARD L. THORNDIKE AND CONNECTIONISM

Thorndike's ultimate goal was a science of education on which all teaching could be based. In his straightforward approach to the problems of education he proclaimed: "A true science of education must be inductive, must be made up from the study of particular facts in answer to thousands of different questions."[3] During his long career, spanning forty years, Thorndike attacked a multitude of psychological questions by gathering objective, verifiable data from which he drew laws of learning. Objectivity was the key; induction from the data was the method. Detailed experimentation, intricate quantitative treatment of results, and subtlety of analysis were abilities in which Thorndike excelled. William James considered Thorndike, more than any of his other students, to have the quality most essential to a scientific man: the ability to see things apart from acquired perspective and personal reference.[4]

Although he was the prototype of the successful applier of scientific methods to educational problems, Thorndike can hardly be credited with beginning the science of education movement. The origins are complex and rooted in the comprehensive changes in American intellectual life around the turn of the century, and nowhere was the impact of new scientific thought more revolutionary than in the psychology of learning. As late as 1870 men of knowledge regarded the human mind much as it had been viewed for centuries. The human mind was considered to set man off from other creatures and, if it existed parallel to corresponding bodily activities, it was still a separate entity. The accepted method of study of the mind was introspection. William T. Harris, a noted educator of the period and a firm supporter of kindergarten, defined introspective psychology as the study of mental phenomena perceived "in one's self and inferred to exist in others."[5] This was the leading method of this time.

While traditional views of mind were, in the 1870s, prevalent in the United States, Wilhelm Max Wundt at Leipzig was employing an objective technique for studying mental life. Wundt carried out experiments in order to understand and measure sense perceptions in scientific terms. He had a number of American students and of these Curti has written: "While no one can dispute the contribution of Wundt's American disciples in establishing objective techniques for the study of mind and divorcing mental phenomena from teleological and supernatural characteristics, the same end was even more strikingly promoted by the gifted pioneers working within the Darwinian scheme of things."[6] Darwin's publications seemed to provide striking evidence that man achieved his intellectual as well as his bodily nature as a product of interactive experience in a physical and social environment. Thus, mind, or behavior, as the new psychologists preferred to call it to divorce it from any metaphysical aspects, could be viewed as a product of long growth and as having a natural rather than miraculous history. The concept that growth, change, and interaction were inherent in a world of nature, which encompassed man as well as all other aspects of the physical and animal world, was a radical idea that transformed psychology into a natural science. It led to a psychological orientation that viewed behavior as part of nature to be studied through observation and understood in relation to other phenomena and to their own evolutionary past.

A growing number of scientists in various parts of the world began to make careful observations and measurements of the way the human organism behaved under controlled conditions. Ivan Pavlov in Russia built a theory of conditioning as a principal aspect of learning on the basis of his study of animals; Francis Galton in England focused upon hereditary factors in genetics; Alfred Binet in France studied memory, attention, and intelligence in children to arrive at a conception of "normal mental age." A whole generation of American psychologists threw themselves into the task of building educational psychology on an objective basis; among these were William James, Lewis Terman, James McKeen Cattell, and, of course, Thorndike.

James, as a real pioneer in developing the evolutionary conception of the human mind, wrote of man as a biological organism whose behavior was built upon certain innate tendencies to react. As a result of the repetition of acts, habits emerged, which increasingly governed behavior. In his *Talks to Teachers on Psychology*, James declared the purpose of education to be organizing the child's conduct so as to fit him for his school environment,[7] a condition that demanded the inculcation of the right habits of action at an early age. James was expansive when he thought about habits: "Sow an action, and you reap a habit; sow a habit, and you reap a character; sow a character, and you reap a destiny."[8] Meanwhile his pupil, Edward Thorndike, was carrying out experiments on animal learning that gave support to James's conception of learning.

The revolutionary nature of Thorndike's experimentation is revealed by the fact that Harvard refused him space to investigate the instinctive behavior of chickens at the university. So it was in the basement of the James's home in Cambridge that Thorndike observed the behavior of animals placed in a problem box. The process by which the animal responses became increasingly more efficient and economical Thorndike called learning, and as a result of his experimentation he formulated laws of learning that had a vast influence on American education. Undergirding the laws was the assumption that human learning proceeds in essentially the same manner as animal learning, an assumption deemed unacceptable before the formulation of evolutionary doctrine. Curti clearly states this aspect of Thorndike's theory: "the evolution of mind from man to animal has no essential breaks; thinking or human self-consciousness and self-control are really secondary results of the tremendous increase in the number, quality, and complexity of associations or bonds which the human animal has acquired by virtue of the greater fineness of his neural organization."[9] The term *mind* for Thorndike, then, referred not to a distinct organ nor an entity with extra psychic existence, but to "the sum total of connections between the situations which life offers and the responses which the man makes."[10]

Laws of Learning

Based on this proposition Thorndike explained learning as a process wherein a specific response was allied to a specific stimulus by a physiological bond in the neural system. This description of the way in which a sense organ may be stimulated so that a "message" tours the circuit and produces a response of muscle or gland utilizes the reflex arc concept long used in biology.[11] Sensations and ideas are built up as connections are established by the reflex arc between a situation S and a response R. Such was the fundamental premise on which Thorndike enunciated laws of learning that governed the forming of neural bonds. The law most central to the process of learning was the law of effect wherein a response is strengthened if followed by a pleasurable effect and weakened if followed by an unpleasant effect. A connection is learned better when satisfaction is the result, but annoyance or pain will tend to prevent learning. Thorndike gave equal weight to both types of outcomes: success or failure, reward or punishment, satisfaction or annoyance to the learner.[12] The law of exercise held that the more frequently a stimulus-induced response is repeated, the longer it will be retained. The third primary law referred to readiness and assumed that, because of the structure of the nervous system, in a given situation certain conduction units (or neurons) were more predisposed to conduct than others. In this situation, to put the action system into operation would bring satisfaction, not to act would bring annoyance.

Thorndike's readiness referred not to the law about growth — the child's reaching a certain maturity level — already discussed; rather, it pertained to a law of preparatory adjustment. Actually it may be considered "an accessory principle which describes a physiological substration for the law of effect."[13] Readiness, for Thorndike, was an action tendency aroused through preparatory adjustments, sets, or attitudes so that fulfillment of the tendency was satisfying, nonfulfillment was annoying. Of Thorndike, Hilgard states that "it would be historically inaccurate to construe his law of readiness as an anticipation of maturational readiness," even though there is "a logical relationship between the two kinds of readiness, because interests and motives mature along with capacities."[14] Different though they may be, the two kinds of readiness probably were joined in the thoughts of early childhood educators and in the vast literature on the readiness that developed in the 1930s and 1940s.

Laws of learning were meant to govern educational practice and Thorndike stated his major position succinctly: "Put together what you wish to put together. Reward good impulses. Conversely: keep apart what you wish to have separate. Let undesirable impulses bring discomfort."[15] Thus, connectionism, as his conception of learning came to be called, presented a view of the child as modifiable. Someone had to be the modifier and the teacher was given the responsibility and power to select the connections to be established and to set the stage for fixing responses. From this position came the description of the learner as a passive organism in the learning process. "The child would be apt to be overlooked as the result of such a procedure, in the eyes of some critics, since by insisting on the analytic and neglecting the synthetic aspects of learning, it would put a premium on skills and habits and come near to denying purposive behavior," explained Curti.[16]

Habit Formation in the Kindergarten

Very early in his career Thorndike's wide-ranging concern for problems, psychological and educational, included the kindergarten. In "Notes on Psychology for Kindergartners"[17] Thorndike presented to the leaders and teachers of the kindergarten movement a discussion of the use of children's natural tendencies for the development of habits and the laws that governed their formation. As he was writing at the turn of the century, much in this thirty-page article was intended to counteract the Froebelian emphasis so prevalent. Thorndike considered physical health to be the prime need in caring for children, for intellectual and moral life depended upon it. The needs of children might vary so drastically that Thorndike wrote: "One can well conceive of a set of children whose teacher might choose as the first gift, a toothbrush, and as the first occupation, sleep."[18] Instead of children sitting around tables or in a circle, seating should be arranged so that the light would come to all children from the side. Purely physical play such as running, jumping, climbing, digging, and paddling were needed to counterbalance all indoor school work or play.

Then Thorndike stated his main hypothesis:

> The psychology of habit is fairly recognized in educational practice in the case of those customary activities which we call behavior, but its fundamental importance throughout the life of ideas and ideals is neglected. The truth is that a human life is a bundle of habits; that what we mean by knowledge is habits of sequence amongst ideas; that what we mean by capacity is the possibility of forming a certain set of habits not actually functioning; that what we mean by interest is a habit not of execution but of intellectual or moral regard. The function of the mind is to form connections between impressions and our responses to them, and the phrase, "habits of thought and action," as used in psychological literature is simply a name for these connections.
>
> The practical import of this is simple enough. It is, in short, that unless we measure our educational work in terms of actual habits formed, we are likely to deceive ourselves with vain hopes of mysterious transformations in the "soul" or "personality" or "development" or "growth" or "spiritual nature." A transformation in the soul or personality, if real, is a change in the ways it acts. A change in development or growth in the mind is a change in its responses to things and people and its own ideas. A change

in spiritual nature, if real, is a change in the habits of thought and action toward the broadest issues of life and the unseen things of God. There is in fact no greater step forward to be made by the teacher or educational leader than to adopt the custom of working directly for concrete habits and measuring his success by their attainment. It must be remembered, of course, that the most obvious habits are not necessarily the most important; that a new gleam in the eye, a new tone of the voice, a new vigor in intellectual work, may in the long run mean more for the cultivation of habits as a whole than some far more striking accomplishment.

The leaders of the kindergarten system who are eager for its introduction as a recognized division of public education everywhere will silence the majority of criticisms and answer the decisive question in the minds of most school officers, if they will present a list of worthy habits, the establishment of which by properly conducted kindergartens they can demonstrate. There is, it must be confessed, in some kindergarten literature an offensive air of speculative exaltation and of unwillingness to talk the matter-of-fact language of practical school men and common sense. This can only obscure the truth and create prejudices, unjust it may be in fact, but all the more harmful.[19]

Thorndike then continued his lengthy discourse by explaining the manner in which habit formation functioned in young children. Let us take for example his explanation of the need for immediacy of reward or discomfort when the law of effect was put into operation with young children.

The closer the response is connected in time with the satisfaction or discomfort, the more readily is the habit formed.

The immature and untrained minds of five-year-olds do not hold in memory the events of a day or an hour well enough to connect rewards and punishments accurately with acts that are past and gone. The younger a child is, the more likely he will be to connect as cause and effect and to retain as habits things and acts that go together in immediate sequence. He steals his playmate's toy; you later find it out by seeing the toy in his possession; you call him to you and administer the rebuke or other punishment. The chances are, with a kindergarten child, more than even that he will form the habit, not of refraining from theft, but of refraining from showing what he steals or even of not coming to you when you call him. The teacher who connects rewards and punishments with the results of certain impulses, will attain only insecure progress in habit formation. The teacher who connects them with delayed detection of the good and bad acts will probably only work the mischief of forming habits of display and deceit. The utmost ingenuity is required to prevent young children from the irrational associations of ideas and undesirable associations of acts with circumstances which follow whenever we fail to connect the incentive or deterrent closely with the impulse.[20]

In summarizing the goals of kindergarten education Thorndike recommended "making as a chief duty of childhood the establishment of worthy habits, especially of obedience, self-help, cheerfulness, modesty, and courage."[21] To attain this positive goal might require the repression of unworthy tendencies as well as the establishment of good habits. Rigid pruning he considered a necessary practice in the kindergarten and to trim away bad behavior he believed that "straightforward inhibition is the honest and economical course."[22] Thus did Thorndike place in the hands of kindergarten teachers the responsibility for molding behavior to bring about "definite, observable, particular changes."[23]

This was the firm recommendation that took form in the conduct curriculum under the leadership of Patty Smith Hill. Each segment of the day in the classroom was analyzed in terms of typical activities that could promote desirable, observable changes in behavior. Changes were not expected to come all at once but in stages, so these were outlined at four different points in a child's growth — three preschool stages and then developments in first grade. By the 1920s nursery schools were beginning to be established in the United States with Miss Hill as an early supporter of nursery education. It was natural for her to include the downward extension of education in a new curriculum plan. Furthermore, leaders in the kindergarten movement, such as Miss Hill, had long thought of early childhood as embracing the primary school years and were committed to the unification of kindergarten-primary education. No definite age levels were designated, for growth was expected to be steady from year to year, but planned experiences may be considered to span nursery school through first grade.

The care given to the analysis of children's block building will illustrate curriculum building, which focused upon desirable changes in thought, feeling, and conduct.

SPECIFIC ACTIVITIES AND CONDUCTS OF THE WORK PERIOD

BLOCK BUILDING

Materials

Group I	Hill blocks (without corner blocks).
	Miscellaneous blocks (large gift blocks in bulk, etc.).
Group II	Materials same as Group I.
Group III	Hill blocks (with corner blocks).
	Miscellaneous blocks.
	Stabuilt blocks.
	Other playthings, such as furniture, toys, etc.
First Grade	Hill blocks.
	Play materials including rope, pulleys, etc.
	Stabuilt blocks.

Group I

Typical Activities	*Desirable Changes in Thought, Feeling, and Conduct*
Taking out blocks and putting them away. (Blocks are kept in large boxes.)	Handling blocks with safety for self and others.
Experimenting with blocks (piling or placing lengthwise, sometimes naming product).	Pleasure in activity. Pleasure in using blocks. Satisfaction in vigorous use of whole body.
Playing with blocks — sliding them on floor or on inclined plane.	Beginning of interest in playing together. Gaining ideas from other children. Learning to share materials.
(Play is largely individual.)	

Group II

Taking out blocks and putting them away.	Continuation of conducts of Group I.
Building alone or in gregarious group.	Growing interest in the work of other children.
Constructing with more definite idea in mind — using more blocks.	Getting ideas through imitation.
Constructing something, calling it "train," "house," etc., and playing with it.	Ability to plan growing out of experimentation.

Group III

Taking out blocks and putting them away.	Continuation of conducts of Group II.
	Handling blocks and building safely.
Working sometimes alone but more often in self-organized co-operative group with definite leader and followers.	Taking building down quietly, safely. Growing ability:
	to work together,
	to plan together,
Constructing with definite purpose — plans usually made before beginning to build.	to interchange ideas in arriving at common purpose, to concentrate on problem for longer period.
	Increasing interest in activity of constructing.
Building for different purposes:	Increasing interest in product.

Building for different purposes:
House   Hospital
Store   Fort
Boats   Wagons

Trains, tracks, etc.
(Interest in play often interferes with
further construction—children play
in boat before it is finished.)
Experimenting with wheels and
rods.

Interest in new way of fastening
blocks together.

Using Stabuilt blocks (largely in experimental way).

Growing dexterity in handling small
blocks.

FIRST GRADE

Taking out blocks and putting them
away.

Continuation of conducts of Group
III, with growth in efficiency.

Working in self-organized co-operative group with chosen leader.

Much more definite planning.

Building with purpose—plans quite
definite and detailed, interest in
plan often lasting for weeks.

Much greater interest in product.

Building for use (playhouse, stage).

(See "Number," Dramatic Play,"
"Hygiene," "Reading.")

Experimenting with wheels, ropes,
and pulleys.

Interest in simple mechanics.

Using Stabuilt blocks in a more definite way—often working from
model.[24]

Not goodness in general but the specifics of desirable behaviors became
the goals of early childhood education in this curriculum plan.

THE MEASUREMENT MOVEMENT AND THE CONCEPT OF FIXED INTELLIGENCE

Thorndike did not view behavior as completely modifiable; he was
well aware of human differences. His study of individual variation was
allied to the problem of the influence of heredity. Like James, Thorndike believed that intellectual individuality rested to a very large extent
on germ plasm heredity. Thorndike's strong emphasis on hereditary
aspects was summed up by Hofstadter when he writes that Thorndike
"did much to spread among educators the eugenists' idea of inherited mental capacity. Thorndike believed that men's absolute achievements can
be affected by environment and training, but their relative achievements
can be accounted for only by original capacity."[25] The reason for this has
been stated by Butts and Cremin in a manner close to Thorndike's own

terminology: "The intellectual faculties are not inherited as a spiritual bequest of man, but intelligence is built up out of the biological action and reaction system of the organism which *is* inherited. The reflex arc based upon an afferent nervous system leading from preceptors to the brain and an efferent or motor nervous system leading from the central nervous system to the muscles or glands is the inherited unit of behavior."[26] Thus, Thorndike's emphasis upon heredity was strong and had important educational consequences; it promoted the development of special curricula for different classes and individuals.[27] At no point in his career was Thorndike an advocate of educational equality, but rather he recommended a curriculum adjusted to abilities. Writing within a few blocks of Harlem and close to the East Side slums, Thorndike did not qualify his position that original nature was more important in determining ability than was environment.[28]

The development of intelligence tests during this same period of time was an important instrument in making influential Thorndike's position on native intelligence. Alfred Binet and Théophile Simon in France first applied the scientists' idea of a scale or graded order to test construction. Their intelligence scale consisted of a series of problems of graded difficulty, each corresponding to a norm of a specific mental level. Children's performance on the tasks presented in this scale, determining mental age, ranged widely and did succeed to a considerable degree in differentiating less able pupils from those more able and thus attracted considerable attention. A group of influential psychologists in America expanded these beginnings into a strong intelligence testing movement. At Stanford University under the leadership of L.M. Terman a famous revision of Binet's scale, known as the Stanford-Binet, established the use of the "intelligence quotient" (I.Q.) — the ratio between mental and chronological age.

The very manner in which the tests were constructed inferred that the average I.Q. from age to age is highly constant; the inference was fixed intelligence. It was assumed that it was inherited capacity that was measured in a way that was not affected significantly by environment or education. Empirical evidence to support this assumption was derived from intercorrelations of test scores and from their predictive ability. Evidence was impressive and so widely accepted that "most of the general textbooks written before World War II tended to present the view that the I.Q. is essentially constant because intelligence is fixed."[29] Faith in nature prevailed.

The scientists' precise use of measuring instruments, so welcome to psychologists wishing to make their work more scientific and efficient, was soon applied to achievement as well. Tests contributed to the dream of building a genuine science of education. Charles Judd, director of the

School of Education at the University of Chicago, urged that the same methods that were applied to problems of mental development could open up every aspect of education to full inspection and evaluation. "Be exact," Judd advised his students. "Standardization is nothing but a systematic effort to deal with educational problems explicitly and in the light of exact information."[30]

It was Thorndike, however, who provided the most frequently quoted statement when he wrote: "Whatever exists at all exists in some amount. To know it thoroughly involves knowing its quantity as well as its quality. Education is concerned with changes in human beings; a change is a difference between two conditions; each of these conditions is known to us only by the products produced by it — things made, words spoken, acts performed, and the like."[31] Thorndike and his students set about using the scale idea for measuring achievement in arithmetic, spelling, reading, language ability — even handwriting and drawing. Other universities quickly became centers of test making, especially the University of Chicago under the leadership of Judd. By 1918 over a hundred standardized tests designed to measure achievement in subject areas were described by Walter S. Monroe in *The Measurement of Educational Products*, the yearbook of the National Society for the Study of Education.[32]

In his address to the leaders of kindergarten, as early as 1903 Thorndike had written in glowing terms about the promise of quantification.

Psychology is passing, and education will soon pass, from the condition of a descriptive to that of a quantitative science. The human mind is being given the quantitative study by exact measurements which has long characterized astronomy, physics and chemistry. The education of a human child will sometime be treated with the respect and care that we now give to recording eclipses or measuring the brightness of stars. The best service to be done by early education, for instance by that of the kindergarten, will then probably be considered the accurate measurement of the mental powers and tendencies of children, and the accurate recording of their progress. At present this is possible in the case of the sense powers, motor ability, the perceptive and associative processes, and some of the more definite and mechanical of the other mental traits. Needless to say, however, such measurements are quite beyond the capacity of kindergarten teachers. It requires as much scientific training to observe and measure complex mental traits as to be an astronomical or physical observer. It would be folly to impute to kindergartners the duty of becoming psychological experts. The leaders of the kindergarten, however, may in wisdom master the elements of quantitative psychology and watch its development in the hope of a day when human thought will give its best, exact quantitative science, to the problems of human life and welfare.[33]

Thorndike certainly included early childhood when he later wrote:

> To measure a product well means so to define its amount that competent persons will know how large it is, with some precision, and that this knowledge may be conveniently recorded and used. This is the general *Credo* of those who, in the last decade, have been busy trying to extend and improve measurements of educational products.[34]

The feverish activity exhibited in test making reached down into the kindergarten. By the 1920s reports were made of new tests of mental abilities to be used with young children.[35] Despite Thorndike's warning about the psychological expertise necessary for the quantification of mental growth, group intelligence tests were constructed and used. Ultimately, reading readiness tests were to be the most influential at the kindergarten level.

All these developments revealed how quickly early childhood leaders were reaching for the new scientific formulations. Although they may not have recognized it, new basic assumptions now supported new curriculum proposals.

Thorndike and His Contemporary World

As a theorist, Thorndike considered and assessed the psychological conceptions of his day. He repudiated the idea of mental discipline — that humanist idea going back to Plato, which held that certain educational subjects strengthened the mind's power to reason logically. Since Thorndike considered learning a matter of establishing connections, it was, for him, more specific than disciplinary. Thus he held that instead of any general transfer of training, transfer is possible from one learning situation to another only to the extent that there are identical elements in the two: "a change in one function alters another only so far as the two functions have as factors identical elements."[36] As this position came to be accepted, education gained a more utilitarian flavor.

Hall's theory of recapitulation came under sharp attack by Thorndike. "This does not at all imply that I think, as a present school of scientists seem to, that because a certain thing has been in phylogeny we ought to repeat it in ontogeny. . . . We ought to make an effort . . . to omit the useless and antiquated and get to the best and most useful as soon as possible; we ought to change what *is* to what *ought to be* as far as we can."[37] Thus, Thorndike proclaimed that man could be changed and for the better; that was the task of education.

Nor did Thorndike find much value in John Dewey's concern for utilizing the child's own interests as an important element of learning. Interest for Thorndike was only valuable insofar as it was incorporated into the law of effect. He wrote to early childhood educators: "The great contribution of the so-called doctrine of interest to modern education has been its recognition, half unconscious indeed, of the fact that any mental activity must be so arranged as to pay the active agent something which he craves, if it is to produce a permanent change in him."[38] In the final analysis Thorndike viewed all methodology as "arrangements for making the good thoughts and acts of profit, and the bad thoughts and acts of disadvantage, to the personal cravings of those educated."[39]

Thorndike did not deny the general American trust in education as the road to social improvement; he believed scientifically educated individuals to be the hope for a better world. Yet the zeal to produce more schooling Thorndike would balance with the realism gained through scientific study. "School education is one of the most important of human institutions," he wrote, "and free schooling for those who can use it for human welfare is one of the first and most beneficent. But we honor education more by understanding it than by praising it, and we should not ask too much from it."[40] Part of the scientific realism Thorndike would apply to education stemmed from evidence of individual differences. While he argued the need to adjust individuals to their environment through strengthening, weakening, or abolishing original tendencies, he was also convinced that this process must be varied according to individual potential. Consider Thorndike's clear statement on this: "Specialization of schools is needed not only to fit pupils for special professions, arts, trades, and the like, but to fit schools to original differences in the pupils. Specialization of instruction for different pupils within one class is needed as well as specialization of the curriculum for different classes. Since human nature does not fall into sharply defined groups, we can literally never be sure of having a dozen pupils who need to be treated exactly alike."[41]

It is not usual to include Thorndike in searching for the theoretical bases of early childhood education. A recent publication dealing with this history and theory affords Thorndike a brief sentence or two.[42] However, in the introduction to this chapter it was established that the reconstructed kindergarten program, developed under the leadership of Patty Smith Hill, was influenced by Thorndike's work. In a systematic analysis of *A Conduct Curriculum for Kindergarten and First Grade*, Charlotte Jammer found that it represented opposing points of view — Dewey's and Thorndike's — and concludes: "Neither view was followed through with clarity, but the weight went to Thorndike. It was much easier to implement the specific suggestions set forth in the long series of objectives and activities than to carry out the generalized principles of the experimental method."[43] The excerpt included confirms this judgment.

Moreover, the leaders of the curriculum reform movement thought of themselves as aligning with the scientific developments in education so influential at that time. They thought of themselves as progressive, as did Thorndike; scientism was one ingredient of the progressive movement, picturing education as an instrument of social improvement.[44] If we include the primary grades as part of early childhood education, as the leaders of the kindergarten movement clearly wished to do at that time, there can be no doubt about Thorndike's influence upon the curriculum both through stimulus-response psychology and through measurement.

There is, however, an even stronger need for educators of young children to understand the origins and assumptions of behavorism. In the 1960s facets of behaviorism were incorporated into early childhood education as never before. As early education was once more viewed as a way to improve society, behavior modification, behavioral objectives, and teaching machines were recommended for some programs. These are rooted in behavioral premises, although not quite as conceived at the turn of the century. Recent developments rest upon the reinforcement theory of B. F. Skinner, the most influential contemporary behaviorist. We will here depart from chronology and turn to reinforcement theory as proposed by Skinner.

REINFORCEMENT THEORY

While the proposals of B.F. Skinner's operant conditioning stem more clearly from the behaviorism of Pavlov and Watson than from Thorndike's connectionism, they still hold a number of significant attitudes and methods in common. For both, psychology is the science of behavior that can be built from the study of overt behavior in animal and man. The assumption of both is that man is neutral and passive and that all behavior can be described in sequential mechanistic terms.[45] Both share the conviction that the information thus derived should form the basis of educational practices. Affirming the relationship between Thorndike's associationism and behaviorism two contemporary psychologists state: "With the addition of a nonintrospective empirical methodology and a carefully restricted lexicon chosen to describe the characteristics of observable stimuli and measurable behavioral responses, associationism fostered behavorism in America."[46]

Skinner's method is a consistent and persistent inductive empiricism applied rigorously in experimentation and observation; he insists upon limiting psychological study to the observable behavior of organisms. He wants to establish laws of behavior, laws relating independent to dependent variables, for he views the ultimate goals of behaviorism to be the prediction and control of behavior. For Skinner the dependent variable is the behavior of the individual organism; the independent variable consists of external conditions that influence the behavior. In evaluating the probability of behavior, the scientist must explore the conditions determining it. "We are concerned, then, with the causes of human behavior. We want to know why men behave as they do. Any condition or event which can be shown to have an effect upon behavior must be taken into account. By discovering and analyzing these causes we can predict behavior; to the extent that we can manipulate them, we can control behavior."[47] This extreme determinism of Skinner is reminiscent of John B. Watson, whose behaviorism was a combination of the ideas of Locke and the experimentation and thinking of Pavlov. Watson accepted the existence of innate organic reflexes such as sucking and breathing and he postulated the existence of innate love, fear, and rage, but virtually all human behavior he believed to be explained by conditioning. The strength of his view of the openness of human behavior to conditioning by the environment is made clear by the following quotation: "Give me a dozen healthy infants, well-formed, and my own special world to bring them up in, and I'll guarantee to take any one at random and train him to become any kind of specialist I might select — doctor, lawyer, artist, merchant-chief, and, yes beggarman and thief, regardless of his talents, penchants, tendencies, abilities, vocations, and the race of his ancestors."[48]

While Watson engaged in some study of human infants (his dissertation in 1903 was "Animal Education: The Psychical Development of the White Rat"), Skinner's experimental work has been carried out on animals — pigeons, rats, dogs, monkeys — and he finds all these organisms showing amazingly similar properties in the learning process. He readily extends these similarities to people for, while he agrees that learning in the everyday life of people is more complicated, it still shares the basic nature of animal learning through operant conditioning.

Operant Conditioning

Skinner has come to believe that the most influential determinant of behavior is reinforcement. The explanation of why reinforcement works is not provided in his writings, but he does offer a step-by-step description of the process. It has to do with the likelihood of a response being repeated in the future: positive reinforcement supplies the condition most favorable to increased probability. A careful definition of such a consequence is given by Bigge and Hunt: "A positive reinforcer is any stimulus the presentation of which strengthens the behavior upon which it is made contingent"[49] In lay language this would refer to a reward. "Stimulus" in this definition does not refer to the classic stimulus of Thorndike's theory, for this "stimulus" follows rather than precedes the act.

While for Skinner the simple unit of behavior is the reflex, he provides for two types of behavior: respondent and operant. Respondent behavior is that which is correlated with a specific eliciting stimuli. Operant behavior departs from the traditional stimulus-response paradigm, for the response comes first and is then reinforced; this is the procedure through which the efficiency of behavior is improved. Skinner's description is simple: "The experimental procedure in operant conditioning is straightforward. We arrange a contingency of reinforcement and expose an organism to it for a given period."[50] In operant learning, the significant element is that which immediately follows an operant — an act or set of acts. Thus Skinner describes the means by which behavior is modified: "Operant conditioning shapes behavior as the sculptor shapes a lump of clay."[51]

Punishment is an ineffective means of controlling behavior in Skinner's opinion. He speaks out forcefully on this issue:

> When you say you punish a child to make him work, you are misusing the word "punish." You are arranging conditions which he can escape from by working. When you punish a child to keep him from misbehaving, however, you are trying to suppress behavior. In my earlier experiments punishment did not suppress behavior as it had been supposed to do. Punishment may only be reducing a current tendency to respond. As soon as punishment is withdrawn, the behavior bounces back. This isn't always the case, because extremely severe punishment may knock behavior out for good, at least as far as we are able to determine. But what is surprising is that if you make common punishing events contingent on behavior, the behavior will recover after the punishment ceases, and the organism will continue to behave, even though it has been rather severely punished. I object to aversive control in general because of its by-products. All sorts of emotions are generated which have negative side effects."[52]

Thus a vigorous repudiation of aversive control is made by Skinner, for he believes its overuse in society and in education has been generally ineffective. It leads to escape or avoidance: "A stimulus is known to be aversive only if its removal is reinforcing."[53] A student given strong punishment may escape by playing hooky or becoming a dropout; he may counterattack by vandalizing school property. Operant conditioning does not generate such negative by-products. The struggle to escape and avoid aversive treatment or to react aggressively toward those who arrange aver-

sive conditions is a pattern Skinner finds in most social aspects of life—
in the family, education, economy, government, religion, and ethics.[54]
He would like to see this minimized and replaced by positive controls.

All human behavior in Skinner's model of man is externally caused and
controlled; he argues against the use of terms that imply unobservable
conditions—"image," "drive," "morale," "interest." "One who readily engages in a given activity," he writes, "is not showing interest, he is showing the effect of reinforcement. We do not give a man a sense of achievement, we reinforce a particular action."[55] It is not the inner man that
has any relevance to Skinner's scheme of things, nor does he consider the
concept of the self essential in any analysis of behavior. There is an alternative upon which he places more reliance: "The concept of self may
have an early advantage in representing a relatively coherent response
system, but it may lead us to expect consistencies and functional integrities
which do not exist. The alternative to the use of the concept is simply to
deal with demonstrated covariations in the strength of responses."[56] As
the inner self is denied, behavior becomes completely available to outside control.

Teaching Machines

There is no question, in Skinner's opinion, that behavior should be controlled; the only question is who should carry out the behavioral engineering. In education teachers are considered the architects and builders of
the children's behavior, and within this building process the teacher's major tool is reinforcement, the foundation upon which programming and
behavior modification have been developed. In programmed instruction
the selected subject matter is broken down into discrete steps so that the
learner can be reinforced after each step. The material is organized in
a logical sequence so that each step is designed to follow the preceding
one. The usual reinforcement in programming is immediate knowledge
of the correctness of the response made.

In an article on "Teaching Machines" Skinner describes the carefully
ordered steps that he considers "optimal conditions for self-instruction":

> Sets of separate presentations or "frames" of visual materials are stored on
> disks, cards, or on tapes. One frame is presented at a time, adjacent frames
> being out of sight. In one type of machine the student composes a response
> by moving printed figures or letters. His setting is compared by the machine
> with a coded response. If the two correspond, the machine automatically
> presents the next frame. If they do not, the response is cleared, and another
> must be composed. The student cannot proceed to a second step until the
> first has been taken.[57]

Such a machine for teaching spelling, arithmetic, and other subjects in the primary grades acts surprisingly like a private tutor in Skinner's opinion. He considers that the comparison holds in several respects: through constant interchange, insisting on mastery, presenting only the material for which the student is ready, assisting the right answer, and reinforcing "the student for every correct response using immediate feedback not only to shape his behavior most efficiently but to maintain it in strength."[58] Skinner views teaching machines as essential to any progressive school of the future.

Behavior Modification

Behavior modification refers to the use of reinforcement to strengthen or weaken a specific behavior of a child. It deals with operants — the overt reactions of the learner — that can be modified through the consequence attached to them. Only the outward manifestations of behavior, not any internal causes of them, are the focus. Desired behavior is reinforced, and thus strengthened, so as to increase the probability of recurrence. To the many natural reinforcers frequently used by teachers — a smile, a nod of the head — the behavior modifier adds a host of tangible reinforcers from candy or crackers to tokens. When tokens are used over a period of time, the system is sometimes referred to as a token economy.

The principle behind behavior modification can be stated succinctly: All behavior is learned, hence all can be modified. Behavior modification is a technique for shaping behavior that rests upon positive reinforcement. A single, specific behavior is pinpointed; behavior means anything a learner does, says, or even thinks so long as it is manifested in action. Then the payoff must be found — the consequence or reward for which the child will work and, in the process, modify his behavior. The child must understand what he has to do to earn the particular reinforcement contingency. Skinner has written: "The conditions the teacher arranges must be powerful enough to compete with those under which the student tends to behave in distracting ways. . . . To straighten out a wholly disruptive classroom, something as obvious as a token economy may be needed."[59]

For improved education, Skinner sees no alternative to improved use of reinforcement. He writes:

> The whole process of becoming competent in any field must be divided into a very large number of very small steps, and reinforcement must be contingent upon the accomplishment of each step. . . . By making each step as small as possible, the frequency of reinforcement can be raised to a max-

imum, while the possibility of aversive consequences of being wrong are reduced to a minimum.[60]

For effective reinforcement Skinner considers the teacher to be "out of date"; mechanical devices are a necessity. This could only free the teacher for other essential functions.

Behavioral Engineering

Skinner's vision of a utopian society must by now have a familiar ring, for it is built on the premises of behavioral engineering. In his scheme of things independent behavior is a value to be taken seriously, not independent action based upon inner direction, but action built in through operant conditioning so that the individual responds appropriately without needing to be told.[61] *Walden Two* presents Skinner's picture of a completely controlled society, in which he believes it will be easy to be good and to achieve excellence.[62] In *Walden Two* the experiences provided in the community systematically establish desirable human behavior and eliminate undesirable traits. Thus Skinner sees the autonomous man, the inner man, the man so long defended by the literature of freedom and dignity, abolished and control turned over to the environment. Man is, indeed, controlled by his environment, but Skinner goes beyond this for he deems it an environment that is largely of man's own making.[63] In this way Skinner expects the advances of behavioral psychology to attain human and societal improvement. "A scientific view of man offers exciting possibilities. We have not yet seen what man can make of man," he concludes.[64]

In 1954 Skinner wrote that nothing stood in the way of the use of mechanized instruction but cultural inertia: the necessary techniques were known; the equipment could be easily provided.[65] Whatever the reason, teaching machines have not been widely accepted in schools. To be sure extensive experimentation with "plug-in instruction" has been part of the research of Patrick Suppes and others at Stanford University in the teaching of both reading and arithmetic.[66] One restraining factor, in the opinion of Wayne K. Howell, a vice president for the Fund for Media Research at Chicago, is that little progress has been made in discriminating between the human functions of education and the machine functions. He writes: "Important instructional decisions are made at the place of confrontation between teacher and pupil; and, unless the new media and technology can conveniently and comfortably find their place in this confrontation, they will surely not make any constructive difference."[67] Such comfortable accommodation seems difficult to make.

Behavior modification, however, seems to have had a more pervasive acceptance as evidenced in journals describing psychological research projects and in teacher-oriented journals commenting on classroom practice. In *Today's Education*, the journal of the National Education Association, a teacher described the use of behavior modification with ten boys who had a history of disruptive behavior in the classroom.[68] The teacher expressed her own satisfaction with the boys' apparent move toward certain specific goals. An article in *Instructor* magazine characterized behavior modification as a "kind and caring way to handle children."[69] *The Journal of Applied Behavior Analysis*, available since 1968, includes a continuous stream of articles pertaining to a vast array of behaviors and to all ages. The titles of articles in a single bound volume (1970) illustrate a variety of applications of behavior modification in work with young children (for example, "The Use of a Token System in Project Head Start," "Modification of Preschool Isolate Behavior: A Case Study," and "The Effects of Teacher Attention on Following Instructions in a Kindergarten Class").[70] To precisely delineated reinforcement was attributed greater skill in handwriting, increased interaction with peers, or more unequivocal following of the teacher's instructions in these articles. Behavior modification is in widespread use, particularly with children labeled as having "special needs."

BEHAVIORISM IN PERSPECTIVE

Revolutionary is not too strong a word to use to describe the ideas championed by all those who have endeavored to build an objective science of psychology. A generation of intellectuals exposed to Darwinian conceptions and Germanic theories of mind seemed waiting to embrace new conceptions of the nature of man and new methods for the investigation of his behavior. The sheer enthusiasm for coming to grips with the scientific approach led them into some false emphases. One such falsity has been the persistent doctrine of fixed intelligence. In view of more recent studies, Thorndike was unjustified in asserting such forceful claims for the role of heredity and in deprecating the influence of environment. That he made his claims in the name of science gave them a strong hold on educational practice for decades.

The crumbling concept of fixed intelligence evidences itself in the literature on intellectual development today. As early as 1952 Arthur Combs defined intelligence as the capacity for effective behavior and stated: "The intelligence of an individual will be dependent upon the richness and variety of perceptions possible to him at a given moment."[71] Benjamin

Bloom's analysis of the effects of environment on intelligence led him to conclude that "intelligence development is in part a function of the environment in which the individual lives" and that extremes of environment, either abundant or deprived, may richly provide for or leave a child devoid of the experiences in certain describable areas of thinking.[72] But it is J. McVicker Hunt's forcefully organized presentation of data from a variety of sources that provides the most conclusive evidence and serves as the foundation of the proclamation: "The assumptions that intelligence is fixed and that its development is predetermined by the genes is no longer tenable."[73] To add to the evidence, the role of experience in learning is a basic premise of Piaget's theory as will be developed later.

Despite the dissenting voice of Arthur Jensen,[74] there is widespread belief that it is in the interchange, the continuous communication, between child and environment that learning depends. Consider, for example, Ira Gordon's statement: "We are shifting in psychology from a notion that intelligence is fixed and immutable and unchangeable to the notion that we can do something about a youngster's intelligence by the nature of the opportunities for experience that we provide for him. . . . We conceptualize that intelligence is behavior, and behavior comes under environmental control just as much as it comes under biological genetic control, and therefore, intelligence is changeable."[75] Such a firm view of intelligence strips away the encrusted beliefs of intelligence as limited by race, class, or sex that had attached themselves to the notion of fixed intelligence. The newer conceptions open up greater educational promise than did the antiequalitarian aspects of the psychology of James and Thorndike, who included both sex and race in their explanations of intellectual growth. The uniqueness of individuals, then, is no longer attributed solely to genetic influence but to continuous involvement in organism-environment interaction. What a radically different concept of the source of the uniqueness of individuals!

On the other hand the behaviorism of Pavlov, Watson, and Skinner must answer to the opposite contention of complete determinism, the idea that the individual can be quite totally structured by behavioral engineering. Even Thorndike's connectionism with its emphasis on specific elements gave life to the idea of indoctrination,[76] but Skinner's behaviorism implies a stricter determinism. Thus, the shaping possibilities of environmental-social-cultural determinism are elevated as the main causative factor of behavior. Note that it is not the interaction of learner and environment but the influence environment can exert to produce predicted behavior that is the essence of behaviorism. It leaves out any capability of man to mold and shape his own destiny. Furthermore, because of the emphasis on making behavior more efficient, critics label it mechanistic and atomistic. Indeed, Skinner's own writing accentuates the mechanistic criticism: "Man has . . . created the machine in his own image. And as a result, the living organism has lost some of its uniqueness. . . . At the same time, we have discovered more about how the living organism works and are better able to see its machine-like properties."[77] The sequential order of presenting stimuli or reinforcing behavior also contributes mechanistic elements. The molecular acquisition of new behaviors in a piece-meal fashion is truly atomistic; any integration of thinking is completely left to chance. The label "additive learning" has been applied to the step-by-step reinforcement procedure. Isolated facts, without a theory to unify them, provide for repetition of responses but not for the interrelated concepts or conceptual models; this procedure focuses on the analytic and neglects the synthesizing aspects of learning.

Effective education for this century cannot be based upon behaviorism in the opinion of Donald Snygg, for it can only teach what is already known, promote conforming behavior, and prepare children to live in a world exactly like the one of the designers.[78] In a world of rapid change where adaptable, creative people are needed to deal with a host of unpredicted problems, these children will be ill-prepared to cope. Furthermore, Snygg considers reinforcement theory an even more difficult one to put into practice than connectionism for it implies a vaguer theory of causation. The teacher can only wait for an operant to appear and then reinforce it; she is not able to make plans to achieve the act.[79]

The behaviorist view of man as a neutral, passive organism governed by external stimuli denies purposive behavior. This conception of man disturbs psychologists for whom the essence of man comes from within and inner direction enables man to choose his behavior freely according to his conscience. Addressing the question of man's nature, John Rich declares: "Our understanding of man is severely limited when interior life is avoided, when the organism is broken into bits and pieces for their amenability to certain forms of investigation, leaving human purposes, values and ideals with no place in the study of human behavior."[80] Is the study of overt behavior the means for learning about the nature of man? Is this the study to which the word science should be exclusively applied? Surely we learn little about the impulsive, alogical behavior and thinking of the young child by molding him into adult standards of response. The failure to respect the subjective life of learners in the manipulation of behavior denies the genuineness of the responses induced. Individuals tend to be treated as objects.

While most academic psychology has had a stimulus-response orientation for decades, faith in its all-encompassing explanation of learning is waning. Hunt describes stimulus-response methodology as opposed to stimulus-response theory in which centralized processes intervene between stimulus and response.[81] Thus Hunt would not discard behaviorism, but he would relegate it to only certain aspects of learning where conditioned responses contribute to the whole.

Since the 1950s speculation about the workings of the mind suddenly has become acceptable again as investigators have turned increasingly to the work of Jean Piaget whose semiclinical interview technique is unaligned with the tradition of measurement and quantification. His work has moved the thinking of psychologists back to the consideration of the mind as an interacting agent rather than the passive responder to presented stimuli. In analyzing instructional psychology in 1977, Wittrock and Lumsdaine observe a notable shift in emphasis in research and theory:

> The current shift emphasizes the study of central cognitive and affective associationistic and holistic processes by which the learner selects, transforms, and encodes the nominal characteristics of experience into functional, meaningful internal representations. A cognitive perspective implies that a behavioral analysis of instruction is often inadequate to explain the effects of instruction upon learning. From a cognitive perspective, to understand the effects of instruction upon learning and memory one must comprehend how learners use their cognitive processes, knowledge, abilities, and interests to transform the nominal stimuli of instruction into functional ones.[82]

Note the active role of the learner in this conception. This leads us into a conception of man as an active interacter with his environment, another view of man with a long history.

6 The Reconstruction of Experience

"The child develops not in isolation," wrote Alice Temple, "but in interactions with situations, which contain or carry subject matter."[1] This statement, written in the decade when the slowly emerging reconstructed kindergarten curriculum was coming to fruition, clearly reflects the influence of John Dewey. A number of other Deweyan ideas are imbedded in Temple's article: purposeful activities stimulate problem solving; experience supplies the motive for growth in reading, writing, and number; social growth develops through experiencing desirable social behavior.[2] On the kindergarten level, we find articulated Dewey's interactive theory of growth, his emphasis on purpose in the learning process, and his belief that social, democratic learnings come in a classroom operating as a small community.

Alice Temple was, in 1929, chairman of the Kindergarten-Primary Department at the University of Chicago, an influential center for early childhood education in the Midwest. The lines of influence upon her thinking extend directly back to the laboratory school established by Dewey. Before joining the university faculty, she served the Chicago Free Kindergarten Association as assistant, then supervising teacher, and finally principal.[3] Here Miss Temple worked with Anna Bryan, an initiator of new educational procedures that broke the patterns of Froebelian materials and methods. Her experimental classroom had drawn the attention of educators of the period, among them Dewey. In the *Elementary School Record* of 1900, Dewey acknowledged his indebtedness to Anna Bryan for her suggestions for new kindergarten practice. The respect was mutual; it is reported that Miss Bryan made continuous use of Dewey's statement of educational philosophy presented in "My Pedagogic Creed" in her teaching in the normal department at Armour Institute where the Chicago Free Kindergarten Association was then located.[4] A close connection was maintained between Dewey's laboratory school and the Kindergarten Association; some of Anna Bryan's students served as assistants in the Dewey sub-primary — the term applied to the earliest classes at the university laboratory school because Dewey's strong disagreement with Froebel's philosophy extended even to the name Froebel had supplied.

Whether or not Alice Temple's appreciation of Dewey's educational ideas stemmed from her work in the Free Kindergarten Association or directly from contacts with Dewey, she staunchly explained the meaning of Dewey's principles for early childhood education. She expected both her kindergarten and the primary grades to profit from a curriculum based upon Dewey's philosophy; one of her persistent themes was the unification of the two school levels. In her articulate presentations Temple captured some of the complexity of Dewey's philosophy, so that her recommendations for classroom practice contained not only suggestions for experience and the utilization of a child's interests but also the meanings of these for child growth. She recognized Dewey's contentions that interest and effort lead to a more potent learning of ideas, and that problem-solving experiences of worth to the child must engage him in subject matter. Knowledge and information she considered one fundamental of education.[5] She is reported to have "put the stamp of sound scholarship on the kindergarten-primary field."[6] It is to her credit that she early gained an understanding of the complex meaning of much that Dewey said and was not enticed into just a superficial application of "experience," "interest," and "activity" for their own sake. She frequently referred to children learning subject matter in the functional manner of Dewey.

The International Kindergarten Union (IKU) served as a battleground for the "conservatives" who maintained a strictly Froebelian perspective, and the "liberals" who wished to reconstruct the program according to contemporary insights. Alice Temple and Patty Smith Hill were prime leaders of the movement to bring the kindergarten in line with new theoretical ideas. But they were by no means alone in this endeavor. The annual meetings of the IKU included, for a number of years, round table discussions on such topics as the advisability of using gifts and occupations, freedom in the curriculum, or the nature of the training of teachers for kindergarten classrooms. In the 1900 discussion, centering around the use of gifts and occupations, out of seven main speakers six held not only to the use of Froebel's materials but to the sequence of use he had prescribed. But among the responders, each limited to a five-minute presentation, the balance went to those recommending a more "liberal" or "progressive" curriculum. The intense feelings of the participants were engaged in the discussion, so that Minnie E. Glidden, chairman for the meeting, warned of the need to be discriminating but tolerant. "We are here today," she stated, "as friends and co-workers. Some of us think along widely diverging lines, yet we are all held together by our interest in the welfare of little children, our high educational aims, and our desire to realize our ideals in our daily living."[7] Small wonder that feelings had to be calmed as the points of view presented were radically different.

The questioning of established patterns of thought was based upon new ideas gleaned from Dewey. At the 1900 meeting Mary Boomer Page rejected the logical use of gifts as meaningless to the child and recommended in its place a concern for the psychological growth of the child.[8] Alice Temple reiterated the emphasis upon a psychological continuity of individual growth rather than sequential ideas and continued to reveal how new materials could relate to the child's interests.[9] Alice Putnam also protested that the kindergarten door should be opened wide to the pure interests of children.[10] For Patty Smith Hill play should give opportunity for expression of the child's own ideas and interests, only then could self-activity be attained.[11] And Bertha Hofer-Hegner protested that the child's needs must come first and attention to a systematic curriculum last.[12] Concern for a psychological continuity of growth, interest as an important element in learning, activity projecting the child's own ideas and images, education related to need: how much these leaders of the kindergarten movement had gained from Dewey even in 1900!

The one article John Dewey aimed directly at kindergarten education, "Froebel's Educational Principles," was published in 1900 also.[13] In the archives at the Washington, D.C., headquarters of the Association for Childhood Education International (the organization that evolved from the International Kindergarten Union), there is a bound volume donated from the library of Patty Smith Hill. It contains a much underlined copy of "Froebel's Educational Principles," replete with marginal notes and this comment by the donor on the cover: "Highly prized by Professor Hill and used constantly for many years with her classes." The contributions of Dewey in these early years to a revised kindergarten program were substantial and turned the thoughts of leaders in early childhood education to the reconstruction of experience and to the classroom as a small community for democratic living.

DEWEY'S REJECTION OF FROEBEL'S CURRICULUM

Symbolism, play, unity, and imitation as they abounded in current Froebelian programs were discarded by Dewey in lieu of experience and method closer to the real world of the child. While Dewey did not use the terms in his article rejecting Froebelian ideas, the advice he gave implies a curriculum based on reconstruction of experience — the reliving and clarifying of ideas on a higher level. In the section on method he outlined the various steps of problem solving and the values that accrue from it.

Dewey accepted play as contributing to learning but completely disagreed with Froebel's planned process when he explained:

> Play is not to be identified with anything which the child externally does. It rather designates his mental attitude in its entirety and in its unity. It is the free play, the interplay, of all the child's powers, thoughts, and physical movements, in embodying, in a satisfying form, his own images and interests. Negatively, it is freedom from economic pressure — the necessities of getting a living and supporting others — and from the fixed responsibilities attaching to the special callings of the adult. Positively, it means that the supreme end of the child is fullness of growth — fullness of realization of his budding powers, a realization which continually carries him on from one plane to another. . . . To state it baldly, the fact that "play" denotes the psychological attitude of the child, not his outward performances, means complete emancipation from the necessity of following any given or prescribed system, or sequence of gifts, plays, or occupations.[14]

Play, for Dewey, must be embedded in the child's own natural impulses and "carry him onto a higher plane of consciousness and action,"[15] These requirements ruled out imitation or dictation by the teacher; they also replaced the "artificial," "abstract" symbolism of the Froebelian program with imaginative play that was really representative for the child. For this the child needed materials as direct and straightforward as possible. Dewey clarified this point about symbols:

> But the principle does not end here — the reality symbolized must also lie within the capacities of the child's own appreciation. It is sometimes thought the use of the imagination is profitable in the degree it stands for very remote metaphysical and spiritual principles. In the great majority of cases it is safe to say that the adult deceives himself. He is conscious of both the reality and the symbol, and hence of the relation between them. But since the truth or reality represented is far beyond the reach of the child, the supposed symbol is not a symbol to him at all. It is simply a positive thing on its own account. Practically about all he gets out of it is its own physical and sensational meaning, plus, very often, a glib facility in phrases and attitudes that he learns are expected of him by the teacher — without, however, any mental counterpart. We often teach insincerity, and instill sentimentalism, and foster sensationalism when we think we are teaching spiritual truths by means of symbols. The realities reproduced, therefore, by the child should be of as familiar, direct, and real a character as possible. It is largely for this reason that in the kindergarten of our School the work centers so largely about the reproduction of home and neighborhood life.[16]

Thus did Dewey explain that symbolic images were derived from the child's own interactive experiences in home and in school.

As a method, Dewey considered the peculiar problem of early education to be the use of the child's natural impulses and instincts and to utilize them so that the child had "an enlarged and deepened consciousness, and increased control of powers of action."[17] This made play a means of educative growth. Providing constructive work for the young child at his level ultimately led to problem-solving techniques:

> It brings the child in contact with a great variety of material: wood, tin, leather, yarn, etc.; it supplies a motive for using these materials in real ways instead of going through exercises having no meaning except a remote symbolic one; it calls into play alertness of the senses and acuteness of observation; it demands clear-cut imagery of the ends to be accomplished, and requires ingenuity and invention in planning; it makes necessary concentrated attention and personal responsibility in execution, while the results are in such tangible form that the child may be led to judge his own work and improve his standards.[18]

Here Dewey gives Anna Bryan credit for countless suggestions regarding materials appropriate for these developments in the Dewey sub-primary classroom. Dewey believed constructive work in areas of particular interest to be the most effective means of securing the two factors that would lead to problem-solving abilities: initiation in the child's own impulse and termination on a higher plane of thought and action. Because of the prevalent use of Froebel's program with its reliance on imitation Dewey flatly stated: "As a general principle no activity should be originated by imitation."[19] For Dewey imitation had serious consequences:

> From the psychological standpoint it may safely be said that when a teacher has to rely upon a series of dictated directions, it is just because the child has no image of his own of what is to be done or why it is to be done. Instead, therefore, of gaining power of control by conforming to directions, he is really losing it — made dependent upon an external source.[20]

As clear mental images were derived only from direct experience, so must democratic group living also be experienced. Dewey agreed with Froebel on the importance of harmonious relationships in the classroom, but he extended the principle of social living when he stated that "the primary business of the school is to train children in cooperative and mutually helpful living; to foster in them the consciousness of mutual interdependence, and to help them practically in making the adjustments that will carry this spirit into overt deed."[21] Democratic group living stemmed not from direction but from direct experience. Thus did Dewey strip away much of the practice derived from Froebel and make clear premises on which new practice could be based. "Froebel's Educational Principles," together with the personal declaration and revolutionary manifesto Dewey called "My Pedagogic Creed," was available by the turn of the century for those searching for new educational practice. Many ideas proposed in these two documents became important elements of Dewey's theory, greatly expanded in subsequent writings.

DEWEY'S INSTRUMENTALISM

Before Dewey arrived at the University of Chicago to head the departments of philosophy, psychology, and education, he had become dissatisfied with German idealism as he had studied it in Hegel's dialectic. He was drawn increasingly to a scientific approach to problems and he welcomed the opportunity of a Laboratory School where he could test and develop psychological and educational hypotheses. The rapid changes in American life — immigration, urbanization, and industrialization — creating a new national climate were largely ignored by the traditional school and Dewey recognized acutely the lack of connection between the child's classroom activities and his life outside the school. Coming to believe, as he did, that education is a deliberate and continuous reconstruction of experience, he used the experimental elementary school as a place to reconstruct and elaborate his own educational ideas through firsthand experience.[22]

The changes in Dewey's thinking reflect the turbulence in intellectual life that accompanied social and economic transitions. He was significantly influenced by William James's *Principles of Psychology*, which evidenced "the association of the new experimental outlook with evolutionary theory in the foundation of American pragmatic philosophy."[23] Evolutionary doctrine, new scientific thought, and James's biological psychology were influential factors in Dewey's development of a new synthesis of ideas. In an essay on the influence of Darwin on philosophy Dewey pointed to an intellectual transformation due to Darwinian logic that "shifts from an intelligence that shaped things once and for all to the particular intelligences which things are even now shaping; shifts from an ultimate goal of good to the direct increments of justice and happiness that intelligent administration of existent conditions may beget and that present carelessness or stupidity will destroy or forego."[24] Thus Dewey rejected absolute, idealistic conceptions of reality in favor of concrete, meaningful experience as a shaper of intelligence and goals. This repudiation of *a priori* principles to be replaced by a philosophy of instrumentalism directed by trial and error is at the heart of Dewey's disagreement with Froebel's kindergarten program based as it was on a fixed and knowable truth.

Dewey attached no superficial meaning to pragmatism, or instrumentalism, as he had preferred to call his philosophy. His use of "pragmatism" referred to the need to consider consequences in determining final meaning and as the test of all thinking. He pointed out that these consequences need not be practical in the popular sense of the word, but they may be "aesthetic, or moral, or political, or religious in quality."[25] For such varied outcomes, experiences needed to be rich and pregnant with meaning for the learner. The quality of the experience, Dewey explained, was the critical factor and thus, "the central problem of education based upon experience is to select the kind of present experiences that live fruitfully and creatively in subsequent experiences."[26] In Dewey's profoundly developed construct of experience as the core of learning, leaders in early childhood education found the fundamental generating power to reform the curriculum. In his small volume entitled *Experience and Education*, Dewey explained how experience could be the moving force in education and in life and related two major ideas he considered inherent in a viable theory of experience: interaction and continuity.

The one permanent frame of reference for Dewey was the organic connection between education and personal experience; one prime characteristic of experience was its interactive nature. Neither the situation nor the states of the learner could be ignored for effective education; this Dewey states forcefully:

> The word "interaction," which has just been used, expressed the second chief principle for interpreting an experience in its educational function and force. It assigns equal rights to both factors in experience — objective and internal conditions. Any normal experience is an interplay of these two sets of conditions. Taken together, or in their interaction, they form what we call a *situation*. The trouble with traditional education was not that it emphasized the external conditions that enter into the control of the experiences but that it paid so little attention to the internal factors which also decide what kind of experience is had.[27]

The relatonship between situation and interaction Dewey further elucidates in this paragraph:

> The statement that individuals live in a world means, in the concrete, that they live in a series of situations. And when it is said that they live *in* these situations, the meaning of the word "in" is different from its meaning when

it is said that pennies are "in" a pocket or paint is "in" a can. It means, once more, that interaction is going on between an individual and objects and other persons. The conceptions of *situation* and of *interaction* are insepa-rable from each other. An experience is always what it is because of a trans-action taking place between an individual and what, at the time, constitutes his environment, whether the latter consists of persons with whom he is talking about some topic or event, the subject talked about being also a part of the situation; or the toys with which he is playing; . . . The envi-ronment, in other words, is whatever conditions interact with personal needs, desires, purposes, and capacities to create the experience which is had.[28]

Note Dewey's explanation of interaction in the educative process; it assigns equal rights to the two factors: the objective aspects of the situa-tion and the internal perceptions of the individual learner. Here Dewey was dealing with the dichotomy of reality as inner experience and outer world, private reality and public truth. Froebel had considered this di-chotomy also when he talked about making the inner-outer and the outer-inner. Dewey brings the two together when he designates learning as "a transaction taking place between the individual and what, at the time, constitutes his environment."[29] The actively learning child was at the core of Dewey's theory and it was learning by doing and undergoing, in-volving both physical and intellectual activity. Doing meant concrete en-gagement with materials and problems in the immediate environment; it also meant transactions with the world of ideas and symbols, but these must relate to personal needs, desires, purposes, and capacities for learn-ing to be meaningful.

The key criteria the educator had for determining experiences was the principle of continuity, which, as stated by Dewey, proposed that "every experience both takes up something from those that have gone before and modifies in some way the quality of those which come after."[30] Dewey never meant that all experiences were educative and would lead toward an effective continuity of growth; indeed, some experiences could be mis-educative and lead toward lack of sensitivity and responsiveness and thereby restrict the richness of subsequent experiences. These the educator should avoid; part of the teacher's role was to determine the appropriate continuity of experience.

On the other hand, if an experience arouses curiosity, strengthens initiative, and sets up desires and purposes that are sufficiently intense to carry a per-son over dead places in the future, continuity works in a very different way. Every experience is a moving force. Its value can be judged only on the ground of what it moves toward and into. The greater maturity of experience which should belong to the adult as educator puts him in a position to evaluate each experience of the young in a way in which the one having the less mature experience cannot do. It is then the business of the educator to see in what direction an experience is heading.[31]

Continuity of learning, as Dewey expressed it in the foregoing excerpt, was also premised upon individual growth and the integration of ideas. Continuous growth was not to be found in sequences of organized subject matter, but in the individual's growing ability to deal with experience, to undergo changes in thinking, and to solve problems with increased insight. As he stated: "In a certain sense every experience should do something to prepare a person for later experiences of a deeper and more expansive quality. That is the key meaning of growth, continuity, reconstruction of experience."[32] Because increasingly intelligent action seemed to be based upon the development of insight, some interpreters consider that in this respect Dewey anticipated the position of Gestalt psychology. Ernest Bayles and Bruce Hood have written: "to think of education as 'continuous reconstruction of experience' is to take it as reconstruction of insight."[33] In other words ideas have been integrated to form a unique, useful perception. Dewey's recognition of the wholeness of learning formed another link to Gestalt psychology. Often, he considered the "collateral learnings" of attitudes, feelings, and values to be of greater import than any precise knowledge gained. Edwin Boring established this link to Gestalt psychology explicitly and explained that Dewey's insistence that coordinated learning is adaptive and purposeful gives him a position in the history of dynamic psychology.[34]

Striking, also, were Dewey's anticipations of some of Piaget's conceptions of learning. In *The Child and the Curriculum* Dewey argued that for effective learning to take place the teacher must begin with the child. "Learning is active," he insisted. "It involves reaching out of the mind. It involves organic assimilation from within. Literally, we must take our stand with the child and our departure from him . . . the only significant method is the method of the mind as it reaches out and assimilates."[35] Assimilation is, for Piaget, a major factor in learning, as we shall see. The constructivist theory that undergirds Piaget's principal ideas was also touched upon by Dewey when he wrote: "A fully integrated personality . . . exists only when successive experiences are integrated with one another. It can be built up only as a world of related objects is constructed."[36]

The organism-environment interaction that Dewey explained as occurring in experiences, he sometimes characterized more precisely as a transaction.[37] The distinguishing factor is that neither aspect is independent: both are parts of a unified transaction. As Bernstein explains

Dewey's refinement of interaction: "In a transaction, the components themselves are subject to change. Their character affects and is affected by the transaction."[38] This more rigorous formulation seems not to have had any immediate response, but it certainly is evident in the literature of early childhood education today.

These psychological premises advanced by Dewey had significant impact on the psychology of education even though his primary contribution is considered to be in philosophy. Of course, his early articles were published at a time when the demarcation between philosophy and psychology was not clear. It is also evident that his philosophical departures demanded a different view of psychology than those prevalent. Neither introspection nor an emerging behaviorism were adequate to support the education Dewey proposed. In an article published in 1896 called "The Reflex Arc Concept in Psychology," Dewey presented what Wayne Dennis calls "a criticism in advance, of behaviorism."[39] In it Dewey objected to the prevailing description of a reflex arc as consisting of three distinct existing elements — sensory stimulus, psychical reception, and motor response. For Dewey these entities were always organically related and responses represented the means or instruments for accomplishing a goal. The learner was active every step of the way: selecting a problem to be solved or establishing a goal to be attained, determining the methods for reaching a solution, putting these in operation, and evaluating the appearance of the solution or goal achievement. This, of course, is defining the educated person as one who uses the pragmatic method in attacking problems. The educated man is one who can use knowledge and skills in the solution of problems, in discriminating judgments, and in acting intelligently in light of them. Goals, interest inherent in these goals, and intelligent action provide central ideas in Dewey's psychology of learning; they define a continuous learner activity. Contrast this with the limited role of the learner in behaviorism. "Is it surprising that the two systems came to be described as presenting a picture of an 'active' learning organism as opposed to that of a 'passive' learning organism?" asks a contemporary psychologist.[40]

The depth of meaning of Dewey's educational recommendations was no more apparent to early childhood leaders than to educators at other levels. They were caught up in many of the shibboleths of the day: the doctrine of interest, felt need, and activity. Yet this sincere search for new ways of working with children and even the less sophisticated interpretations of Dewey's philosophy implied radical changes in curriculum. A classroom permitting physical activity on the part of children freed them from the sendentary manipulation of small gift blocks around tables divided into one-inch grooves. Leaders discussed free play endlessly and searched for materials that would allow the child to express his own interests and ideas. Patty Smith Hill defined free play: "In free play the self makes its own choices, selections and decisions, and thus absolute freedom is given to the play of the child's images and volition in expressing them."[41] She continued by explaining the manifold functions of play as it contributes to individuality. By 1909, when the "Report of the Committee of Nineteen" was presented to the International Kindergarten Union, play and activity were linked to problem solving: "When mind is consciously exercised in the solution of a problem it is creatively self-active. In its broadest sense therefore, creative self-activity is exercised whenever an end is set up and means are selected for its realization."[42] Leaders in kindergarten education had moved from a Froebelian to a Deweyan view of self-activity. Even these clear statements of Dewey's ideas did not make them easily operable in a school setting.

With education as the reconstruction of experience taken seriously, the home and family life seemed an appropriate starting point in the kindergarten. At this time the housekeeping corner became a permanent part of the classroom so that the children could recreate their knowledge of family living in a larger setting. One observer of the Dewey sub-primary classroom at the University of Chicago laboratory school found children using pieces of wood, spools, and paper to make furniture for play houses.[43] Another report described the morning lunchtime in which the children took entire charge of food preparation, serving each other, and washing and putting away the dishes.[44] At a later time and in another setting Louise Alder extended the reliving of experiences out into the community, while emphasizing the need to stay close to the child's experiencing:

> We no longer talk of "The Carpenter," but each child sets to work to find out how his home was built, and then he applies as many of the principles as possible to the making and furnishing of houses for the doll family. We no longer talk of "The Grocer" and "The Farmer" but are led to observe the activities of these men in an attempt to solve the big problem of Where We Get Our Food! The problems chosen for the child's solution must be connected with his own living and his own experience in a very intimate way, and the solution of them must lead him to real thinking, to putting forth interested and earnest effort. It will not mean listening to long explanations of things, but the actual handling of things, of experimenting, of doing in order to discover.[45]

EDUCATION AND DEMOCRACY

As children were engaging in the reconstruction of experience they were part of that small classroom community that Dewey envisioned as the training ground for democracy. In his allegiance to democratic values

Dewey called on the school to release the full potentialities of group life. When the organization centered around cooperative, productive work, the principles of shared interests and responsibility prevailed. Each individual contributed through open inquiring, reflective thinking, and moving toward a commonly accepted goal. It followed that the locus of authority existed within the community of learners who lived and worked together and where each had a participant voice. Even young children could participate in community experiences adapted to the conditions of childhood. The school thus operated would help the individual attain his potential for social contributions. It was in the workings of the social whole that intellectual and social self-realization developed. Dewey also conceived this form of education to be the basis for effective social change.

Convinced that rapid social and economic changes in the United States demanded a restructuring of social institutions, Dewey placed his faith in the educative process. In a Platonic sense, Dewey cast the school as a lever of social change. Early in his career, when asked to state his pedagogic creed, he declared that "education is the fundamental method of social progress and reform." The teacher, he claimed, could act as "the prophet of the true God and the usherer in of the true kingdom of God" by "the formation of the proper social life" and "the securing of the right social growth."[46] Small wonder that Dewey's philosophy of education was so welcomed by leaders in the kindergarten field. They had long believed that by starting with the child early they could set him on the right path in life. Dewey reconfirmed their belief and provided a definite process to bring it to fulfillment.

This hope that the younger generation could ultimately rebuild social organizations was based upon the conception of guiding and encouraging them toward more intelligently creative lives. When Dewey spoke of the school as a society, he expected it to approximate a more ideal set of values, not to mirror the existing values of society. If the child would experience the type of training that enabled him to be self-directive and critically evaluative from a very early age, effective social reform would follow. The school's role, then, was one of promoting the realization of creative individuality. Dewey's social conception, as he explained it to an audience of parents and other interested persons at the University Elementary School in April 1899, united individual growth and social progress. "Only by being true to the full growth of all the individuals who make it up," he stated, "can society by any chance be true to itself."[47] The natural interest of parents for the advancement of their child was admirable in Dewey's view but their outlook needed to be enlarged. Dewey would extend that concern: "What the best and wisest parent wants for his own child, that must the community want for all its children. Any other ideal for our schools is narrow and unlovely; acted upon, it destroys our democracy."[48]

Seventeen years separate *The School and Society* from *Democracy and Education*, Dewey's more extended explanation of the relationship between the educative process and social behavior.[49] By this time Dewey was a professor at Teachers College, Columbia University, involved in his long and fruitful career there. He had left the University of Chicago after disagreements with its president. Actually his time in Chicago was brief, but for early childhood education his years directing the Laboratory School were potent; it provided the time and the setting to observe his democratic conception of education in action — even to be a participant.

The social view of mind and self did not originate in Dewey's writings. Sociologists, social historians, and social philosophers began to apply the evolutionary concept of growth and change to social institutions as well as individuals and Dewey, as a student of the history of philosophy, was acquainted with contemporary developments. He had studied the pre-Darwinian evolutionary speculation of Herbert Spencer, the survival of the fittest struggle proposed by William Graham Sumner, the social nature of the self presented by George Herbert Mead, and many other such proposals set in motion by Spencer's *The Study of Sociology*.[50] But Dewey entertained a thoroughly radical social point of view as early as 1888, as is shown by a paper in which he argued that economic aristocracy was incompatible with democracy.[51] For above all, Dewey was American in his democratic vision of a way in life in which opportunities for participation in common tasks eventuated in the sharing of the fruits of the common labor. In the evolutionary spirit he emphasized the unfinished nature of society and stressed the possibility of remaking both man and society for the better through the application of the pragmatic method of testing ideas. Dewey's belief in the efficacy of intelligence and education in social change was fully expounded in *Democracy and Education*. At one point he wrote:

> A democracy is more than a form of government; it is primarily a mode of social living, of conjoint communicated experience. The extension in space of the number of individuals who participate in an interest so that each has to refer his own action to that of others, and to consider the action of others to give point and direction to his own, is equivalent to breaking down those barriers of class, race, and national territory which kept men from perceiving the full import of their activity. These more numerous and more varied points of contact denote a great diversity of stimuli to which an individual has to respond; they consequently put a premium on variation in his action. They secure a liberation of powers which remain suppressed as long as the incitations to action are partial, as they must be

in a group which in its exclusiveness shuts out many interests. . . . A society which is mobile, which is full of channels for the distribution of a change occurring anywhere, must see to it that its members are educated to personal initiative and adaptability.[52]

"Powers" that are liberated, "personal initiative and adaptability," and creative individuality Dewey saw as the ideal characteristics of persons devoted to social change. Such characteristics developed under the careful guidance of the teacher who gave direction to learning and promoted order. In the continual reconstruction of experience Dewey anticipated a progression away from the child's immature immediate experiences to those that become more systematic and pregnant with meaning, those that brought the child into contact with subject matter in an orderly manner. The freedom for learning advocated by Dewey was never anarchic behavior but a freeing of the intellect to act purposively, to make effective choices. Only as these characteristics were carefully and deliberately cultivated through appropriate educational experiences could the ideal society become a concrete reality. Instead of recommending complete freedom for the child, Dewey challenged what he considered a reflection of "sentimental idealization of the child's naive caprices and performances."[53] Much later, Dewey castigated schools under the influence of Freudian psychology that "indulged pupils in unrestrained freedom of action and speech, of manners and lack of manners."[54] Responsibility to the social group clearly accompanied freedom, for while Dewey preached the effectiveness of intelligence as an instrument in modifying social institutions, he brought to the pragmatic argument "an unusually strong consciousness of its social import and an urgent sense of the social responsibility" it entailed.[55]

Dewey's basic faith in intelligent and rational thought obscured irrational forces that might govern man's motives or conduct. In *My Pedagogic Creed* Dewey had stated: "I believe that if we can only secure right habits of action and thought, with reference to the good, the true, and the beautiful, the emotions will for the most part take care of themselves."[56] Some critics believe Dewey to have been insufficiently moved by the Freudian emphasis upon the emotions and unconscious motivations.[57]

Dewey's analysis of behavior motivates us once again to consider the role of education in the community. Moral behavior was determined by a set of values learned from, and modified by, experience, for democratic social living required the development of a code of relations with peers and teachers in the school society. Ideally, in the classroom, the system of controls would rest upon social necessity and a rational adjustment of any conflicts. Values would also accrue from a study of the life activities of man, with the youngest children investigating their own immediate environment. In a statement written with his daughter, Evelyn, Dewey strongly affirmed the "moral advantages of the active form of education" that called "for the positive virtues — energy, initiative, and originality." Beyond that "the first business of the public school is to teach the child to live in the world in which he finds himself, to understand his share in it," thus the experiences would have meaning for the learner in terms of his own environment.[58]

This dual conception of the process of value formation through experiencing democratic social relationships and through gaining increasing ability to understand and reconstruct environmental experiences departed radically from Froebel's conception of moral growth. It was hard for some teachers to divorce themselves from the Froebelian conviction that for the building of positive values the child ought to be continually presented with the models of ideal behavior. In one round table discussion on "Programs," Geraldine O'Grady, who taught in a mission kindergarten in New York City, pointed out that if children were given freedom to play they might dramatize a policeman taking a drunken man to jail. The Froebelian position was proposed by a member from Chicago who suggested such play be replaced by the ideal of the soldier or a knight. Annie M. Perry of Boston commented that putting the life of a policeman before the child, something so everyday and common, would tend to lower their ideals. But Alice Temple answered that the ideal of the policeman was quite within the good environment of the city child, therefore, the teacher could help to give strength and vigor to the policeman's part and keep it close to the child's experience. When the chairman of the meeting polled the group, there emerged a strong feeling that experiences needed to be close to the child's environment.[59] Members were at least moving toward the Deweyan view that "the school must relate morality to the actual conditions and problems of community life if it is to enable the child to contribute to the betterment of society."[60]

Leaders clearly and directly articulated Dewey's deeper meaning of moral development derived from children's participation in that miniature school community where they pursued common goals of interest to a group. In 1909 in the "Report of the Committee of Nineteen" the liberals stated their conviction in this way: "Since the moral development of children is affected largely by co-operation, co-operative efforts of various kinds should form an important phase of kindergarten procedure. The co-operation in question may be that of a small group or of all the children for some common end of real interest and value."[61] They clearly believed this to be a distinct possibility.

For no other thinker of the period can we trace the changing thought of leaders in the field of early childhood education as closely as to Dewey and the principles he set forth. The evidence for this comes not only from the discussion of his ideas and the use of his terminology but in the transformation of the curriculum. In the organization of the classroom, the selection of experiences to be undertaken, the new kinds of materials to be provided, the freedom for the child to pursue his interests, and the new conception of the teacher's role, we find reflections of Dewey's recommendations. It was a gradual transformation, debated every step of the way, but by 1925 few evidences of the Froebelian kindergarten remained.

Other influences modified a pure Deweyan stance, to be sure. Child study as it followed the initial impetus given to it by G. Stanley Hall formed a continual source of new insights about chldren. By the 1920s the impact of Edward Thorndike was strongly evident, particularly in the new curriculum that emerged under the leadership of Patty Smith Hill (already discussed). Another book, published two years later and written by Alice Temple and her coauthor Samuel Chester Parker, held more closely to the Deweyan conception of learning as problem solving and based recommendations on a quotation from Dewey that "to maintain the state of doubt and to carry on systematic and protracted inquiry — these are the essentials of thinking."[62] Interestingly, their "scientific justification" for the unification of kindergarten and first-grade teaching, however, was the overlapping of mental ages of children of the two age levels as determined by intelligence tests.[63]

DEWEY'S LEGACY TO EARLY CHILDHOOD EDUCATION

Did Dewey's philosophy of education have a pragmatic attractiveness as suggested by Oscar Handlin?[64] Certainly this designation can be accepted for early childhood education, for Dewey's ideas were pervasive as they revealed the shortcomings of both kindergarten and primary education in the form each had in the 1890s. As Dewey stripped away formerly prized curriculum premises he supplied new proposals meaningful to emerging leaders. His very terms *growth, interaction, continuity,* and *unity* were criticized as vague by some critics, but they had great meaning for those working with young children. Take, for example, new meanings given to the term *unity* by Dewey. The Froebelian metaphysical sense of unity he discarded, but Richard Peters has characterized Dewey's educational theory as exhibiting a "passion for unification."[65] Like Hegel, Dewey could not tolerate dualism, therefore he continually endeavored to synthesize educational aspects that on the surface appeared irreconcilable. In his encyclopedic range over vast areas of thought and action, Dewey sought to bring together the child and his experience, the school and society, interest and effort in education. The titles of his books reveal his quest to bring compatible elements into a unified educational program. If he stood for unification in the conception of education in general, Dewey also extended it to the education of the individual child. He would break down divisions between the home and the school as the child experienced them. In dealing with authentic situations and problems the whole of learning and thinking became a unified process never fragmented into isolated subjects or bits of knowledge. Furthermore, all aspects of the learning child would be involved: his interest, effort, interactions with others, experimentation, evaluative abilities — all contributing to a reasoned solution to the problem at hand. Thus the idea of unity, so meaningful to kindergarten teachers, was transformed for them by Dewey.

Probably the overriding aspect of the appeal of Dewey's philosophy for early childhood leaders was his optimistic social conception; with his emphasis on rationality, he expected reason to reform the world.[66] A faith in human nature led Dewey to envision man as a shaper and evaluator of his own destiny.[67] The shared interests, open communication, and practical experiences dominating life in the miniature community of the school made for a quality of life valuable in itself, but served also "as a springboard for social progress."[68] Dewey's confidence in the common school and its influence on learners was shared by early childhood educators, particularly because Dewey took a long view of education; he anticipated no quick pay-offs. While the moral purpose of education was to prepare persons as worthy members of society, education was not simply a preparation for what would be useful later. Each critical stage of development was valued for the kind of growth appropriate to it. "From the very start therefore the child would become acquainted with, and through his life learn even better, the relationship of knowledge to conduct. That was the most worthy function of his schooling"; Handlin thus summarized Dewey's emphasis as gleaned from a number of sources.[69] For early childhood educators the betterment of society began with the young child.

Such an encompassing vision for education has led some critics to propose that it has not yet been realized.[70] Certainly some of Dewey's critiques of education are still fitting today. An overemphasis on the mere symbols of knowledge ungrounded in firsthand experience is a prevalent aspect of current education. The quantification of educational outcomes dominates curricular planning in a manner repudiated by Dewey. While recognizing some minimal value in measurement, Dewey found norms hostile to the aims of the school as he delineated them. Firmly he stated: "*Quality* of activity and consequence is more important for the teacher than any quantitative element."[71] Freed intelligence and democratic functioning rested upon experiences whose qualities embodied these possible outcomes. That many failed to capture the importance of quality impelled Barbara Biber to write: "Perhaps if Dewey's conceptualization of *experience* had been fully understood, the pendulum might not have had to perform wide, wasteful swings as we have experienced" them in the curriculum for young children.[72] Yet within the progressive education movement Biber recognized crosscurrents that weakened its impact. For, as she wrote, "within the goal to 'educate the whole child,' two divergent positions emerged: to develop intelligence as a basis for personal and social effectiveness *vs.* to channel emotional forces into productive thinking and acting."[73] The first course was Dewey's theoretical position, the second stemmed from depth psychology — that concern for the emotional processes and the development of personality not within Dewey's framework for education yet growing rapidly in the same decades. These two crosscurrents remained unintegrated in progressive education and led Biber "to see within the progressive movement itself the embryonic stage of a cognitive-affective dichotomy even though the heart of the movement had been its opposition to the traditionalist's myopic concern for intellectual achievement."[74]

THE IMPACT OF THE INDUCTIVE METHOD

If we look back at all the theoretical formulations gaining momentum around the turn of the century: objective child study, a connectionist theory of learning, a democratic conception of education, they have one common link — their evolutionary base. When one realizes that each of these new directions of thought and investigation has links forged closely to Darwin's *The Origin of Species*, the impact of this publication is startling, indeed. For since this time much child study has adhered closely to the gathering of observational, objective data (the scientific method) and early childhood has relied heavily on child study for knowledge about the young child. Behaviorism, so prevalent in education today and reaching down into early childhood with increased emphasis, has no foundation without the acceptance of evolutionary doctrine. Even Dewey's social conception of education is premised upon growth, change, and reconstruction. Few ideas in the history of education have had such a widespread influence. Gone was any reliance on metaphysical deductive thinking; the inductive method had garnered man's allegiance.

But the concern for the inner, the subjective life that seemed to be at odds with Dewey's rationalism, had also been moving forward since Sigmund Freud's early psychoanalytic investigations in the last decades of the nineteenth century. We must now turn to his work and its influence on early childhood education.

7 The Psychoanalytic View of Man

The kindergarten embraced Dewey's principles of education, turned to child study for assistance, and, to some extent, added connectionism as a directive for the curriculum; it was the nursery school that most readily accepted psychoanalytic thinking. During the decade of the 1920s nursery schools replaced the kindergarten as the first rung of the educational ladder. One U.S. Office of Education bulletin reported the number of nursery schools increasing from three to 262 between 1920 and 1930.[1] The years under five became discussed as that period of life when some of the child's most fundamental and lasting attitudes toward life were formed. The nursery school could function to alleviate the misdirected efforts of parents — inhibitors permanently preventing the child from effectively using his powers.[2] At Walden School in New York City more emphasis was placed on the early years, for "Analytic Psychology in probing the mysteries of the adult psyche finds that tendencies and attributes previously assumed as inherent in the 'personality' of the individual are the result of the emotional colorings of the earliest years."[3] Therefore the role of the school was grounded on an understanding of the "naturally irrational child," an understanding that would help the teacher to discern the child's inner conflicts and identifications, and to fulfill his needs. Harriet Johnson, who in 1917 with Caroline Pratt and Lucy Sprague Mitchell organized the Bureau of Educational Experiments in New York City, wrote that the nursery school must foster creative, dynamic personality. Deep within outward manifestations of affectivity she found attitudes and interests developing early. "They will be the driving force of the organism throughout life," she stated, "and are roused, developed and modified by the interaction of organism and environment."[4]

The pioneer nursery school in England had as its main impetus the determination to provide healthy conditions and physical care for children of the poor. At the Deptford School Clinic in London the nursery school was started by two sisters, Rachel and Margaret McMillan, in 1908. The vision of education founded on physical nurture was later expanded to embrace other areas of growth, particularly the affective. Mental health was added to the physical, as it was deemed important for the nursery school to provide the child with the means and opportunity to express his own feelings and ideas, also to supply an atmosphere of love and sympathy.[5] Another British educator wrote of just beginning to realize the great danger inherent in the repression of the appetites and instincts of the young. Olive Wheeler argued that the nursery school could prevent the unnatural repression of primitive impulses and avoid overrepressive discipline "which drives impulses below the threshold of consciousness, where they tend to organize themselves into a sort of secondary, antisocial personality."[6]

Not all nursery schools incorporated analytic thinking at this early date; some centers were established to promote child study research. As previously discussed, the Yale Clinic of Child Development was engaged in establishing norms of development with children. Gesell himself reported on 500 children studied to determine levels of motor development, language, adaptive behavior, and personal habits and conduct. The individual differences the study revealed, Gesell attributed to the conditioning environment. "It is almost dismaying to note how promptly and how relentlessly the conditioning process begins. It begins literally at birth," he wrote.[7] Still other nursery schools rested upon the belief that habit formation was the essence of early training. Rose Alschuler wrote in this vein when she stated her belief that "the fabric of life is made up of a network of habits, and that the pattern of the fabric in each life is started with the beginning of life itself. Nervous stability is often given or taken away through the habits established in the first two years."[8] Eating, sleeping, even responsiveness to others she described as largely a matter of early habit training. A basic book on nursery school described the environment as providing for many kinds of habit training.[9]

Despite the variety of theoretical strands in evidence at the nursery school level, Ilse Forest, making an historical and critical study published in 1927, found psychoanalysis strongly influencing preschool education both in England and the United States.[10] Particularly did she find the Freudian concept of discipline to be the criteria for dealing with nursery school behavior. For, of course, this entire new emphasis stemmed from the work of Sigmund Freud which we will now investigate.

FREUDIAN PSYCHOLOGY

Darwin and Freud stand out as architects of present-day conceptions of man to the point where psychologists scarcely consider behavior uninfluenced by their views. Both basic conceptions had sweep and brilliance that produced dismay and dissension. Darwin's beliefs formed the basis for others to build psychological theories; Freud built his own ideas into an explanation of the structure and dynamics of personality. While Bruner considers Freud's doctrine the more daring and revolutionary insight, he believes Freud to be inconceivable without Darwin.[11] Darwin's evolutionism laid the ground for viewing life as a struggle and for relating this struggle to the life-generating processes.[12]

It was essentially Freud's way of conceiving man, his metaphor, his imagery that drew opposition. He destroyed the serenity of Rousseau's conception of man as essentially good by reviving a demonic view of the child that had been absent from psychology for a century and a half.[13] Freud pictured the individual as a battleground for conflicting urges; he presented man as engaged in a continual struggle between unconscious, instinctual trends and the socially responsible ego. The instinctual urges Freud highlighted were essentially sexual and aggressive. The irrational in man became a focus of study for Freud in a manner anathema to the scientists of his day. While the opposition to Darwin's ideas stemmed mainly from the clergy, Freud's opponents up to about 1910 were actually "a Who's Who of psychiatry and neurology."[14] It was Freud's introduction of a wholly new factor — the unconscious forces of behavior in human thinking — that drew such marked repulsion.

FREUD—THE MAN AND THE CLINICAL METHOD

To understand Freud is to recognize the dominating factors in his life. He was a Viennese Jew living in a prudish Victorian society where anti-Semitism was epidemic. The general atmosphere of Victorian Vienna no doubt supplied the source of his emphasis upon the sexual drive. He was the oldest of seven surviving children, and with the family hopes centered upon him, he developed a commitment to achievement. Indeed, without apology, Freud hoped to be a genius.[15] It is probably significant that he considered life to be hard rather than easy.[16] In his early career in medicine he soon challenged the scientific assumptions on which German medicine was based and these challenges led his thought into new psychological channels. His biographer, Ernest Jones, attributes to Freud an extraordinary respect for what he calls the "single fact" — the single observation that seems inconsistent with other data or general knowledge. Linked with the intellectual quality of judgment, Jones explains Freud's attention to the single fact, his intuitive insights, as the mind of a genius at work.[17] These insights led Freud to an emancipation from current practice into the inception of the psychoanalytical method. The term "psychoanalysis" was first employed in 1896 in papers published in French and in German, but Freud had earlier talked about the "psychical analysis" of neurotic behavior.[18]

Psychoanalysis looked inward, not in the manner of the previous notion of introspection in which consciousness was examined, but in inferences gained in order to interpret elements of the unconscious. Clues appeared through hypnosis, dreams, free association, and slips of the tongue, which Freud used clinically as revealing connections to the causes of maladjustment; the clinical technique was clearly one of inference from obtainable clues. Freud embarked upon an extensive period of self-analysis based upon an interpretation of his own dreams, material readily available to him and most used in his books. "His self-analysis proceeded simultaneously with the composition of his magnum opus, *The Interpretation of Dreams*, in which he records many details," wrote Jones and concluded that the interpretation of dreams was the part of his work in which Freud had the greatest confidence.[19]

None of the statistical devices so greatly attracting the attention of American psychologists were applicable to Freud's work. Although, throughout his life, Freud held intellectual integrity as an essential aspect of science, he could not be tied to tedious exactitude. Precise measurement of details was not part of his nature, which was more devoted to revolutionary tendencies that burst the bonds of conventions.[20] The commitment of the mainstream of psychology to exact scientific measurement did not encourage interest in naturalistic observation, "let alone the 'rough and ready' observations and theorizing characteristic of psychoanalysis."[21] The wide use of the clinical method was one of Freud's contributions, although this was not acceptable to many scientists at the time.

A further deflection from the mainstream of psychology was Freud's emphasis upon the unconscious, for enlightened leaders such as James and Dewey emphasized the rational and organized ego as a perfectly natural expression of evolutionary human development. Freud, however, did not equate mental functioning solely with consciousness; for him "mental" consisted of somatic processes, largely unconscious.[22] Indeed, the probing of the unconscious was so central to psychoanalysis that Jones calls "investigation of the unconscious" a "fair definition of psychoanalysis."[23] The overcoming of the individual's natural resistance to this exposure was part of the process. Hence, the consistently favored method has been that of reconstruction: the past of the individual reconstructed from free association and dreams, yielding causal connections to the determinants of behavior. Psychoanalysis stands on the proposition that the crucial determinants of behavior are unconscious, for the life tendencies are conceived to be deeper, more primordial than phenomena of consciousness.

These determinants, however, can be inferred from what is amenable to observation. Every dream, every odd remark, every whim, every word association are claimed to spring basically from tensions within. Psychoanalysis becomes a tension-reducing process; it begins with force and ends with the dissipation of force.[24]

BASIC PREMISES

Freudianism was deeply imbued with the principles of causality and determinism. Freud asserted that all behavior was ultimately drive determined, with drive "defined as a causal agent inherent in the organism."[25] Behavior broadly included feeling, thought, and overt behavior, both normal and pathological, which was to be considered as integrated and indivisible. Every behavioral phenomenon was considered to hold perceptual, memorial, cognitive, motor, and feeling components; thus behavior must be viewed as multifaceted and multiply determined. Since no behavior stood in isolation, but within the framework of a total personality, as an element of a genetic system, much of what existed in the present could only be understood through an exploration of its antecedents. The probing for determinants inevitably included memories going back into childhood. The process pointed with increasing evidence to experiences in childhood as the most important single influence on personal development.

Since Freud found a remarkable number of significant memories concerned with sexual experiences, he gradually concluded that sexual factors exerted a strong influence in neuroses. This became an important and most controversial theme in his writings. Psychosexuality Freud defined broadly in a manner that made it not synonymous with sex. For example, Freud linked thumb sucking to satisfaction gained through an erogenous zone.[26] Startlingly radical, Freud's theory of infantile sexuality portrayed a far more complicated and hidden child than Gesell's work. What Freud presented was an individual forced to deal with conflicting urges from infancy and thus deprived of innocence.

The Structure of Personality

From the basic premises set forth Freud built a structure of personality, explained the dynamics of behavior, and outlined stages of development. The three major interactive systems — the id, ego, and super-ego — represent roughly the biological, psychological, and moral components. The id, the original system embracing everything inherited and present at birth, was designated as the reservoir of psychic energy in close touch with the body. The id experienced increases of energy as tension, which must be discharged for this it could not tolerate. Release of tension might come from reflex action or from the formation of images of a product that removes the tension. An example might be the hunger urge that would be satisfied with food or allayed by images of food to come. The function of the id was to obey the pleasure principle and to render the psychic apparatus as a whole free from excitation.[27] One need of the organism was to develop a new process in relation to reality; that new mechanism was labeled the ego.

The ego was conceived as the organized subdivision of personality standing between the id and the external world. The central role of the ego was designated as binding the mobil energy of the id under the jurisdiction of the reality principle. The purpose was to maintain life, to inhibit the discharge of excitation until environmental conditions were appropriate. The ego controlled all cognitive aspects and all relation to the environment. Under the guidance of the reality principle the ego sought to gratify the wishes of the id in a manner that did not violate the dictates of reality. In Freud's words: "It has the task of self-preservation. As regards *external* events, it performs that task by becoming aware of stimuli, by storing up experiences about them (in the memory), by avoiding excessively strong stimuli (through flight), by dealing with moderate stimuli (through adaptation) and finally by learning to bring about expedient changes in the external world to its own advantage (through activity)."[28]

The super-ego, the last province to be formed, represented morality. It reflected the standards of society and strove for perfection in balancing right and wrong. As a consequence of the praise and punishment of parents, the growth of the super-ego resulted in a conscience that judged behavior and set standards. The process of development was proposed as introjection through which the individual took on as part of himself the standards of his parents. The super-ego was thus described as modeled on the earliest parental images received through commands, accusations, and threats. The super-ego punished the ego through guilt and rewarded it with pride. "The details of the relation between the ego and the super-ego become completely intelligible," wrote Freud, "if they are carried back to the child's attitude toward his parents. This parental influence of course includes in its operation not only the personalities of the actual parents but also the family, racial and national traditions handed on through them, as well as the demands of the immediate social milieu which they represent. In the same way, the super-ego, in the course of an individual's development, receives contributions from later successors and substitutes of his parents, such as teachers and models in public life of admired social ideals."[29] Through Freud's writings it was clear that the early years were most important for the development of the super-ego, this moral arm of the person.

Of course, the boundaries between these structural divisions were never sharp; like areas of color, they were shaded to work together in harmony. But this ideal was not always in evidence and a neurotic individual was described as one in which the systems were in opposition. When the ego had difficulty managing the large number of built-up tensions, it resorted to defense mechanisms.

The propelling force of individual behavior Freud designated as psychic energy. In his day psychology was as much concerned with instincts and energy as was physiology; the needs of the id Freud called instincts — "the somatic demands upon mental life."[30] These basically biological forces aimed always at the satisfaction of instinctual needs. Besides the life-preserving life instincts and the aggressive tendencies of the death instincts, Freud elevated the sex instinct to a high level of importance. A number of bodily erogenous zones were included; the oral, anal, and genital he considered to exercise a decisive influence upon life and to be manifested shortly after birth. The term *libido*, used frequently by Freud, referred to a relatively fixed quantity of energy held by individuals that related primarily to their sex drive.[31] So central to Freud's theory was his conception of the sexual drive that his proposed stages of development were based upon it.

Psychoanalytic Stages of Development and the Avoidance of Negative Defense Mechanisms

A series of dynamically differentiated stages that a child passed through in attaining adulthood were outlined by Freud. The stages were not conceived as completely distinct and ages of transition varied, but the dynamics grew out of Freud's position on infantile sexuality. Responses to the child's behavior in these stages were alleged to be decisive in the development of personality; this was considered particularly true during the first three stages, which covered the first four or five years of life. The oral stage, with the libido localized in the mouth and oral regions, dominated the first months when the infant was dependent upon the mother. Proper oral gratification became linked to the manner of feeding and weaning. Around the age of two the second stage began when libidinal pressures moved to the anal region, thus making the process of toilet training significant for personality development. A repressive regimen produced far-reaching effects, according to Freud, as responses gained at this time were generalized in later behavior. The important aspect of the phallic stage (3–6 years) was the resolution of the Oedipus complex. The strength of the super-ego came into play to form a bulwark against incest. These three significant stages of early childhood were to be further resolved in the subsequent latency and genital periods in which socialization grew and interest became more focused on others.

Early childhood was thus elevated to a period of life of great significance. Putting this point forcefully Kazin writes: "the greatest and most beautiful effect of Freudianism is the increasing awareness of childhood as the most important single influence on personal development."[32] Those drawn to early childhood education profoundly cherished childhood and welcomed the theory that highlighted its importance. Their insistent optimism about infant innocence and human perfectibility grasped "the thesis that permissiveness would free the child of conflict and neurosis."[33] The essential pessimism of Freud's view, which held that the child must inevitably face the confrontation between his urges and reality, was hidden behind the possibility of alleviating the difficulties the child experienced. No doubt Freud's writings made it possible for teachers and parents to be more humane and more sensitive to the child's seemingly irrational behavior. Kessen writes that "the true novelty of psychoanalysis is its respect for the ambiguities and incoherence of childhood."[34]

Permissiveness was the result of efforts to avoid the dire effects suggested by Freud from repression of the child's natural instincts. When the ego became flooded with anxiety it lost the ability to cope effectively and resorted to the use of defense mechanisms that always operated unconsciously. Repression, projection, reaction formation, fixation, and regression might be part of "normal" behavior but when carried to extremes they served as evidence of neurotic or psychotic behavior. All these major defense mechanisms tended to falsify or distort reality: repression by forcing the alarming out of consciousness, projection by attributing to others the traits and characteristics objectionable to the self, reaction formation by placing in consciousness the opposite of impulse, fixation and regression by holding to a specific level or returning to an earlier level of development. Hopefully, these defense mechanisms would be minimized if the child experienced a less restrictive and repressive anxiety-producing environment.

Since growth produced tension, character formation required more positive dynamics for the reduction of tension. Two major methods for dealing with conflictual situations were designated as identification and displacement. In identification the individual took over the characteristics of others and incorporated them as part of the self. This patterning of behavior extended throughout the life cycle, but parents were deemed the most important identification figures, especially during early child-hood. Displacement was the substitution of the original object choice by another one more acceptable to society. Food, for example, the original object of hunger, might be replaced by the collection of recipes. Sublimation, a special form of displacement, occurred when higher cultural achievements took the place of the immediate objects of instinct. Freud pointed out that the development of civilization was made possible by the direction of instinctual energy into culturally creative channels. Indeed, Freud described the artist as one urged on by clamorous instinctual needs to turn away from reality and transfer "all his interest, and all his libido too, on the creation of his wishes in the life of phantasy."[35]

FREUD'S LECTURES IN AMERICA

In September 1909 Freud delivered five lectures on psychoanalysis at Clark University in Worcester, Massachusetts. He had been invited by G. Stanley Hall on the occasion of the celebration of the university's twentieth year. Freud himself declared that the invitation to give these lectures was the first official recognition of his young study. Each of the lectures, given on five successive days, was "composed in half an hour's walk before hand in [Sandor] Ferenczi's company — an illustration of how harmoniously flowing his thoughts must have been," reported Ernest Jones, who was also present at the time.[36] On his return to Vienna Freud was induced to write these extemporaneous speeches and Jones assures us that Freud's verbal memory was so good that the printed version did not depart much from the original delivery. In the first lecture Freud established his conviction about the psychological meanings underlying specific symptoms; this was followed the second day by a discussion of repression and symptom formation. The third and fourth lectures dealt with psychic determinism, especially dreams, and infantile sexuality. Freud concluded his note-less extempore remarks by focusing on transference and resistance.[37]

In these lectures Freud presented, concisely and lucidly, a number of his major impressions concerning the curing of nervous disorders and some of his direct statements may serve to elucidate his meanings. He described the method of psychoanalysis as seeking to bring to conscious recognition the aspects of mental life that were repressed. To attain this state, "the arrogance of consciousness" must be overcome, for Freud described a patient under treatment as subject to two forces operating against each other: "on the one hand his conscious endeavour to bring into consciousness the forgotten idea in his unconscious, and on the other hand, the resistance . . . striving to prevent what was repressed or its derivative from thus becoming conscious."[38] Freud then described the method of free-association in which the subject was instructed to "say whatever comes into his head, even if he considers it incorrect or irrelevant or nonsensical, and above all if he finds it disagreeable to let himself think about what has occurred to him."[39] With this direction carried out Freud felt sure of obtaining the material that would reveal repressed complexes.

The difficulty of getting directly to repressions compelled Freud to investigate the technique of making jokes for he believed they often held significant allusions. He illustrated this with an example.

> Two not particularly scrupulous business men had succeeded, by dint of a series of highly risky enterprises, in amassing a large fortune, and they were now making efforts to push their way into good society. One method, which struck them as a likely one, was to have their portraits painted by the most celebrated and highly-paid artist in the city, whose pictures had an immense reputation. The precious canvases were shown for the first time at a large evening party, and the two hosts themselves led the most influential connoisseur and art critic up to the wall on which the portraits were hanging side by side. He studied the works for a long time, and then, shaking his head, as though there was something he had missed, pointed to the gap between the pictures and asked quietly: "But where's the Saviour?" I see you are all much amused at this joke. Let us now proceed to examine it. Clearly what the connoisseur meant to say was: "You are a couple of rogues, like the two thieves between whom the Saviour was crucified." But he did not say this. Instead he made a remark which seems at first strangely inappropriate and irrelevant, but which we recognize a moment later as an *allusion* to the insult that he had in mind and as a perfect substitute for it. We cannot expect to find in jokes *all* the characteristics that we have attributed to the ideas occurring to our patients, but we must stress the identity of the *motive* for the joke and for the idea. Why did the critic not tell the rogues straight out what he wanted to say? Because he had excellent counter-motives working against his desire to say it to their faces. There are risks attendant upon insulting people who are one's hosts and who have at their command the fists of a large domestic staff. . . . That was the reason why the critic did not express the insult he had in mind directly but in the form of an "allusion accompanied by omission"; and the same state of things is responsible for our patients' producing a more or less distorted *substitute* instead of the forgotten idea we are in search of.[40]

Thus did Freud hope to clarify to his audience, generally unacquainted with psychoanalysis, the subtlety required in obtaining and analyzing clues to the mechanisms of the unconscious.

Dreams, and their interpretation, however, were given in his lectures the most extensive description. Freud approached this topic hesitantly:

I must admit, Ladies and Gentlemen, that I hesitated for a long time whether, instead of giving you this condensed general survey of the whole field of psycho-analysis, it might not be better to present you with a detailed account of dream-interpretation. I was held back by a purely subjective and seemingly secondary motive. It seemed to me almost indecent in a country which is devoted to practical aims to make my appearance as a "dream-interpreter," before you could possibly know the importance that can attach to that antiquated and derided art. The interpretation of dreams is in fact the royal road to a knowledge of the unconscious; it is the securest foundation of psycho-analysis and the field in which every worker must acquire his convictions and seek his training. If I am asked how one can become a psycho-analyst, I reply: "By studying one's own dreams." Every opponent of psycho-analysis hitherto has, with a nice discrimination, either evaded any consideration of *The Interpretation of Dreams*, or has sought to skirt over it with the most superficial objections. If, on the contrary, you can accept the solutions of the problems of dream-life, the novelties with which psycho-analysis confronts your minds will offer you no further difficulties.[41]

The dreams of adults have become so thoroughly subject to distortions that the psychoanalysts must distinguish the "manifest content" of the dream from the "latent dream thoughts" present in the unconscious. Such distinctions led Freud to a consideration of the repressions occurring in childhood and their relationship to sexuality as a determinant.

You will also learn with astonishment from the analysis of dreams (and most convincingly from that of your own) what an unsuspectedly great part is played in human development by impressions and experiences of early childhood. In dream-life the child that is in man pursues its existence, as it were, and retains all its characteristics and wishful impulses, even such as have become unserviceable in later life. There will be brought home to you with irresistible force the many developments, repressions, sublimations and reaction-formations, by means of which a child with a quite other innate endowment grows into what we call a normal man, the bearer, and in part the victim, of the civilizaton that has been so painfully acquired.

I should like you to notice, too, that the analysis of dreams has shown us that the unconscious makes use of a particular symbolism, especially for representing sexual complexes. This symbolism varies partly from individual to individual; but partly it is laid down in a typical form and seems to coincide with the symbolism which, as we suspect, underlies our myths and fairy tales.[42]

In his fourth lecture Freud discussed his view of infantile sexuality, but not without some consideration for the alarm it might produce in his listeners. "Put away your doubts," he admonished them, "and join me in a consideration of infantile sexuality from the earliest age."[43] He recognized that his wide use of the term, related in its earliest phases to kinds of pleasurable feelings independent of the reproductive function, was an unaccustomed one. To limit the term narrowly, however, meant, in Freud's view, to miss much that was significant about early behavior.

> It means that you are sacrificing an understanding of the perversions and the connection between the perversions, the neuroses and normal sexual life; and you are making it impossible for you to recognize in its true significance the easily observable beginnings of the somatic and mental erotic life of children. But however you may choose to decide the verbal usage, you should bear firmly in mind that psycho-analysts understand sexuality in the full sense to which one is led by a consideration of infantile sexuality.[44]

Here is evident the strong determinism of psychoanalysis, for in every case the analyst expected to find sufficient motives for every behavioral occurrence in an analysis of the early years.

The significance of childhood for Freud was as a source of the impressions and events that determined the later onset of illness. "It is only experiences in childhood that explain susceptibility to later traumas and it is only by uncovering these almost invariably forgotten memory-traces and by making them conscious that we acquire the power to get rid of the symptoms," Freud answered his audience.[45] And he ended his fourth lecture at Clark University with this statement: "You can, if you like, regard psycho-analytic treatment as no more than a prolongation of education for the purpose of overcoming the residues of childhood."[46]

It is not possible to know the direct impact of these particular lectures on early childhood education. Their value here has been in the clarity and brevity with which Freud stated basic premises.

ASSESSMENT OF PSYCHOANALYSIS

Freud pointed psychology in a completely new direction, the recognition that behavior is not propelled by rational thought alone, and in doing so he ventured into completely new territory. Even psychologists and therapists who have parted with many of the specifics of Freudian psychology credit him with providing for the first time a perspective on the inner workings of psychic processes. He opened up areas for discussion that had previously been hidden in the attitudes and restrictions of Victorian society: the unconscious, human sexual life, and neurotic behavior.

In the expansion of this theory, all of it derived from his own clinical work with patients suffering from hysteria, nervous disorders, and character difficulties, Freud depicted a structure of personality, the dynamics of functioning, and stages of development. As encompassing as this may seem it must be examined in the light of its single base — retrospective analysis that elevated early childhood to a place of prime significance. For the antecedent — consequent relationship dominates Freudian theory; what man is results from early childhood influences. Furthermore, man is caught up in infantile strivings to serve the pleasure principle — the pursuit of pleasurable excitement and the avoidance of pain; nowhere in Freud's system is there a recognition of a loftier motivational system. A purposive individual who pursues ideals and social goals in the face of hardships hardly fits into Freud's conception. Small wonder that Dewey rejected psychoanalytic thinking.

For all the importance Freud attached to early childhood, he spent relatively little time working directly with children. True, one of his most celebrated cases was that of "Little Hans," for the analysis of the phobia of a five-year-old boy confirmed for Freud the early sexual instincts he had postulated from retrospective stories of adults. From a contemporary, Abraham Brill, we learn also that Freud's relationship with his own children was one of subdued freedom and congeniality. A recent biographer has written that each of Freud's three sons and three daughters developed as an unstressed and stable individual.[47] But "Freud tended to regard the child as an adult in matters of cognition," writes Howard Gardner, who adds that Freud was inclined to ignore such cognitive aspects as concept formation, moral judgment, problem solving, and logical reasoning, either inferring their presence at an early age or viewing them as defense mechanisms.[48] Summarizing this analysis Gardner points out that despite the power Freud attributed to early childhood his view of the child was as an immature, simpler adult. Lacking crucial information, Freud believed the young child able to conceptualize certain complex notions. Indeed, some of his statements such as those on infantile narcissism and children's ideas of sex seem untenable in the light of new understandings on the gradual development of a sense of self and the child's gradual emergence into representational thought that subsequent theory has revealed.

With all its complexity Freud's view of man was exceedingly pessimistic. Of this Rich contends: "The problem with Freud is that he built a theory of human nature by studying man at his worst," for what he gleaned about man was from those in serious difficulty rather than man at his best.[49] To consider man unalterably tied to a picture of conflict provided scant hope for the individual or for mankind. The fact that at heart man was considered irrational, unsocialized, and destructive of others and self was so basic a belief of psychoanalysis that it was accepted without question by its followers. The child did not escape this demonic view, for no matter how his parents or teachers tried to alleviate basic conflicts, "Freud's child must inevitably face the confrontation of his wishes, unbearable to parents and inevitably unbearable to him, with the facts of the world."[50]

PLAY, DISCIPLINE, AND CREATIVE EXPRESSION

Teachers of young children did engage in efforts to alleviate the basic psychic conflicts of childhood. The effects of Freudian postulates can be found particularly in connection with play, discipline, and creative expression. Play, valued since the days of Froebel, took on deeper psychological meanings as it was deemed important for the child to experience individual play or very loosely organized group play without the application of obvious pressure or coercion.[51] Play served the double function of providing an outlet for deep emotional needs and of supplying the teacher with clues to those needs. "It is doubtless impossible to estimate just how far a rich play life enables children to live through and resolve the conflicts involved in the early processes of growing up," wrote Harriet Johnson, an early advocate of this point of view.[52] The wise and observant teacher could find the play of even two- and three-year-olds revealing impulsive tendencies based upon deep emotional urges.

The end point of any control of the child's behavior, Ilse Forest declared, is a well-adjusted personality.[53] The requirements for adjustment were a sense of security and lack of repressive discipline; the danger of repression was the force that thwarted urges retained as unconscious motives of conduct. The overzealous emphasis on certain habits might well lead to unfortunate reactions; repressive toilet training could no longer be justified.

The most far-reaching utilization of the psychoanalytic view of man occurred in the area of creativity for sublimation was proposed by Freud as a major means of reducing inner conflict. Sublimation, a special displacement in which an original object choice was replaced by a more socially acceptable choice, accounted for the great creative acts performed in the cultural sphere. To educators, however, the process of sublimation became a method of reducing personal conflict and the task of education one of sublimating the child's repressed emotions into socially useful channels. All artistic expression could serve this purpose. A survey of preschool education in 1927 revealed increased interest in character education and in encouraging creative expression in children.[54] Opportunities for free expression became viewed as an insistent demand of childhood and children's creations a sure guide to understanding them. Overt behavior presented only part of the emotional life of the child; the deep springs beneath the surface required an outlet. In order for these deeper emotions to become stable and satisfying, "normal living depends upon their finding natural channels or contributing their flow to the more placid streams of conscious conduct."[55] Play materials provided tools for expression; blocks could be a medium for the expression of feelings; painting and drawing revealed unconscious urges.

Preschool education was not alone in espousing creative expression as an essential of the curriculum. In an interpretive survey of pioneering schools written in 1929, Harold Rugg found a number of new schools where the teaching was directed by child interest. The change of curriculum Rugg attributed to a change in purpose, that of growth through self-expression.[56] So pervasive did this function of the school become that he believed it redirected the whole progressive education movement. Rugg's major publication on curriculum published in 1928 and written with Ann Shumaker was an interpretive survey of schools in which self-expression triumphed.[57] The crux of progressive education was no longer the social reformism proposed by Dewey but the advancement of self-expression as a means of personal growth; for "in creative self-expression they found the quintessential meaning of the progressive education movement," at that time, stated Cremin.[58]

Creative writing flourished under Hughes Mearns' sympathetic encouragement and stimulation of older children at Lincoln School, the demonstration school at Teachers College. Mearns, an associate of Rugg at Teachers College, Columbia University, did not limit his philosophy of self-expression to creative writing alone; he expanded it to embrace the entire curriculum. In powerful language Mearns described the creative curriculum as one in which "personality develops with the springing certainty of a dry seed dropped onto moist earth."[59] He argued that curriculum regarded as the development of creative power made for great artists, great scholars, and thinkers; it produced distinction. The method Mearns offered for promoting the creative impulse he considered to be most observable in young children and most readily flourishing in play. The spirit of play—unrestrained, outpouring, genuinely engrossing—was evidence of creativeness and needed cultivation.[60]

For all these instances of the direct application of Freudian ideas in the classroom, many teachers remained untouched by its doctrines. So educated were they in the beliefs of connectionism that the chief influence of Freud came indirectly, "through gradual public acceptance of the psychoanalytical image of the child."[61] Its concepts have gradually penetrated popular thought, although often in unclear form, making not only a new vocabulary but a mode of considering and judging man. Certainly psychoanalysis has exerted a subtle, indirect, almost unnoticed effect upon child-rearing practices and classroom climate. Few who employ the vocabulary and accept its premises understand the sources of the theory or the view of man it entails.

Psychologists have not agreed upon Freud's position regarding nature or nurture as the propelling force of development. Two writers propose that he was "simultaneously neither and both a nativist and nurturist," for Freud pointed to the genetic-experiential origins of mental disease.[62] On the other hand, Freud insisted that the explanatory principles of behavior were rooted in the organism, in the instinctual drives. He always emphasized the organic and physical rather than the social and cultural.[63] So it is unclear how much Freud himself would have accepted these modifications in the curriculum as a means of fostering a healthier personality.

The psychoanalytic system necessarily outgrew Freud. It has been estimated that Freud's precise movement broke apart even before the First World War.[64] Two students of Freud parted with him early; Carl Jung because he rejected Freud's pansexualism, Felix Adler because of his insistence that power feelings, not sex, were prime motivators. The major change, however, that was felt in early childhood education was the break with Freud's exclusively biological approach and the elevation of the surrounding culture as the source of the dynamics and desires of behavior. Eric Fromm, for example, tended to emphasize personal relatedness to others. Looking for the origins of anxiety and frustration in the pressures and conflicts that arise in social situations, Erik Erikson, Daniel Prescott, Lawrence Frank, and later James Hymes, Jr., interpreted this point of view so directly and so persuasively for early childhood educators that it became a dominant influence in the next decades.

8 Focus on Affective Growth

By the middle decades of the twentieth century the expanding provision of education for young children may be characterized by the strong focus placed on each child's affective development. It was not, however, Freud's vision that was attached to early childhood education for in the hands of neo-Freudians his theory had undergone a metamorphosis. Urie Bronfenbrenner has called the striking change that occurred a "socialization" in which the genesis of behavior was no longer viewed as *within* but *without* the child. "The biological and instinctual bases of the theory," wrote Bronfenbrenner, "have been set aside, and the social aspects have been further developed through the fields of cultural anthropology and sociology."[1] With such a monumental revision of theory Bronfenbrenner suggested that Freud might have had difficulty in recognizing many ideas as originally his own.

The major modification made in Freud's theory enabled neo-Freudians and educators to ally psychoanalysis to their firmly held view of infant innocence and of the perfectibility of man. Kessen states: "The essential pessimism of Freud's view was hidden behind a thesis that permissiveness would free the child of conflict and neurosis."[2] As neo-Freudians dropped the exclusive biological approach of Freud they concentrated on the culture as a source of the dynamics of behavior. Many spoke directly to early childhood educators in a way that helped to build a new sensitivity to the depth and power of emotional responses. The inner struggles of the child as he grew up in a culture that inevitably produced conflict, his desire for independence even when dependence was a necessity, and his need for support in holding strong emotions in check: all these ambivalences of development, and many more, were eloquently explained. These new explanations were destined to have a pervasive influence on early childhood education through the 1960s and because they diverge so crucially from some of Freud's basic premises, they need to be investigated at this point. Influential interpreters will be used illustratively for they elaborated the psychological needs of the child as they arose in his interaction with cultural demands. There was no clearer interpreter of this point of view than Lawrence Frank.

120

LAWRENCE K. FRANK AND CHILD DEVELOPMENT

Beginning with the decade of the 1920s the child development movement in the United States became a potent force with Lawrence Frank
wielding considerable influence upon aspects of the developing science.
Frank began his career as an economist whose entrance into the field of
human growth was spurred by early studies of human welfare in New
York City and New York state. His work as an economist brought him
into contact with Wesley Clair Mitchell, the founder of the business-cycle
theory, but it was Mitchell's wife, Lucy Sprague Mitchell, who had the
strong and lasting effect on Frank's life. Mrs. Mitchell's interest in children
and research compelled her to establish, with Harriet Johnson, the Bureau
of Educational Experiments (which later became known as Bank Street
School and currently as the Bank Street College of Education), as a
scheme for combining research and experimental education. Frank followed closely the work of this bureau and became convinced of the need
for systematic and intensive study of child growth and development. He
recognized that a sound program of child rearing and child care was dependent upon research in this field and he was able to translate these
beliefs into action through the Laura Spelman Rockefeller Memorial, a
liaison that Frank recalled in the following manner:

> In the spring of 1923 Beardsley Ruml, the newly appointed director of the
> Rockefeller Memorial, told me he was perplexed by the question of how
> the Memorial could usefully expend a million or so a year for the benefit
> of children. . . . When I proposed the child study program and indicated
> how it could be implemented through research centers and fellowships for
> the training of personnel and by a concurrent program of parent educa-
> tion all over the country, Ruml asked me to undertake the development
> of this program and persuaded the trustees to approve and make the grants
> that I proposed.[3]

Under the aegis of the Spelman Memorial, child study institutes were established at Teachers College, Columbia University, in 1924; the University of Minnesota in 1925; and the University of California, Berkeley, in
1927. Other institutes were enlarged, as at the Iowa Child Welfare Research Station and the Clinic of Child Development at Yale under the
direction of Arnold Gesell. This was the beginning of a movement that
expanded greatly with Spelman Memorial funds and from other sources.

Not only the available funds but the professional climate of the era supported Frank's work. Frank, himself, recognized the rapid expansion of
child study as an outgrowth "of the growing awareness of the importance
of childhood and the increasing concern for the improvement in the nur-

ture and education of children as aroused by Dewey and Parker, by Hall, and also by Freud . . . whose theories emphasizing the crucial significance of early childhood were being discussed in the 1920s."[4] This auspicious climate for establishing a child development movement included a faith in science as providing a solution to problems and an aura of business optimism that generated the resources. The 1919 White House Conference on Children and Youth took pains to point out how alarmingly poor was the physical and educational showing of World War I army recruits. Improved care of the nation's children was a necessity. Not surprisingly the answer to the problem seemed to rest in the scientific knowledge of child development and the use of the type of care this knowledge indicated.

Frank's efforts to support the building of authoritative knowledge of the child and for deriving effective prescriptions for child care were matched by his grasp of available theoretical knowledge, which he conveyed through lectures and articles. His many contacts with researchers, developmental specialists, and all engaged in the human sciences, together with his ability to organize and generalize the concepts of others, supported his communications with substance. His dissemination of ideas permeated the field of child development to the point where the following remark seemed to fit: "I am sure that someone must have quoted you the recently made remark that theories of child development in America followed the age of the Frank children, and as the Frank children grew older, the theories changed."[5] Frank was a synthesizer of ideas with a pervasive conviction that persons were ongoing coherences and that imaginative, disciplined, undiscouraged work would reveal the significant changes across the developmental span. In his writings he presented a broad view of ideas, increasingly integrating new knowledge as it became available so that by the end of his career his writing encompassed a number of theoretical positions.

The Fundamental Needs of the Child

In 1937 when Frank eloquently presented his views to the National Conference for Nursery Education in Nashville, Tennessee, he spoke mainly as a neo-Freudian. Later published in *Mental Hygiene* magazine, this speech, "The Fundamental Needs of the Child," became influential in teacher preparation.[6] As a convincing interpreter of depth psychology as it related to early socialization, Frank, in this article, explained that the gradual molding of behavior to conform to acceptable societal patterns inevitably held frustrations and anxiety. Frank had faith, however, that if children were given affectionate reassurance and tolerance for individual, temperamental differences in the early years, they would become well-adjusted, creative, happy, peaceful adults.

Frank opened his persuasive and well-reasoned speech to nursery school educators with a recognition of the momentous step taken in discussing *the needs of the child* as a basis for his nurture. Anthropological studies had revealed the general practice of centuries of molding a child into "the image prescribed by the culture as the only right form for a man or a woman."[7] All over the world the nurture and education of children tended to be "dictated by religious, ethical and moral ideas, by political and economic requirements, by social class lines, [which] ended by an extraordinary variety of ideas and purposes all more or less remote from the child himself."[8] It was Frank's intention to redress this lack of consideration for the child's needs in the socialization process by delineating the effect of certain coercions and pressures exerted upon the child. While only a fragmentary knowledge of child needs was available, since the process of growth was only undergoing study, Frank offered a positive generalization:

> Probably the most general statement that we can make about the child's needs is that he should be protected from distortions, from unnecessary deprivations and exploitations by adults-parents, teachers and nurses, physicians, psychologists, and others engaged in dealing with children.[9]

In the rest of the article he went on to describe specific needs and the manner in which the child could be protected.

Foremost among fundamental needs Frank proposed acceptance of each child as an individual person with full recognition and appreciation of idiosyncratic temperamental make-up and differing needs. Frank strongly expressed this point:

> It is not without reason, therefore, that we stress this primary and inalienable need of the child to be accepted as a unique individual, or, if the parents cannot or will not accord that acceptance, the need to be protected and reinforced against the destructive, warping influence of these parental biases. Every child suffers to a greater or less extent from this denial of his own personal, temperamental individuality, because even the most emancipated parents are not wholly free from the desire to see their children conform to the images they have constructed. Moreover, every teacher has these partialities, often unconscious, which incline her toward one child and away from another. Further, the child himself is subject to the strong desire to be like the parents, however out of harmony with his own make-up such an identification may be. It is interesting to see how the recognition of individual differences is resisted even by professionally trained per-

sons, such as teachers, who will accept the fact of such differences with respect to mental capacity, as shown by standardized mental tests, but deny it with respect to personality, temperament, physical maturity, and other obvious characteristics.[10]

Recognition of individual growth necessarily refuted any emphasis upon chronological age standards.

Following Freud's insistence that the handling of feeding and toilet training in the early years might account for personality twists or give rise to persistent needs, Frank included these specifics in his discussion, always linking his recommendations to the nursery school situation. Breast-feeding and the "affectionate cuddling" that accompanied it formed a source of "belongingness" and deprivation might be mitigated for the bottle-fed baby if his feeding also included warmth and security. But for all children weaning needed careful consideration.

> But even the breast-fed infant must sooner or later lose that happiness and comfort and face the process of weaning, which may create anxiety and irritability if too abruptly or roughly handled. During weaning the child needs additional reassurances and comforting to prevent acute feelings of insecurity and anxiety and to lessen the loss of sucking. Every deprivation is a threat to the child, a source of anxiety which can be mitigated by affectionate reassurance which makes him feel that the deprivation is not a punishment and that he is still loved. The important question for nursery schools to ask is what can they do for the children who have been deprived of breast-feeding or unwisely weaned, and who need to be reassured and protected, helped to outgrow their anxiety, and aided with affectionate reassurance.[11]

Eliminations and their regularization presented possible traumas for the child for he was asked to surrender his own physiological autonomy when toilet-training began. Frank found the concern of many parents for early toilet training to raise a question for nursery schools about their own role in providing reassurance for the anxious child and in making toilet functions an unemotional subject and action. Certainly nursery schools should not be guilty of aggravating the child's insecurity by rigid rules or making a fuss over "slips" in toileting. Thus was Freud's attention to oral and anal erogenous zones reflected in Frank's interpretation. However, Frank went beyond overt handling of these situations to point out the importance of "the emotional tone or attitude" of the adults for "the child reacts to the tone or attitude and feels the tenseness or overemphasis or dislike in the adult's voice and handling."[12] These could provide the source of reassurance or of trauma.

Each of the fundamental and recurring problems of early childhood — sibling rivalry, controlling emotions, fears, grief, taking on sex roles, learning the inviolabilities of the culture, accepting authority — was dealt with at length by Frank, as were the child's needs engendered by these situations.

In all circumstances arousing strong emotions constant patience, simplified enlightenment, and supportive reassurance were the continued requirements if the child was to escape confusion and anxiety and possible lifelong unhappiness. Of the young child's induction into the regularities of group life Frank wrote:

> These lessons are indeed formidable, and the young child struggling with the complicated customs of group life faces a heavy task for which he needs endless patience and sympathetic teaching. How often a little mistake over private property, which he is just beginning to understand, evokes sudden and immediate punishment, with accusations of "thief" and "liar" and other terrifying characterizations. When we realize that these early lessons in observing the inviolabilities are the most essential steps in preparing for group living, perhaps we shall devise more desirable and effective methods of teaching them, and shall remember to provide toleration and reassurance for the bewildered child who is attempting to assimilate the cumulative customs of thousands of years. It is little wonder that the learning of these inviolabilities, involving as they do repeated frustrations and a form of negative conditioning that inhibits the response to biologically adequate stimuli of objects and persons, should so frequently impair the child's whole adult life, causing him to face every encounter and every negotiation with timidity or anxiety, or to be intensely preoccupied with getting the better of every one in all situations.[13]

Such dire results, however, need not follow if the authority figure was benevolent and helpful.

The requirements for promoting healthy personalities were, then, the security of stable, persistently uniform situations, the support of endless patience and tolerance, and, above all, the strength given by dependable human relations. These fundamental requirements, which included no repressive policies, no routinization, and no withdrawal of love for any reason, could be supplied by the nursery school. Indeed, Frank viewed the nursery school as a prime agency for mental health.

> The opportunity in pre-school education to build wholesome, sane, cooperative, and mature personalities, and to determine the future of our culture, is unlimited. The discharge of that responsibility lies in helping the young child to meet the persistent life tasks and to fulfill his insistent needs.

But the nursery school cannot do this alone. It must have collaboration from the kindergarten and the grade schools, and it must find some way of co-operating with the home and the family, despite the frequent blindness and resistance of the parents. If nursery-school teachers were to realize that they are like parents, with their personal peculiarities, their emotional resistance and susceptibilities, their ignorance and rigid convictions — which may be just as undesirable for the child as the home practices they deprecate — perhaps such a realization would make them more tolerant and more willing to seek a basis of collaboration in meeting the fundamental needs of the child.[14]

Play and the Emotions

Not surprisingly, Frank could be counted among persons valuing play as an essential for mental health. He was instrumental in forming the quintessential publication on the significance of play for emotional adjustment, *Understanding Children's Play*. Large numbers of teachers and directors of nursery schools and day care centers were involved in recording children's play experiences, which were then interpreted to reveal the child's emotional and social development. Some indication of the number and range of individuals contributing to the study was provided in the acknowledgments that preceded the text: ninety-three teachers and directors of nursery schools were assisted by numerous students, volunteers, photographers, and toy suppliers, all listed by name. This extensive study was carried out by the Caroline Zachry Institute under a grant provided by the National Institute of Mental Health in 1947. Frank organized and supervised the project, which was directed by Ruth E. Hartley. Finally, the vast amount of data collected was condensed and revised for publication by Robert M. Goldenson.

Frank proposed that a major insight was revealed by the vast array of records and comments: to understand the language of play is to come close to the minds and hearts of children. "The inner workings of young children have a philosophy and a poetry of their own," he wrote, "and, like all philosophy and poetry, they can be appreciated and understood only by minds properly keyed and attuned to them."[15] The material collected and presented was just for the purpose of aiding adults to resonate more understandingly with the basic emotional development of the child and to recognize the difficulties to be coped with in the course of that development. The New York State Mental Health Authority provided a grant so that early childhood educators could discuss the findings of the study. All teachers could profit because "play activities are equally significant for relatively untroubled youngsters and for the many children who have suffered deprivations, frustrations, neglect, bad treatment, or exposure to crises and disturbance in the family — for example, desertion, divorce, alcoholism, prolonged absence of the father in military service, or enforced absence of the mother for gainful employment."[16]

The project and its publication contributed importantly to teachers' understanding of the benefits a child might experience in play with blocks, water, clay, finger paint, other graphic materials, and in dramatic play. The direct observational vignettes enlivened the play experiences, the interpretations illumined their hidden meanings for the adjustment of the child involved. While Frank later added the intellectual contributions of play in his discussions of the values of play to individual growth, in the late 1940s and early 1950s the concern for emotional adjustment transcended all others.

The book dramatically underscored the general and specific values of play. In general terms it was stated: "By permitting the child to play fully in a setting of security and acceptance, we enable him to deal satisfactorily and healthfully with his most urgent problems."[17] Specific benefits were attributed to each type of play experience. Illustratively, dramatic play enabled the expression of pressing needs: "Some children sought in play the warmth and affection they failed to find at home; others, who were being insistently urged toward 'mature' behavior, often adopted infantile roles."[18] Illustratively, Warren's actions, in the descriptive vignette that followed the generalization, graphically evidenced the latter interpretation. Blocks could become the means for a child to diffuse hostile or aggressive behavior. Jules's three-year-old throwing and kicking of blocks illustrated their use as a safety valve, for "youngsters who are under great internal pressure often feel compelled to use blocks 'explosively' before they can use them constructively."[19] Clay was described as serving as a protective shield for an inhibited or anxious child while still providing group membership in a common activity. An excerpt concerning John showed clay to be an "almost magical tongue-loosening" medium producing a flow of talk including "references to figures significant" in his private world.[20] Thus, the very practical illustrations of children at play, vignettes recognizable by a nursery school or kindergarten teacher, sustained the interest of the reader while vividly documenting the theoretical statements.

Because Frank was a synthesizer of ideas of child growth and was committed to the wholeness of growth, he was one of the early incorporators of some of the theory of Jean Piaget. Frank eventually included Piaget's revelation of the child's integral use of symbols as an important aspect of their play. The play of the young child was based upon themes in which his immediate concerns were focused and symbolically played out. As Frank went on to describe the child's symbolic play:

The degree to which he can utilize symbols reveals his increasing capacity for transforming his infantile organic needs and direct primary sensorimotor relations into the patterns of our adult world, using ideas and concepts and symbols for transforming his functions and establishing new relations to the increasingly orderly, meaningful world he is learning to perceive and respond to. This calls for the capacity to sustain, build up and defer the release of tensions which are essentially enhanced or augmented physiological functional responses to events. The child uses his own symbolic play for communicating with himself, especially the self of his early primary sensorimotor experiences that he must progressively renounce to live in the adult world.[21]

Note Frank's incorporation of the value of symbols in play for their contribution to resolving the conflicts engendered by adjusting to life in the consensual world. Play, for Frank, was above all a means of understanding and adjusting each unique personality to a perplexing world. His influence in this realm was extensive.

HELPING TEACHERS UNDERSTAND CHILDREN

The work of Daniel A. Prescott vividly illustrated the extension of the understandings of depth psychology to teachers of the primary grades. Teachers' lack of comprehension of vast areas of knowledge about child growth impelled the American Council on Education to establish, in the 1940s, the Commission on Teacher Education to redress this omission. Prescott, then a faculty member of the University of Chicago, was selected to head up the work of the commission. At the collaboration center, situated on the University of Chicago campus, a vast store of research data was collected and synthesized for use in teacher education. Furthermore, the commission provided staff representatives to go to specific schools to work directly with teachers in a manner designed to improve their interactions with children. One project of this nature was reported in detail in a book published in 1945 called *Helping Teachers Understand Children*.[22] The consultants from the commission staff who served this particular school system in connection with its program of child study were Daniel Prescott, Caroline Tryon, and Fritz Redl. With engrossing detail the book depicted the changes wrought in teacher attitudes and concerns for children over a three-year period.

What immediately startled the consultants was the teachers' bald lack of sensitivity to the underlying motives and feelings attached to children's behavior. The early questions asked of the consultants came in this form: "What would you do with a child that steals? How would you handle lazy children? . . . How would you treat cheating?"[23] The questions indicated the teachers' search for general procedures, applicable to all children, that would prevent unwanted behavior. They also revealed a great need to understand why children behaved as they did. The early anecdotal accounts of children's behavior written early in the study were expressions of teachers' judgments concerning the child's behavior and of their emotional acceptance or rejection of the child as a person. Both questions and anecdotal accounts laid bare the teachers' great need to focus upon a child as an individual, to understand the world of the child from his point of view, and to build an acceptance of all children emotionally. This the consultants set out to do.

A strong determinism undergirded the work of the specialists in charge; they wished teachers to recognize the causes of behavior as embedded in societal conditions. A prime requisite for understanding children was the attitude that all behavior is caused, expressed in this way:

> We believe, in the first place, that teachers who understand children think of their behavior as being caused. They see a youngster's present actions as based upon his past experience, as shaped by his present situation, and as influenced by his desires and hopes for the future. This view of human behavior holds that a child's actions can be undertood if his relevant past experience is known, if his present situation is analyzed in terms of what it means to him, and if his desires and hopes for the future are taken into consideration. It also implies that every girl and boy is educable, that unacceptable behavior can be changed, and that desirable and effective action can be evoked. This, we think, can be accomplished by arranging conditions and situations that are appropriate to the child's developmental level, capacities, and personal needs; by maintaining relationships with him that are supporting and reassuring; and by providing him with experiences that help him to understand the world and people around him, and that indicate effective ways of acting which he himself can perfect. This point of view is in sharp contrast with the more common conception of child behavior as capricious and impulsive and therefore to be controlled by adults without reference to its causes. We believe that teachers find in the idea that behavior is motivated and understandable a more reasonable and effective hypothesis for their daily work with children.[24]

The corollary that followed such a position was the great need to search for the causes of behavior. An understanding teacher gathered and organized information about his pupils and then used it to support the uniqueness of each child; a genuine acceptance of each child as independently valuable was a prerequisite to building basic understanding.

The child study procedure outlined above was followed by the consultants with groups of teachers. The causes of an individual child's behavior were ferreted out in the home, in school, in the peer group, in early records — wherever the teacher could gain insights. The search was accompanied by an explanatory framework of scientific knowledge imparted to the teachers through lectures, films, and child development literature. Important knowledge was to be found in "more than half a dozen different sciences including biology, physiology, pediatrics, anthropology, sociology, psychoanalysis and psychiatry as well as the more usual psychology and education."[25] Child study had become by this time a more complex and multidisciplinary endeavor, and while it was not possible for a teacher to gain expert knowledge in each contributing science, a working knowledge of their cardinal principles was deemed essential. Continuous sessions over the three-year period conveyed these basic principles.

Put simply, the study attempted to change teachers' attitudes toward children and to increase their understanding of behavior and its motivations. The child study experts stated their aims in this manner:

> To sum up, our definition of understanding a child includes contrasting subjective and objective elements. On the one hand, it calls for the subjective acceptance and valuing of individual boys and girls — emotionally and philosophically rooted and serving to reassure and afford security to all children, even when they misbehave. On the other hand, it also implies objectivity in the use of sound procedures and knowledge to interpret the causes of a child's acts, to appraise his adjustment problems and personal needs, and to work out practical ways of helping him master his developmental tasks.[26]

The contrast between the anecdotal accounts written by teachers before and after the child study program attested to the success of the study. Frequently a teacher selected for intensive study a child whose behavior was reprehensible to her. An understanding of the child and the environmental causes of behavior, the life tasks the child faced, and the negative forces marring his achievements, led invariably to an empathetic understanding and frequently a real liking for the child.

Striking changes occurred in teachers' attitudes toward what they had formerly considered "problem behavior." In assessing her own modified views a teacher stated directly:

> I placed whispering, restlessness, profanity, and rudeness at the head of my list of undesirable types of behavior. My studies have shown me that unsocialness, unhappiness, sullenness, shyness, and bullying are more detrimental than those I considered very harmful. The causes of these forms of behavior are hard to detect and often overlooked because they are the

child's own problems. They are worrying him and may cause him untold misery in the future.[27]

For the teachers involved in the study the aims of education were expanded to include the child's sense of adequacy and personal worth, his belongingness in the group, and his sense of security in personal relationships.

In later years Prescott became a member of the Institute for Child Study at the University of Maryland and was involved in continuous field work to promote the understanding among educators that he believed necessary to guide the personal development of each child. The major deterministic quality of Prescott's recommendations turned thought to the unconscious motivations of behavior — the emotional drives. He considered the climate of affection, social background, and self-defensive and adjustment processes essential factors needing attention when educational decisions about the child were made. These considerations led Prescott to strike out boldly against aspects of schools that negated the natural processes of growth and adjustment. One such undesirable practice was the enforcement of "grade-level standards," which deleteriously affected the development of many children. Prescott martialed the evidence of psychological theory and of research to support this position.[28]

While Prescott worked consistently to influence education to make full use "of scientific knowledge and of the scientific method" so that all "valuable human material no longer will be damaged accidentally or left undeveloped,"[29] he recognized firmly that philsophical and ethical values must underlie the use of scientific information. He stated: "The purposes which scientific knowledge can serve do not adhere in the knowledge itself. They depend rather upon the philosophical, religious, and social assumptions about the meaning of life and about the nature of valid human self-realization."[30] Then he delineated with care the basic philosophical and social assumptions that supported the child study program. The breadth of his view exhibited a melding of the philosophical and psychological to form a view of man as "a creature with special value and significance in the universe" and "as a creative being."[31]

ERIK H. ERIKSON'S STAGES OF DEVELOPMENT

Erik H. Erikson's theoretical position shares Freud's view of development as marked by conflict. Stages, however, as proposed by Erikson, are transformed from psychosexual to psychosocial issues, or crises inherent within a particular period of growth. Every individual must some-how confront and resolve each pivotal struggle with the manner of resolu-tion producing important consequences for the remainder of life. The arena of struggle Erikson designates as not stemming from the individual but held within the person's relationship to society. The resolution takes place between the child's own wishes and feelings and the needs and re-quirements of the social setting.

Deeply involved in psychoanalysis himself, Erikson has written of the first psychoanalyst: "In Freud, a genius turned a new instrument of obser-vation back on his childhood, back on all childhood. He invented a spe-cific method for the detection of that which universally spoils the genius of the child in every human being. In teaching us to recognize the dai-monic evil in children, he urged us not to smother the creatively good. Since then, the nature of growth in childhood has been studied by in-genious observers over the world: never before has mankind known more about its own past — phylogenetic and ontogenetic."[32] Erikson has devot-ed much of his work to the demonstration of the ways in which the ego's development is inextricably bound with the nature of social organization, to show the relationship between ontogeny and phylogeny. The many years engaged in studying children living in different circumstances and different cultures have served as a base for Erikson to demonstrate the impact of society upon the ego, thus linking child study and anthro-pology. His great contribution has been the proposal of a theory of the self and of identity in touch with both the individual's own organism and society.

Erikson paralleled Frank and Prescott in linking ego development to the series of orientations taking place between the self and the social world. The quotation above shows, however, that Erikson did not take on the view of infantile innocence held by the others. But Erikson was much closer to Freud's whole theory in his training and outlook and re-mained faithful to both the theory and the man, with only one major ex-ception — the impact of cultural influences.

Erikson, whose growing years were spent in Germany, began by in-vestigating a career as an art teacher. During a time in Florence, Italy he met Peter Blos, who later became a recognized psychoanalyst. When Blos was invited to direct a school in Vienna in which there were children undergoing analysis, he invited Erikson to join him. In this setting Erikson became acquainted with Freud, who opened up psychoanalytic training to him. Precisely at this time Freud's daughter Anna was searching for people to help her develop psychoanalysis for children. Erikson found this group and made the work with children his specialty. Of this Erikson has said: "I feel lucky that as a clinician I started with child patients and young people under Anna Freud."[33] When Hitler came to power, Vienna no longer afforded analysts a comfortable location to carry out their work; Erikson moved to the United States. First at Harvard and later at Yale he became associated with outstanding anthropologists; these associations led to his work with the Sioux and Yurok Indians, which provided the opportunity to study child-rearing practices in a self-contained society. The Indian culture opened up new horizons for investigation, yet Erikson was fascinated to find that all the childhood problems seriously studied on the basis of pathological development in Western culture were spontaneously and seriously talked about by the Indians also. "They referred to our stages as decisive steps in the making of a good Sioux Indian or a good Yurok Indian. . . . I think this contributed eventually to my imagery of basic human strengths."[34] For basic human strengths, which Erikson sometimes calls virtues, are the outcome of the successful resolution of conflict and are necessary in human adaptation. Virtue, for Erikson is "something vital, that animates, and is 'the soul' of something."[35] Erikson used the term *virtue* somewhat challengingly "to point to an evolutionary basis of man's lofty moralism."[36]

After numerous other experiences, including participation in a longitudinal study of child guidance at the University of California in Berkeley and work at the Menninger Foundation in Topeka, Kansas, Erikson's basic framework of ideas was set forth in his first book, *Childhood and Society*, which included his synthesis of developmental and social tasks.[37] This conceptualization of eight stages in the growth of a healthy personality was presented in a paper at the Midcentury White House Conference on Children and Youth in 1950. The main theme of the conference was "healthy personality" and in adhering to the theme Erikson set out to formulate, instead of the pathological potentials of early development, the personality gains possible at each stage of growth. The presentation at the White House conference was republished widely and even though the form was shortened, it was an expansive document.[38]

Erikson's scheme of development is a tripartite one viewing the individual as an organism, an ego, and a member of society and thereby involved simultaneously in three processes of organization—"the somatic process, the ego process, and the societal process."[39] For positive ego identity and social health, the ego, at any given stage, must be "strong enough to integrate the timetable of the organism with the structure of social institutions."[40] The accruing sense of ego strength was conceived as the successful outcome of the individual surmounting the crises arising in each developmental phase. The model is also one of epigenesis; the eight stages are part of a hierarchy in which one aspect develops on top of another rather than in a sequence. This simple configuration, *epi* meaning "upon" and *genesis* meaning "emergent," explains the hierarchical view.

The Stages Explained

The first four stages outlined by Erikson proved to be particularly meaningful to early childhood educators for they covered the ages from birth through the early elementary grades. One may consider these stages as a series of dichotomous resolutions; on the one hand desirable qualities might be the outcome, on the other dangers resulted that might have pervasive influence in later life. The first dichotomy dealt with the growth of a sense of trust versus mistrust. The favorable outcome would be trust in the environment and the future; the unfavorable result would present fear of the future and suspicion regarding environmental circumstances.

The powerful influence of Freud was evident in the opening statement in Erikson's chapter on "Eight Stages of Man." He began: "The first demonstration of social trust in the baby is the ease of his feeding, the depth of his sleep, the relaxation of his bowels."[41] The foundation of ego identity was trust built in the first oral stage. If the conditions preferred by parents, or other caretakers, were not conducive to building trust, the absence of basic trust might lead to a lack of wider meaningful belongingness. The child either became aware of the world as a stable and encouraging place to be or as a threatening, frustrating place where no trust was possible. Upon the ensuing outcome rested the child's relationship to others and his approach to the circumstances of his life.

Erikson drew upon his analytic experience to support this basic contention when addressing the Midcentury White House Conference on Children and Youth.

> Studies of mentally ill individuals and observations of infants who have been grossly deprived of affection suggest that trust is an early-formed and important element in the healthy personality. Psychiatrists find again and again that the most serious illnesses occur in patients who have been sorely neglected or abused or otherwise deprived of love in infancy. Similarly, it is a common finding of psychological and social investigators that individuals diagnosed as a "psychopathic personality" were so unloved in infancy that they have no reason to trust the human race and, therefore, no sense of responsibility toward their fellow men.[42]

Only when the sense of trust became reasonably well established could the child respond to the desire asserting itself between the ages of twelve to fifteen months to act boldly, explore, and become more independent.

> What is at stake throughout the struggle of these years is the child's sense of autonomy, the sense that he is an independent human being and yet one who is able to use the help and guidance of others in important matters.

This stage of development becomes decisive for the ratio between love and hate, between cooperation and wilfulness, for freedom of self-expression and its renunciation in the make-up of the individual. The favorable outcome is self-control without loss of self-esteem. The unfavorable outcome is doubt and shame.[43]

The sense of autonomy was to result from solving the problem of asserting himself as an individual and of overcoming conflicting forces — the need for dependency or a fear of overreaching his powers. Accelerated maturation sets the stage for experimentation and for reaching out; Erikson described it as holding on and letting go — with hands, eyes, mouth, and sphincters. Much of the struggle was apt to focus on sphincter control for this period roughly coincided with Freud's anal phase. Shame and doubt were the undesirable outcomes when this stage was unfavorably resolved. Erikson wrote forcefully about shame:

Visual shame precedes auditory guilt, which is a sense of badness to be had all by oneself when nobody watches and when everything is quiet — except the voice of the superego. Such shaming exploits an increasing sense of being small, which can develop only as the child stands up and as awareness permits him to note the relative measures of size and power. . . . Doubt is the brother of shame.[44]

Hopefully, however, the child would emerge from this stage with a sense of self-control without any loss of self-esteem but rather a lasting sense of good will and pride. Too much shaming did not eventuate in a genuine sense of propriety but in a secret determination to get away with things unseen, perhaps to result in defiant shamelessness.

A new miracle of vigorous unfolding characterized the initiative expressed in the third stage of development, which was also coupled with the danger of "a sense of guilt over the goals contemplated and the acts initiated in one's exuberant enjoyment of new locomotor and mental powers."[45] Linked by Erikson to Freud's phallic stage, he discussed the role of infant genitalial impulses, castration, and oedipal leanings with their vast potential for engendering guilt. Coupled with this was the child's readiness to learn, to make things cooperatively, and to share a sense of obligation.

This developmental stage has great assets as well as great dangers. At no time in life is the individual more ready to learn avidly and quickly, to become big in the sense of sharing obligation and performance. If during this preschool period the child can get some sense of the various roles and functions that he can perform as an adult, he will be ready to progress joyfully to the next stage, in which he will find pleasurable accomplishment in activities less fraught with phantasy and fear.[46]

The first three stages as outlined formed the base for personality development; the sense of trust, the growth of autonomy, the sense of initiative achieved, later conflicts were resolved more readily. There are, however, five other dichotomies to be considered. The sense of accomplishment designated in the fourth stage, beginning about age six and extending for five or six years, was derived from directing abundant energies into constructive work. Diligent experimentation with materials, efforts to use cultural tools and symbols, and interest in production eventuated in a sense of industry accompanied by competence and a strong sense of self. With the opposite side of the polarity, the unsuccessful resolution, the child lapsed into a sense of inferiority. Coinciding with the stage Freud designated as a period of latency when violent drives were normally dormant, Erikson viewed it as a socially decisive stage in which the sense of technological ethos of the culture evolved. Indeed, the social orientation of this period was significant for the child and for society.

> In contrast to the preceding stages and to the succeeding ones, this stage does not consist of a swing from a violent inner upheaval to a new mastery. Under reasonably favorable circumstances this is a period of calm, steady growth, especially if the problems of the previous stages have been well worked through. Despite its unspectacular character, this is a very important period, for in it is laid a firm basis for responsible citizenship. It is during this period that children acquire not only knowledge and skills that make for good workmanship but also the ability to cooperate and play fair and otherwise follow the rules of the larger social game.[47]

Other conflicts designated by Erikson extended from adolescence to old age and included a sense of identity versus role confusion, a sense of intimacy versus isolation, a sense of generativeness versus stagnation, and a sense of integrity versus despair. The resolution of these conflicts might well be determined by the outcomes of struggles in early childhood.

A Healthy Balance

Balance was a key word in Erikson's conception of the growth of a healthy personality, for Erikson never conceived of all elements of each pivotal struggle as being positive or of a conflict to be resolved for all time. However, a sensitive balance needed to be achieved between the child's own desires and aspirations and those of his environmental surround in order for a positive sense of self to evolve; the end-state was the mental health of the person. The need was for a favorable ratio of basic trust over mistrust, of autonomous will over shame and doubt that were called for by Erikson. The development of trust, although coming into ascendance and meeting its crisis and resolution during the first stage, was described in the second edition of Erikson's book as extending to the last stage where "we would expect trust to have developed into the most mature *faith* that an aging person can muster in his cultural setting and historical period."[48]

Although Erikson did not dwell on the conditions required to aid the positive ratio of healthy virtues, supportive requirements are threaded throughout his discussions. Trust depended largely on "the quality of the maternal relationship" and on the sensitivity of the responses to the child's needs. As the child began to exercise autonomy, all outer control had to be "firmly reassuring" in order for the child to suffer no lack of self-esteem. The sense of initiative flowered where control was neither excessive nor permissive, but where the child had "ideal prototypes" to emulate in parents and teachers. Much encouragement and leeway needed to be offered to the child's show of enterprise. For the sense of industry to successfully develop, the wider society had to admit the child into the world of skills and tools. Conditions needed were those that mitigated against inadequacy and "inferiority."

Sensitivity, reassurance, carefully considered control, a balance of success in undertakings: these conditions take us back to the recommendations of Frank and Prescott. The conditions that aid in the growth of healthy personality converge in the advice the three theorists gave to the caretakers of the young. While these theorists did not share a similar view of the child or present their position in the same manner, the essential provisions for mental health are strikingly identical.

Play, for Erikson as it was for Frank, was proposed as the child's means of dealing with the complexities of his life and of gaining mastery over his reality. Erikson has called play "the royal road to the understanding of the infantile ego's efforts at synthesis."[49] While the adult might use play as a means of sidestepping into an unreal reality, Erikson viewed the playing child as advancing toward a new stage in viewing the world. He could argue with William Blake that "the child's toys and the old man's reasons are the fruits of two seasons."[50] Indeed, for the disturbed child play activities gave evidence of the capacity for the ego to find release and self-care.[51] Play therapy formed a prominent part in Erikson's work with children. The form of play, used by the child, enabled him to create "model situations" for planning and experimenting in which he was in complete control. In clarifying options and anticipating outcomes in his model realm, the child thus dealt with affective failures and hopes.

Erikson in the Field of Psychology

"In spite of his protests to the contrary, Erikson's thinking presents a decisive departure, and an advance beyond, Freudian psychology," wrote Henry Maier, who pointed out three areas of divergence.[52] First, Erikson shifted from the emphasis on the id to the ego and its synthesizing capacity. Erikson himself described *Childhood and Society* as "a psychoanalytic book on the relation of the ego to society."[53] Second, Erikson concerned himself with the dynamics of sociocultural relationships in the family and beyond. Third, Erikson responded to the demands of his time by pointing out the possibilities within the development of each individual to triumph over the psychological hazards of living today. Erikson recognized change in theory as essential when he said, "I realized only gradually that any original observation already implies a change in theory. An observer of a different generation, in a different scientific climate, cannot avoid developing a field if it is a vital one."[54]

Without doubt it is the vitality with which Erikson has infused his own theoretical stance that has made it one frequently incorporated into books on human development and readily referred to in early childhood education. For example, Howard Gardner's well-designed and synthesizing text on human development draws heavily on some of Erikson's contributions to elucidate stagewise progressions and to explain many aspects of growth.[55] Robert Biehler includes Erikson's work at some length as a basic theory of development.[56] Interestingly, he relates Erikson's position to the use of behavior modification and cautions that too much control of a child's behavior may push the resolution of conflicts toward a negative balance, toward distrust, doubt, guilt, and inferiority.[57] He concludes that wisdom lies in using behavior modification sparingly.

A CURRICULUM FOR MENTAL HEALTH

The concept of play as an autotherapeutic measure of childhood permeated the literature of early education in the 1940s and 1950s. In a chapter on "The Child at Play," Roma Gans, Celia Stendler, and Millie Almy, three specialists in the field, supported play as a child's means of maintaining equilibrium.[58] "For the child himself," wrote Emma Sheehy, another leader in the field, "one of the more important values in make-believe play is that it contributes to his ego support. He can be himself and the self he wants to be."[59] The "self" of the child, the inner feeling aspects of the developing personality, concerned these writers, since "from living in his particular background, each child has begun to form concepts about his 'self,' about adults and what may be experienced from them, about other children, and about the world of things."[60] Play revealed and extended the self.

An emotional climate in the classroom that fostered healthy personality was a focus for much discussion. The early swing to extreme permissiveness was somewhat abated, but it was extremely important to help the child feel good about himself.[61] The classroom atmosphere was viewed as an influencer of behavior. A well-balanced program of activities planned with due consideration to the children's emotional needs could do much to promote good adjustment. For the young child confidence in his environment and security in his relations with others promoted healthy adjustment. John E. Anderson, director of the Institute of Child Welfare at the University of Minnesota, expressed it this way: "The child needs confidence in the teacher but should not be dependent upon her. Much of the skill of a good teacher centers on her ability to build up feelings of confidence in children, without making them dependent. In a stable and emotionally balanced environment, self-expression, creative efforts, and learning are facilitated."[62]

The most eloquent expression of the significance of children's feelings was to be found in the literature of creative expression. "The teacher," wrote Natalie Cole, "should give children confidence and respect for their painting."[63] The teacher's role, Cole implied, was drawing out the child's inner feelings. With the tools of praise and encouragement, the teacher could remove layers of frustration and defeat and free the child's creativity. She concluded: "How infinitely worthwhile, helping a child to find inner harmony through new means of expression."[64]

"The child who uses creative activity as an emotional outlet will gain freedom and flexibility as a result of the release of unnecessary tensions," concluded Viktor Lowenfeld.[65] He described the developing stages in art expression as the changing relationship of the child to his environment, which included emotional as well as mental growth. Lowenfeld's conviction of the integrating process in artistic expression led him to state: "The great contribution of free art expression to our educational system and to our society is the emphasis on the individual and on his own potential creative abilities and above all the power of art to integrate harmoniously all the components of growth which are responsible for a well-balanced human being."[66] Daniel Mendelowitz echoed this strong position on the contributions of creative expression toward healthy personality.[67]

Rhythmic movement was found to be equally therapeutic; free movement born of imagination and emotional impulse eliminated self-consciousness. Big, unrestricted movements of the whole body cultivated a sense of freedom and happiness in individual tempo, asserted Maria Bird, a follower of Émile Jacques Dalcroz.[68] As Emma Sheehy put it later, the twisting, turning, wriggling movements of childhood "spring from feelings and needs that are strong within them. The expression of these in movement has vitality and, if we give it encouragement and support, its own unique form evolves."[69]

Placing child study in perspective John Anderson found that "in the early 1940's psychoanalytic concepts, particularly relating to the effect of deprivation and institutionalization or the relation of early handling of the child and subsequent development, began to appear and much concern, both experimentally and theoretically, for the last decade and a half, has centered in that area."[70] It can be stated, also, that psychoanalytic concepts of adjustment, socialization, and emotional development were of great concern in the education of the young child. A positive philosophy of the importance of the early years for personality formation was a guiding force in developing curriculum. As D. Bruce Gardner firmly summarized it: "During the 40's and 50's the heavy emphasis on affective, personal-social development reached a high peak."[71]

References to Erikson's basic formulations persist today. In summarizing the relevance of psychodynamic concepts to the education of the preschool child, Biber and Franklin state Erikson's thesis as one of six major points to be utilized in curriculum development:

> Growth and mastering involves conflict. The inner life of the growing child is a play of forces between urgent drives and impulses, contradictory impulses within the self and demanding reality outside the self. The resolution of these conflicts bears the imprint of the quality of interaction with the salient life figures and the demands of the culture.[72]

Basic attitudinal patterns and modes of interacting that promote ego strength continue to be a major concern in the education of the young child. The value of constant patience, simplified enlightenment, supportive reassurance, and tolerance, as part of the emotional climate essential for stable personality development, has been firmly established in early childhood education.

9 The Child Development Point of View

Rapidly accumulating data on child growth impelled psychologists and educators to request a unified point of view. Diverse studies and theoretical positions had been immediately incorporated into curriculum planning often in a fragmented manner, as we have seen. Now the demand was for an integration of known understandings as a basis for a curriculum appropriate to the child. Pointing up this need John Anderson wrote: "Insight into the nature of the child as he is and is to be underlies the practical principles of early childhood education. In recent years hundreds of studies involving observations and experiments on children of all ages have been made. This vast and growing scientific literature, with its many implications for education, very much needs interpretation"[1] Interpretations of the implications of the child development point of view and of research findings in the field of child study were forthcoming in the 1940s and 1950s in a two-step process. In the 1940s maturation was the key concept utilized in describing growth and applied to curriculum planning. By the 1950s many postulates of analytic theory were superimposed on the earlier position to bring about a new unified view.

THE CHILD DEVELOPMENT APPROACH OF THE 1940s

Arthur Jersild presented the definitive statement of the relationship between child development and the curriculum when he wrote: "The child development approach to the curriculum means an effort to apply to the education of children the lessons learned from the study of children themselves."[2] Fundamental concomitants to this approach, Jersild set forth as "a spirit of inquiry" and "an attitude of respect for children." Jersild's own spirit of inquiry and respect for children was grounded in his double focus: psychology and education. Early in his career he held appointments in the departments of psychology at Columbia University and the University of Wisconsin. These were followed by his professorship in education at Teachers College, Columbia University, but he consulted and wrote

141

as a psychologist. For each *Manual of Child Psychology* (1946 and 1954), edited by Leonard Carmichael, Jersild wrote chapters that have been considered "important sources of normative data."[3] Some of his normative research was on fears and anxiety, so it was inevitable that he would become interested in psychoanalysis and move in the direction of writing books of another nature: *In Search of Self* and *When Teachers Face Themselves*.[4]

When *Child Development and the Curriculum* was published, however, Jersild was holding to the maturational emphasis and stage theory. Actually the book was the outcome of a major research project initiated in 1943 by the staff of the Horace Mann–Lincoln Institute of School Experimentation. A committee of institute staff members, under the chairmanship of Jersild, was formed "to undertake the task of analyzing and interpreting the child development field as it relates to curriculum."[5] A preliminary draft gained the response of not only members of the institute but teachers and administrators of a number of widely scattered associated schools. Designed for teachers the result captured the developmental approach of the age firmly and convincingly.

Respect for the process of growth dominated the point of view. One of the first paragraphs underscored the maturational position:

> The child development approach assumes the child's right to be a child. Nature has decreed that a human creature shall be a child a long time before he becomes a man. This period of childhood is also the period which fathers the man that is to be. One of the greatest temptations which confront an adult in dealing with a child is to try to tamper with the process of the child's own development. Such tampering may take many forms, ranging from efforts to keep the child from growing up to impatient efforts to make him grow up faster than his own nature permits.[6]

A holistic concern for all avenues of development was also professed; holistic here meaning a view that included all aspects of growth: social, emotional, physical, and mental. The fragmentation of this approach was not yet recognized.

> By reason of his concern about the interplay of many forces in human growth and behavior, the student of child development recognizes, for example, that it is important for the child to master intellectual skills, such as reading and arithmetic. But he recognizes also the importance of the child's mastery of everyday manual and bodily skills. He further emphasizes the importance of the child's emotional well-being, which not only is crucial to his happiness as a person but also plays a decisive role in determining his moral conduct and his behavior as a citizen.[7]

From these basic statements principles of child development were applied to curriculum practice. Selection of experiences was wisest if "in keeping with the child's capacities and potentialities at that level and the forms of behavior dominant at that particular period of life."[8] Norms were accepted as useful "in defining approximately what may be expected at a given level of maturity in a given activity" and also as "a corrective against trying to push one aspect of the child's development at the expense of others."[9] A recognition of the abuse of norms and the effect of rigid standards on an individual child was also included as readiness was considered.

Although growth was viewed as continuous, certain aspects of development were considered preeminent at various periods of life. For this reason the book was organized around broad stages: infancy, the preschool years, the elementary school child, and adolescence. The first periods were included to give teachers of elementary and high schools, considered the largest proportion of teachers, an understanding of earlier development. The infant and preschool child's social abilities, motor development, intellectual growth, engagement in make-believe, expressions in art, and emotional states were depicted in a normative manner so that adults working with them and those dealing with later years could approach each child with enlarged perceptions. Jersild considered much established by the age of six:

> This does not mean that the child's ways of behaving are rigidly set by the age of about six. In the process of maturation beyond the age of six new capacities and drives emerge as well as new hurdles and hazards. . . . But the impact of the new will be influenced strongly by what has gone before.[10]

Assessment of the developmental point of view at this period of time rests upon the nature of child development information elevated as significant for curriculum building. The concept of stage theory adhered to as maturation, which Jersild distinguished from learning, formed the basis for the preponderance of curriculum recommendations. The normative emphasis was pervasive. Referring to the preschool child, Jersild wrote: "In their dealings with others, children move by progressive steps that are more or less characteristic of all children."[11] His use of prevalent research can be illustrated in the discussion of the attention span of the young child: "In one investigation, the average duration in minutes of sustained attention arose from 6.9 minutes at two years to 12.6 at five; in another study, there was a rise from 9.4 to 23.82 for the same period; in a third, there was a rise from 2.5 at two to 5.6 at four. It is interesting to note that according to these studies, all utilizing different settings and criteria, the attention span approximately doubles from age two to age four."[12] Norms of growth raised the question of the timeliness of certain educational procedure, so readiness, or the child's ability to profit from certain studies, was persistently pursued. Discussions of I.Q. permeated the chapters as an infallible measure of individual intelligence.

Supporting Evidence

An analysis of another contemporary publication revealed similar emphases in child development presentations. The thirty-eighth yearbook of the National Society for the Study of Education also dealt with the use of child development data to support curriculum development. The tone of this volume is set by an opening statement concerning the aim of the yearbook: "To confront a child with tasks for which he is not ready, with the implication that he should succeed, gives him a feeling of failure, undermines his security. Instead, we must guide him into those learning situations that he can attack effectively and with sufficient success to yield satisfaction, encouragement, and growth."[13] Maturation, readiness, and level of development were key words as specialists viewed subject areas of the curriculum to discern the optimal time for a given learning or activity as a function of mental and physiological maturity. Research gave support to a psychological arrangement of subject matter, rather than a logical approach. "Developmental or normative studies are of distinct value in determining the readiness of children for instruction, as well as for indicating the appropriate time for systematic practice," wrote a noted researcher of the time.[14]

The same major concerns were evident in Leonard Carmichael's *Manual of Psychology*, that huge compendium incorporating reviews of vast numbers of studies categorized according to levels of growth (the neonate, the infant, the adolescent), to areas of growth (physical, social, language growth), or to special needs (the "feeble-minded" child, the gifted child). In an analysis of methodology utilized in research reported in the volume published in 1946, John Anderson found the normative, cross-sectional approach prevailing; much of the literature was concerned with picturing development and thus many norms were based on chronological age. This led Anderson to conclude that the modern point of view pictured the child "engaged in an on-going process of development that is irreversible."[15]

Having carried out a classic study on early training, Myrtle McGraw did not subscribe to the current desire to separate learning from maturation.[16] She felt that putting maturation in juxtaposition to learning produced only a cumbersome conceptual framework with not very fruitful results. Yet she wrote in 1946: "Both theoretically and empirically there is every reason to believe that behavior development moves according to law and order." She continued by defining various influences on growth:

> Both from embryological studies and from studies of infant behavior, developmental evidence has accumulated which suggests that critical periods occur in the growth of any phenomenon when it is most susceptible to definite kinds of stimulation. The critical period for one activity may occur at one time in the life of an individual and at another time for a different activity. The major factor contributing to an alteration in behavior may at one time be the status of neurostructural components, at another time variations in anatomical dimensions, and at another time personal or individual experience.[17]

In a retrospective statement McGraw implied that many child developmentalists had an age-conscious focus during the 1930s and 1940s.[18]

The stronghold of mental measurement at this period of time was attested by Florence Goodenough in her chapter on "The Measurement of Mental Growth in Childhood." "Within the short space of a quarter of a century," she wrote, "the literature on mental growth has become so voluminous that a mere listing of titles requires an entire book."[19] Dipping into some of this voluminous literature, Goodenough goes on to discuss the quantification of intelligence and studies of mental growth curves. The other chapter dealing with mental growth was one by Harold Jones that considered environmental influences; these influences, however, were measured by mental test scores.[20]

In the 1946 edition of Carmichael's *Manual* the one counteracting position to all the piecemeal study of child behavior was Kurt Lewin's chapter dealing with the psychological field or life-space. He argued for a more total view of behavior, one that looked "for factors which can be inserted as constant values into the variables of the equations which represent psychological laws."[21] For Lewin this required a deeper understanding of individual behavior involving motivational concepts such as "level of aspiration" or "satiation." Here Lewin pointed to the need to consider more than overt behavior. His was a rather lone voice in 1946 when the actual content of chapters suggested a "disdain for speculative theorizing and the emphasis on gathering objective facts."[22] While some of the research reviewed in various chapters used Freud's theory as a frame of reference for its design and execution, the theory per se was given little recognition.

INCORPORATING THE PSYCHOANALYTIC POSITION

The theoretical reticence about Freud's contributions existing in the 1946 *Manual of Child Psychology* became drastically modified in the 1954 edition. Take Jersild's own chapter on "Emotional Development" for example. In 1946 he included two paragraphs on psychoanalytic theory pointing out the insistence of Freud, Susan Isaacs, and Melanie Klein on the child's inner longings and proclivity to anxiety. Jersild concluded: "In the present state of knowledge, pronouncements such as the foregoing cannot be taken as statements of fact based upon tested scientific data."[23] While he included studies centering on constructs that had their origin in Freud's work (such as feeding, weaning, maternal separation, and sibling rivalry), Jersild was reflecting the general rejection of theorizing. Not so in the 1954 *Manual* when Jersild called for a theory of motivation. The following paragraph revealed the great change in Jersild's assimilation of depth psychology.

> Emotion is involved in the whole business of living. The most obvious occasions for emotion are those involving bodily harm or threat of violence or of being overwhelmed. But emotion may also be elicited by any condition which thwarts or threatens or which furthers or enhances the gratification of a person's needs, as he perceives them, or the realization of his goals, or which blocks or expedites a disposition to action or behavior tendency (recognized or unrecognized, "conscious" or "unconscious") which he has acquired in the process of adapting himself to the demands of life. Emotion is involved in anything in which a person sees himself involved. For this reason, to understand the child's emotion it is necessary to take account not only of the objective stimulus situation but also the subjective system known as the self which, while not directly observable to others, is to the person himself the most important reality of existence.[24]

The self had here taken on an important role in personality development as Jersild opened up his view to accept unconscious motivations and inner drives. In incorporating references to Abraham Maslow, Karen Horney, and Eric Fromm throughout his chapter, Jersild revealed how much his thinking was being modified from his earlier normative position. He later became convinced that teachers needed to be directed toward self-understanding and he initiated group efforts to achieve this understanding at Teachers College.

In summarizing trends in psychological thinking in 1954 Harold Anderson recognized the growth of attention to Freudian psychoanalysis and the discovery of the whole child in the total situation.[25] The latter development Anderson attributed to the writings of a number of people, including Lewin and Frank. Lewin wrote: "Without theories it is impossible in psychology, as in any other science, to proceed beyond the mere collection and description of facts which have no predictive value. It is impossible to handle problems of conditions or effects without characterizing the dynamic properties behind the surface of the directly observable *phenotypical* properties."[26] In order to encompass relevant environmental forces, Lewin offered again the construct of psychological field and analyzed the various forces directing a specific behavior. In a forward-looking addendum to Lewin's chapter Sibylle Escalona examined research that showed interest shifting from "the validation of general laws by experimental procedures in laboratory situations to the discovery of constellations of variables as they occur in life situations, by means of controlled observations under field conditions."[27] Furthermore, Escalona considered the convergence of a number of disciplines — sociology, social psychology, physiology, anthropology — to have forced child study to comprehend the child as a whole. The trend toward the integration of various disciplines was corroborated by Harold Anderson.[28] By the 1950s new theory and new data were available to the educator.

INCLUDING THE AFFECTIVE
IN THE DEVELOPMENTAL VIEW

A new theoretical addition demanded a reconsideration of child development and the curriculum. Evolving trends were incorporated into the quintessential developmental curriculum book of the 1950s. Mental health, especially as it was influenced by parents and teachers, formed the central cores of A *Child Development Point of View* by James Hymes.[29] Respect for a child's inherent rate of growth was a matter of essential logic to Hymes. He considered "growth the boss," something that "cannot be speeded up." He called for functional learning as did Dewey and deemed interest the secret ingredient in effective learning. But the influence pervading every page was the concern for feelings, attitudes, and values. The need for trust, the need to love, the growth of independence, the necessity for self-esteem: these formed the basis of a fruitful, life-enhancing learning situation in Hymes's view.

Written in an easy, even chatty, style for parents and teachers, the book had six printings in two years. Undergirding the comfortable direct recommendations was a profoundly substantive theoretical stance. Moreover it aimed toward prevention:

> The stresses and strains in today's living have stirred a wide interest in mental health. In particular, the call everywhere is for preventive efforts — those which build strength into people.
>
> Many persons profess to work in this key area of prevention. Too much that goes on under this good name, however, concentrates on the early diagnosis and treatment of difficulties. Important as this work is, the focus is still on ill health. The preventive task is left undone.
>
> In contrast, good classroom teachers rarely call their work "mental health," preventive or otherwise. Yet, more than they know, good teachers are hard at work building strength. In faculty meetings, workshops, in-service, and college courses teachers are studying children. In their classrooms they are acting on their knowledge to build good feelings into children. This is health. This is prevention. This is the goal *A Child Development Point of View* aims to further.[30]

Hymes could also be labeled a psychologist-educator, for he characterized himself as "trying to be something of a bridge between child development and children's experiences in school."[31] Hymes devoted many years to this task as editor of *Progressive Education* magazine, as member of the Institute for Child Study at the University of Maryland, as a frequent lecturer at educational meetings, and as a writer. His writing was distinguished by the easy style that made significant theoretical statements readily accessible to teachers.

Take, for example, the need for the growth of a sense of basic trust. Hymes presented the direct implication for teachers in this manner:

> The first statement Child Development can make about children is a very direct one. It comes to you straight from the shoulder: *Your youngsters have to think you are a "honey."* Tops! A "peach"! They cannot think of you simply as "Teacher" or as one more adult with whom they are stuck. They cannot have a lukewarm feeling or a passive "She's O.K. . . . I guess." If you want to get the best work out of boys and girls, if you want good discipline, if you want the best for them, they must think you are something special.[32]

Similar statements dealt with the need for first-rate models of identification, the development of a positive self-concept, the importance of success in learning, and other basic postulates.

Most of all Hymes expressed exuberant optimism for the ultimate attainment of widespread mental health. Armed with developmental insights teachers and parents could help children reach the highest attainments.

Child Development's most cheering fact is that the decent way of working with children is also the most efficient way! Decency pays off. When you are friendly, when you help children to feel able and growing, you get the best out of youngsters. You make it easy for them to mature. You provide stabilizers and strengtheners for their growth. You make more sure that the time will come when youngsters are sturdy, sound, healthy citizens. You deserve to feel right; children will feel right; our nation, with its great stake in children, can feel both safe and proud. Youngsters whose basic needs are met are free to learn at their best, free to grow to their peaks.

What is that best? How high are those peaks? No one knows for sure, but this much is completely certain: *As the human grows he heads more and more in the direction that makes good human living possible.*[33]

INFLUENCING THE CURRICULUM

The forthright insistence of Jersild and Hymes that curriculum be grounded in developmental knowledge is no longer startling, but it was hailed as a major breakthrough in education. So significant had scientific knowledge of the crucial years of infancy and early childhood grown that Lawrence Frank welcomed it as an approach to mitigating social problems and difficulties: "In the longer perspective of years to come it is probable that emergence of child development research and the diffusion of what might be called the child development view point will be regarded as one of the more significant developments of the twentieth century, for here, concretely and practically, is being shown how at last man can take charge of his own destiny and begin to build the kind of organisms and personalities through whom alone the enduring human values and aspirations may be achieved."[34] Willard Olson, too, encouraged recognition of development as a master concept in the field of education, formal and informal.[35]

Recognition of the incompleteness of data on development was expressed by child psychologists themselves, as well as an awareness that somehow the wholeness of growth must be accounted for in the complexity of behavior over time. John Anderson believed that an essential domain of developmental theory was the placing of all the segmented data into a manifold whole.[36] Dale Harris suggested that once developmental principles could explain behavior in living systems generally, an accounting could be made of the organizing processes in behaviors that are mediated symbolically. This, he agreed, constituted a considerable reach into the future.[37] Heinz Werner was not satisfied with general principles of growth as the sole outcome: "The original aim of developmental theory, directed toward the study of universal genetic changes, is still one of its main concerns; but side by side with this concern, the conviction has been growing in recent years that developmental conceptualization, in order to reaffirm its truly organismic character, has to expand its orbit of interest to include as a central problem the study of individuality."[38]

While psychologists were evaluating the status of the developmental point of view and speculating on future areas for research, early childhood educators were incorporating the developmental position in their writings on curriculum. Readiness permeated recommendations made. In the late 1950s Ilse Forest wrote of the concept of readiness as "pivotal in today's discussion of the curriculum for young children."[39] She was convinced that studies of human development underscored the fact that in the achievement of any skill, the development of structure must precede the development of function. No support was given by Forest for teachers to sit back and wait for conditions of readiness to appear, but she did expect "constructive accommodations to the limitations of immaturity."[40] Most frequently attached to the process of learning to read, reading readiness delineated an optimum time for specific learnings and suggested that attempts to teach before this stage was reached were usually laborious and unsuccessful.[41] Teachers could do little about physiological readiness, noted Nila Banton Smith, they just needed to respect it.[42] But teachers could provide experiential readiness that would fill the empty shell of symbols with the meat of meaning.[43]

With characteristic zeal early childhood educators continued to incorporate developmental growth patterns into their publications. Normative research based the presentation of characteristics proposed by Myrtle Imhoff for each separate age level from four to eight, which she then followed by implications, again for each age level.[44] More commonly, characteristics of young children were categorized under the headings of physical, social, emotional, and mental development.[45] To these were added the needs of the developing personality: trust, respect, acceptance, and self-confidence.[46] All were strong evidences that the spirit of inquiry into developmental aspects of growth and the respect for children valued by Jersild and Hymes were having effects upon the education of the young child.

10 The Study of Cognition

Some psychologists are now calling Jean Piaget the giant of developmental psychology in the realm of cognition, the one who has added more knowledge about cognitive development than any other person.[1] This appellation has been bestowed only recently. Although Piaget began investigating children's thinking in the 1920s, the major recognition of his work was delayed until the 1960s. During the extended period of time that Piaget investigated cognition he "put together a psychological corpus of considerable magnitude and scope," including a detailed theory of intellectual development from birth to maturity, work on perceptual functioning, various sorties into logic and genetic epistomology, and "as buttress for the theoretical superstructure, a large and diverse body of ingenious experiments."[2] The magnitude of Piaget's work engenders awe; the provocative quality of much of the theory produces diverse reactions among American psychologists. By this time, however, most view his work as a major psychological thrust.

RECOGNITION OF PIAGET'S WORK

At least part of the reason for the long delay in recognizing Piaget's contributions was the controversy regarding his means for obtaining data, which were so at odds with the emphasis on scientific, statistical treatment of findings governing research in the United States. Researchers in psychology concerned themselves with sampling techniques, tests of reliability, experimental controls, and statistical treatment of data. These were not notable elements in Piaget's studies. In David Russell's evaluation of Piaget's work in 1956 a major portion of the criticism was methodological, especially decrying the failure to utilize scientific methods of child study and questioning Piaget's definition of terms.[3]

Piaget consistently employed a semiclinical interview technique, which Russell called a "type of rather peculiar play situation."[4] But careful consideration was given by Piaget to the selection of method in investigating children's thinking and the semiclinical technique evolved gradually. Piaget's earlier use of the standardized test procedure at the Binet laboratory in Paris led him to reject the testing approach as too rigid to uncover the epigenesis of thought that he sought. Naturalistic investigation, used widely with infants, he found to be ultimately too unwieldy. So he devised the semiclinical method with the aim of following the child's thinking without deforming it by suggestions or by imposing an adult viewpoint. As Piaget began to employ this method it relied heavily on verbal interaction but it was gradually modified to include the use of concrete objects. The examiner's questions referred to the objects or events that the child had before him; the child's response could often be through the manipulation of these objects so that language was supported by action. Questioning by the examiner was flexible in order to follow the child's line of thinking and provide a wide range of information.

Another source of neglect of Piaget's work was his continual blending of empirical description with theoretical speculation. Large portions of Piaget's publications consisted of lengthy theorizing on the meaning of data, often couched in complex logico-mathematical terminology. While this constituted a particularly fruitful procedure for Piaget that led him to ingenious new insights, it was anathema to psychologists seeking to build a science of human behavior.

The delayed recognition of Piaget's work meant that it did not have a gradual and cumulative impact upon American psychologists; rather, his "tower of books and articles has fallen almost pell-mell" onto his colleagues in the United States within a brief span of years.[5] The pace of publication and translation has been rapid. The vast and complex material to be ingested made its assimilation difficult and Piaget's whole theory liable to superficial interpretation.

American psychologists and educators had not been unconcerned with intellectual growth, although many of them were highly focused on the affective. In a survey published in 1960 Charles D. Smock found a revival of interest in "higher mental processes" superceding psychologists' absorption in the quantification of intelligence. Smock found neither Piaget nor Heinz Werner, a member of the psychology department at Clark University concerned with an organismic view of growth, "a particularly potent influence in the *recent* revival of interest in cognition."[6] Study was oriented toward systematic research relevant to perception, concept formation, and problem solving. David Russell's book, *Children's Thinking*, may serve to illustrate these studies. In summarizing knowledge on children's concepts Russell wrote: "Children develop breadth and depth in their concepts only after much first hand and vicarious experience in the area involved."[7] Concerning problem solving he stated that this ability increases with age in terms of both speed and accuracy. "This does not mean," he concluded, "that problem-solving abilities change with age, but it does mean that older children and adolescents are often more sensitive to a problem as such and have more experience to bring to bear upon proposed solutions and upon criticism of these solutions."[8] Russell strongly emphasized that developmental changes in thinking were essentially quantitative — more experience, clearer perceptions, expanded concepts — rather than a qualitative change in intellectual growth. "There is no evidence that mental abilities differ in kind," he insisted, "but rather the component parts of mental abilities differ in degree and in relation to one another at different age levels."[9] Here, Russell was refecting the contemporary viewpoint, which failed to accommodate Piaget's position, emphasizing qualitative changes in thinking, as we shall see.

Educators' approach to cognition mirrored the emphasis of psychologists. In texts for teachers of young children, intellectual growth was examined along with physical, social, and emotional areas of development. The child's engrossing exploration of the world, his concentration upon the "here and now" as opposed to abstractions, his rapid growth of language, as well as his vivid imagination were all noted.[10] In many schools for the young child a systematic effort was made to create a learning environment in which the child's expanding conceptual organization grew from encounters that promoted the formulating of relationships. Problem solving, as Dewey had presented it, in which the functional context of learning prevailed, was a major means for expanding relational thinking. City and Country School and Bank Street School for Children maintained this point of view.[11] Reiterating that problem solving and searching for solutions were particularly urgent in a world of change where knowledge was accumulating at a rapid rate, Lucile Lindberg wrote in 1961: "What he [the child] has discovered, he can see in context and understand its relationship to other learnings, sensing many shades of meaning involved."[12] Little of Piaget's conceptualization was incorporated into these concerns for cognitive growth, although some of these ideas were congruent with his writings.

The turning point in a more general positive reception of Piaget's theory came in the 1960s, more from a sociological than a psychological breakthrough. Society, in the concern to alleviate the problems of the poor, turned to education. The assumption supporting faith in education was that something could be done about a child's intellectual effectiveness by the nature of the experiences provided him. Such an emphasis rested upon mitigating confidence in maturation or unfolding as the prime element in cognitive growth and elevating the role of interactions with the environment. Allied to this was the crumbling concept of intelligence as fixed. Faith in nurture rested upon a transactional view of learning and development, which called for the accompanying view of man as active and competence-oriented. Not only does Piaget's theory embrace the latter point of view, it has been instrumental in provoking a more general acceptance of an active organism position.

Furthermore, there need be no long waiting period for the child's readiness to respond to the environment, for Piaget offered a strong contrast to the generally held belief of a newborn as a helpless and essentially passive being. He characterized the infant as active and as an initiator of behavior. The changes that take place between birth and around eighteen to twenty-two months of age, the period of sensorimotor intelligence, are continuous adaptations through coordinating actions to the surrounding milieu. During this period of time, through his interlocking coordination of actions tied closely to his environment, the child reaches the first basic invariant of knowledge: object permanence — the perception that the object "out there" is independent in its existence from his actions.

Under this influence studies of intellectual growth in infancy have increased, leading to the possible conclusion that "not only rate but also direction of development may be determined by the environment" of a particular infant.[13] Programs searching for an environment to maximize cognitive functioning were the result of testing this possibility. Spurred on by concern for the child labeled economically deprived that surfaced in the 1960s, infant programs were designed to identify environmental elements that could enhance the child's cognitive capacities.[14] Finally, then, infancy was included in the educative process. For years educators, including Froebel, Rousseau, Gesell, Frank, and many others, had recommended that more attention be given to the education of infants. Now, under the impetus of new conceptions of cognitive growth, programs for infants became a reality. Education had reached down to the earliest days of life.

GENETIC EPISTEMOLOGY

Piaget in his decades of research, conceptualization, and publication had no such direct outcome in mind. Rather, his life was a continuous search to understand the epigenesis of intelligence, how humans obtain knowledge of the world. Through acute observation in determining the child's understanding of the physical, social, and moral world at successive age levels, Piaget hoped to answer questions about the child's approach to "reality." Philosophical questions were thus tied to his empirical investigations, so he preferred to be called a genetic epistemologist. Therefore, as a philosopher of science, Piaget's writing culminated in the formulation of a genetic epistemology to demonstrate that the perennial philosophical question of knowledge acquisition may be fruitfully studied by the empirical methods of developmental psychology.

Detailed scientific observations were part of Piaget's studies from his precocious childhood. In his first papers, published at the age of ten, he described a partly albino sparrow he had observed in a public park.[15] By the age of twenty-one he had published twenty papers on mollusks and related zoological matters as a result of his work with the director of the natural history museum in Neuchatel, Switzerland.[16] As his interest changed to study of the child, which he originally planned to do for a few years before devoting the remainder of his career to purely epistemological problems, he provided extensive observations either in a naturalistic or semiclinical setting. He spent years watching his own three children, carefully observing their use of eyes, ears, hands, and legs in the first months of life and throughout the sensorimotor period. Many publications report studies of children in the preoperational period, that long age range that extends from about the ages of eighteen to twenty-four months to around six to eight years of age. What distinguishes Piaget's observations, with all their acuteness and scientific orientation, is the ingenious interpretation that he was able to give them.

In understanding the man, as well as the theory, psychologists have asked why Piaget was led to this intensive study and extensive publication at such an early age and have found the answer in his home life. His years with a father of a scientific frame of mind and a mother with a decided mental illness turned him to all-absorbing intellectual preoccupations that shut out anxiety infiltrations. In his *Autobiographie* he wrote:

> My father . . . is a man of painstaking and critical mind, who dislikes hastily improvised generalizations, and is not afraid of starting a fight when he finds historic truth twisted to fit respectable traditions. Among other things he taught me the value of systematic work, even in small matters. My mother was very intelligent, energetic, and fundamentally a very kind person; her rather neurotic temperament, however, made our family life somewhat troublesome. One of the direct consequences of the situation was that I started to forego playing for serious work very early; this I obviously did as much to imitate my father as to take refuge in both a private and a nonfictitious world. Indeed, I have always detested any departure from reality, an attitude which I relate to the second important influential factor in my early life, VIZ., My mother's poor mental health.[17]

Because Piaget also happened to be a genius, his coping was creatively transformed so that his many volumes became "a monument to the child that died early in childhood and was replaced by an intellectual paragon."[18] The outcome of this creative coping, which is now heralded as providing us with more understanding of cognitive growth than we ever had before, Anthony calls an "affectless monolith." But he extends this judgment by stating that in bridging the inner dissociation felt by Piaget and which he speaks about with understanding, Piaget erected a "magnificent theoretical edifice — one completely comprehensive, self-contained, internally consistent, without loose ends or unfilled spaces, and vigorously freed from affect: no place at all for anxiety to permeate."[19]

Piaget was not unaware of psychoanalysis as a way of dealing with mental illness or the feelings arising from dealing with it. It is clear that he read Freud and Jung and spent a time at Bleuler's psychiatric clinic in Zurich. Piaget even gave a lecture in 1922 at the Congress of Psychoanalysis in Berlin with Freud on the lecture platform. But this flirtation with Freudian theory was short lived; as Piaget's own theory began to take form and direction, references to psychoanalysis disappeared. At a later time Piaget stated that the term *unconscious* is as applicable to mental phenomena as to emotional life. "The unconscious," he pointed out, "is whatever is not conceptualized."[20] Freud's psychosexual stages Piaget found disturbing as they were essentially determined by a single predominant characteristic.

The reader is not to assume from all this that Piaget discarded the emotions as insignficant in the developmental process. When questioned he responded: "affectivity is central. Affectivity is the motor of any conduct."[21] In some of his writings Piaget demonstrated the manner in which feelings and thoughts interact in growth. For example, the child still tied to concrete experience, "does not experience as social feelings anything more than interindividual affects."[22] The child is sensitive to his family, his place of residence, his language and customs, but his intellectual development does not yet allow him to understand or feel notions of nationality, social justice, or civic courage. "This is to be expected," explained Piaget, "since, in the 7–11 year-old child, logic is applied only to concrete and manipulable objects. There is no operation available at this level which would make it possible for the child to elaborate an ideal which goes beyond the empirically given."[23] But at thirteen to fifteen years of age a transformation takes place both intellectually and affectively when feelings relative to ideals are added to interindividual feelings. The interactive nature of these developments Piaget stated firmly:

> The fundamental affective acquisitions of adolescence parallel the intellectual acquisitions. To understand the role of formal structures of thought in the life of the adolescent, we found that in the last analysis we had to place them in his total personality. But, in return, we found that we could not completely understand the growth of his personality without including

the transformations in his thinking; thus we had to come back to the development of formal structures.[24]

The key word to describe the intellectual growth used by Piaget in the preceding quotation is "structure," in this case formal structures, as thirteen- to fifteen-year-olds would generally have attained the stage of formal operations. Piaget described intellectual development as a constructivist process; knowledge is not a mere registration or reading of the external environment, it is constructed progressively. Each individual's "reality" is always something constructed in part according to the determinants of previously developed schemes or structures. Gruber and Vonèche interpret Piaget's structures as "not things or beliefs, but coherent sets of mental operations which can be applied to things or beliefs or to anything else in the individual's psychological space."[25] An operation or mental action is an interiorized scheme of action that allows the individual to act on the environment mentally, as in seriation or classification. In this sense Piaget can be considered a structuralist for it is the continual acting on, the evolving of structures that he focused on. "Piaget's concern has always been to show how action is interiorized, transformed into mental life, and he insists that in the course of this transformation action becomes qualitatively distinct from its primitive origins. As actions become operations, they form structured groups that give to thought its flexibility, its versatility, its ability to deal with novelty, its creativity," write two recent interpreters with Piaget's approval.[26]

In a Woodbridge lecture delivered by Piaget at Columbia University in 1968 Piaget presented genetic epistemology from his point of view:

> In sum, genetic epistemology deals with both the formation and the meaning of knowledge. We can formulate our problem in the following terms: by what means does the human mind go from a stage of less sufficient knowledge to a state of higher knowledge? The decision of what is lower or less adequate knowledge, and what is higher knowledge, has of course formal and normative aspects. It is not up to psychologists to determine whether or not a certain state of knowledge is superior to another state. That decision is one for logicians or for specialists within a given realm of science. . . . Our problem, from the point of view of psychology and from the point of view of genetic epistemology, is to explain how the transition is made from a lower level of knowledge to a level that is judged to be higher. The nature of these transitions is a factual question. . . .
> The fundamental hypothesis of genetic epistemology is that there is a parallelism between the progress made in the logic and rational organization of knowledge and the corresponding formative psychological process.[27]

Knowledge, according to Piaget, consisted of a system of transformations that become progressively adequate as the individual constructs for himself a system of transformations that correspond, more or less adequately, to reality.

> For the genetic epistemologist, knowledge results from continuous construction, since in each act of understanding, some degree of invention is involved; in development, the passage from one stage to the next is always characterized by the formation of new structures which did not exist before, either in the external world or in the subject's mind.[28]

The individual's role in building his own structures of thought is reiterated over and over in Piaget's theory. Firm understanding, particularly in the area of logico-mathematical structures, is attained only by the child's own invention.

THE ACTIVE ORGANISM POSITION

Piaget gave depth and meaning to the active organism position inherent in his work. Many of his terms were used to explain the individual's role in his own intellectual growth. For example, he repeatedly uses the terms *assimilation* and *accommodation*: twin processes subsumed under his distinctive term, *equilibration*.

Intellectual assimilation, roughly comparable to biological assimilation, is the mechanism whereby reality data are incorporated into the individual's thought structure. In this sense every newly established piece of data is integrated into existing schemes and the organizing activity of the individual must be considered just as important as the external stimuli. Stimuli have meaning to the individual only to the degree that he can assimilate them by means of existing structures.[29] As schemes or structures are modified to the demands of reality, accommodation takes place. In Piaget's words: "The filtering or modification of the input is called *assimilation*; the modification of internal schemes to fit reality is called *accommodation*.[30] From this point of view all mental life tends progressively to assimilate the surrounding environment. At all stages of development "the mind fulfills the same function, which is to incorporate the universe to itself, but the nature of assimilation varies, *i.e.*, the successive modes of incorporation evolve from those of perception and movement to those of higher mental operations."[31] In this view the progressive organization of mental development appears to be an ever more precise adaptation to reality or a general psychological equilibrium.

Equilibration is the term Piaget used to indicate an individual's active seeking of a satisfying state of equilibrium. He defined it as "the search for a better and better equilibrium in the sense of an extended field, in the sense of an increase in the number of possible compositions, and in the sense of a growth in coherence."[32] Since only the individual can extend his field or establish coherence, equilibration has been roughly translated as self-regulation or self-correction. So important did Piaget consider equilibration in the growth of intelligence that he ranked it as one of the four factors that explain development. The other factors are maturation, direct physical experience, and social transmission. Of these he considers equilibration to be pedogogically fundamental.[33]

STAGES OF DEVELOPMENT

Like many of the psychologists influencing early childhood education, Piaget proposed a sequence of stages of development; in his case they are stages all children go through in arriving at the ability to think logically. Age, as designated by Piaget, is simply a point of reference, for he recognized variations in levels of attainment; his work was not normative. But he did expect each child to experience a lawful succession of relatively stable structures of knowing that characterize growth from stage to stage; in other words, the order of development is considered invariant. This came about as Piaget investigated various forms of knowing, for in revealing the gradations of thought related to principal modes of human experience — space, time, number, for example — he "laid bare a complex succession of preforms and precursors for the most mundane and obvious of cognitions."[34]

Piaget designated three major periods of development — sensorimotor, concrete operations, and formal operations. For the early childhood educator the substages of concrete operations are significant because both include the early childhood years, with the preoperational substage the period of genesis of operations followed by the substage of concrete operations as the period of attainment. The key word, of course, in distinguishing stages is "operation," that mental ability to know an object by acting on it, modifying or transforming it, and to understand the process of transformation. The essence of knowledge in Piaget's theory is an interiorized action, such as classification, seriation, numbering, which modifies an object of knowledge or integrates it into a known system.

Each stage, as Piaget discussed them, has a period of genesis and a period of attainment with distinct transformations occurring as the ability to operate expands. In the earliest period when sensorimotor schemes are generalized and coordinated, the significant development is that of object permanence. Later the path of preoperational thinking involves a slow structuring on the operational plane of logico-mathematical reasoning and an assiduous adapting to the use of symbols. The child in the period of concrete operations, from about the age of seven to around eleven or twelve, has a cognitive superstructure that consists of tightly knit ensembles of reversible operations that enable him to mentally organize and stabilize the surrounding world of objects and events to a degree impossible to a younger child. At least he can do so when the objects and events are within his perceptual field. Reversibility, the ability to think back to an original starting point, is a critical development he has attained. With the achievement of formal operations around the age of eleven or twelve, truly abstract thinking is possible so that logical deductions and generalizations can be made without reference to empirical evidence.

A sense of orderly and coherent change is conveyed as Piaget wrote that each stage "extends the preceding period, reconstructs it on a new level, and later surpasses it to an even greater degree."[35] Continuity of mental growth is assured as each structure "results from the preceding one, integrating it as a subordinate structure, and prepares for the subsequent one, into which it is sooner or later itself integrated."[36] Yet changes in intellectual capacity are not just quantitative but qualitative in nature. Newly formed cognitive structures enable the child to think in a qualitatively distinct manner about certain life problems. Each stage represents a different organization of experience, information, and knowledge that leads to a very different view of the world. For example, most children in the early preoperational stage believe the amount of juice changes when poured into a container with different dimensions. They may center upon the height or width of the new container and fail to see how a corresponding dimension compensates. For the child who has attained conservation of liquid, who understands that quantity is not changed when simply transferred, the world takes on a greater sense of stability and the view of the world comes closer to that of an adult. Or the learner in the stage of formal operations, who no longer needs to use concrete objects to support his thinking, can understand metaphor and is more capable of giving meaning to extensions in time and space. Innumerable examples from Piaget's writings illustrate the child's qualitatively different manner of making sense of his world at distinct stages of development.

Yet, interestingly, the integrative nature of all learning is reinforced in Piaget's theory. In pursuing the epigenesis of thought he has revealed the great number of developmental aspects that are related to cognitive growth: the nature of social interaction, the use of language, growth into the symbolic world, an evolving sense of moral judgment, to name a few. All, in Piaget's view, are inextricably tied to the child's growing intellectual abilities. Until the child gains a degree of flexibility in his thinking he has difficulty taking into account the point of view of another person, thus egocentricity marks much of his thought. Piaget has delineated the manner in which a child's play contributes to symbolization. Through intellectual development, as well as appropriate social experiences, the older child arrives at a morality of social concern and cooperation. All are examples of growth that does not proceed singly.

PREOPERATIONAL THOUGHT

Let us turn now to that long period labeled by many interpreters of Piaget as the period of preoperational thought, although Piaget spoke of it as a subperiod in reaching concrete operations. At any rate, period or subperiod, it embraces the early childhood years. In Flavell's opinion Piaget gives us an "enriched understanding" of "that interesting but often baffling age range."[37] The theory provides insights into the impulsive, sometimes alogical behavior and thinking of the young child.

Structures of Thought

Probably the most informative way to think of the preoperational thought is as a subdivision of larger attainments, for that helps us to focus on the transitional nature of the period and the substantive growth taking place. It is easy to think of it as a time when the individual lacks functional operativity in many areas: conservation is not fully established; the ability to think in terms of a hierarchy of classification has not been developed; seriation may be carried out only intuitively. But more helpful is the consideration of the tremendous growth taking place. Piaget has written: "What is most striking about this long period of preparation for and formation of the concrete operations is the functional unity (within each subperiod) that binds cognitive, playful, affective, social and moral reactions into a whole. Indeed, if we compare the preoperatory subperiod between two and seven or eight with the subperiod of completion between seven or eight and eleven or twelve, we see the unfolding of a long, integrated process that may be characterized as a transition from subjective centering in all areas to a decentering that is at once cognitive, social, and moral."[38]

From Piaget's view cognitive growth is an extended process of decentration, of removing limits that deform an objective view of the world.

Centration may be defined as a subjective focusing on a single aspect or mode of perception. During the sensorimotor period, for example, the child gradually comes to separate the world into self and non-self; he decenters a degree from an entirely subjective view. The preoperational child tends to center on one aspect of a physical entity at a time. When a ball of clay is rolled into the form of a sausage, for example, he may respond that the sausage has more clay because it is longer and thus fails to take other dimensions into account. Not until he has gained reversibility does he decenter from immediate perception and gain the understanding of physical transformations. The final decentering appears when formal operations are achieved and the learner has decentered from perception and action and no longer requires empirical evidence to support operations. He can, then, reason on the basis of hypotheses and propositions.

Because the preoperational child is only decentering perceptually, his cognitive life, like his affective one, tends to be unstable, discontinuous, moment by moment. His thought, neither truly inductive nor deductive, is inclined to be transductive, proceeding from particular to particular and making associative "and" connections rather than true causal relations. Therefore, at this period, he is the slave rather than the master of changes in configuration and his perceptions seem to embroil him in contradictions. Piaget has stated that "although logical structures are not fully developed at the preoperational stage, we do find what can be called semi-logic."[39] What operativity exists tends to be irreversible and in a very literal sense it can be considered "a half logic." But as the child repeatedly acts on things and situations the decentering takes place and this allows him to mentally reverse, at first intuitively and finally to operate in the logico-mathematical mode with full recognition of the justification for his responses. Much greater flexibility has been attained and the child is then in the later substage called concrete operations.

The preoperational child's well-recognized curiosity leads him to constant manipulation, to repeated actions on things and people. A growing awareness of the properties of objects results from the continual acting upon them: touching, lifting, arranging, and sorting. The child is making sense out of his world, understanding the larger physical environment and his place in it. Figurative knowledge, which focuses on the external, figural aspect of an object or event in a static manner, expands rapidly. Operational knowledge, the characteristic interiorized generalizable action, only gradually emerges, its roots in the coordination of actions but its attainment dependent upon "reflective abstraction." The logical, mathematical structures of seriation, classification, and numbers, for example, which Piaget researched extensively, are based in the general coordination of actions but the level of operation is ultimately determined by "the mental process of reflection, that is, at the level of thought [in which] a reorganization takes place."[40] An operation is one that "can be carried out in thought as well as executed materially" and is distinguished by reversibility.[41] Most children at the preoperational substage are working at the figurative level and building toward reflective abstraction.

The Symbolic Function

One of the ingenious insights of Piaget has been to reveal how the child's proclivity for play during the preoperational substage contributes first to gaining meaning from his array of life experiences, and second to the process of symbolization. Play is a means of relating to new realities the child is discovering and gradually constructing for himself. "He must start," wrote Piaget, "by laboriously incorporating them within himself and into his own activity," thus, play is viewed as an "assimilation of reality to the self."[42] Gradually, as deforming centration declines and objectivity increases, play becomes more adapted to others and to reality. Then the symbolic play, so engrossing to the preoperational child, idiosyncratic in nature and including minimal collective extensions to others, gives way at about the age of seven or eight to games with rules that entail common obligations.

While symbolic play is at its height the child becomes adept at designating objects and actions as symbols. It is noteworthy that the book we know as *Play, Dreams and Imitation in Childhood* has the original French title *La Formation du Symbole Chez L'Enfant: Imitation, Jeu et Reve; Image et Representation.* Piaget referred to the book as *La Formation du Symbole* — symbol formation — for during the preoperational subperiod he considers the major focus to be not only the rapid development of language but other aspects of the symbolic function.[43] This symbolic function, which Piaget eventually called the semiotic function to utilize the term employed by linguists, uses play, dreams, and imitation as the means, but the goal goes beyond them to the ability to function symbolically. In make-believe fashion the child allows some things (symbols) to stand for others and, in thus building the ability to see things as representational, forms a basic component of the thought processes.

This generalized ability to make the act of reference — to use an object or action to evoke or refer to another — rests not upon codified symbols that the whole culture can share but upon idiosyncratic, more or less private symbols determined by the child's direct experience. Barbara Biber captures the nature of this development in the following statement:

> It is during the preschool years that the human mind performs its greatest magic: the child is freed from dependence on sensory-perceptual-motor ex-

perience as the sole channel of communication with his environment. The evolution of the capacity to deal with experience symbolically represents the key extensor process of the maturing organism. It manifests itself in every medium of expression known to man, and runs the full course from the simplest gestural representations to advanced levels of abstraction. The string held to the ear is "telephoning" to the child who is nowhere near a three-syllable word in his vocabulary; the spinning five-year-old who drops to the floor in delicious exhaustion is the astronaut in orbit; from the crayon lines of the three-year-old a "face" appears; the clay in the hands of the four-year-old walks like a dog; the left-over strips of lath in the wood-box are regenerated, to live again as a helicopter. Symbolizing through gesture, through two-dimensional and three-dimensional representation, are natural child modes of reiterating the more meaningful aspects of experience, thereby strengthening the joining lines between the inner self and the outer world. Equally exciting to the child, and ultimately the keystone of his ability to deal effectively with the complexity of human living, is his gradual mastery of the word and the idea as tools for symbolically organizing experience.[44]

By ingeniously discovering the unifying symbolic character of such different activities as images, play, imitation, and language, Piaget revealed the relationship between a whole series of behavioral abilities gaining strength in the preoperational period. All part of symbolic (or semiotic) functioning, their coherence was presented by Piaget in this way:

> In spite of the astonishing diversity of its manifestations, the semiotic function presents a remarkable unity. Whether it is a question of deferred imitation, symbolic play, drawing, mental images and image-memories or language, this function allows the representational evocation of objects and events not perceived at that particular moment. The semiotic function makes thought possible by providing it with an unlimited field of application, in contrast to the restricted boundaries of sensori-motor action and perception. Reciprocally, it evolves under the guidance of thought, or representative intelligence. Neither imitation nor play nor drawing nor image nor language nor even memory (to which we might have attributed a capacity for spontaneous reproduction comparable to that of perception) can develop or be organized without the constant help of the structuration characteristic of intelligence.[45]

The ability to represent and understand the representations of others widens the knowing life of the child to an unprecedented degree.

While both symbolic play and language develop during the same time span in the life of the child, Piaget clearly distinguished their origins. Symbolic play, reaching its apogee between two to three and five to six, provides an affective and cognitive means for the child to assimilate reality to the self without coercions and sanctions, through symbols that he has constructed — the symbols that relate to his experience as Piaget put it:

> The child . . . needs a means of self-expression, that is, a system of signifiers constructed by him and capable of being bent to his wishes. Such is the system of symbols characteristic of symbolic play. These symbols are borrowed from imitation as instruments, but not used to accurately picture external reality. Rather, imitation serves as a means of evocation to achieve playful assimilation of reality to the self, as is play in general, but an assimilation made possible (and reinforced) by a symbolic "language" that is developed by the self and is capable of being modified according to its needs.[46]

Language, however, is not indigenous to the child but is presented from without by society: "the essential instrument of social adaptation is language, which is not invented by the child but transmitted to him in ready-made, compulsory, and collective forms."[47]

Piaget distinguished the two types of symbol systems by giving them separate terms. Symbols he considered those invented by the individual by himself; those imposed by society he called signs. "Signs, on the other hand, being conventional, are necessarily collective. The child receives them, therefore, through the medium of imitation, but this time as an acquisition of external models. However, he immediately fashions them to suit himself and uses them."[48]

By broadening the conception of symbol formation and adaptation, Piaget has provided a whole new view of the manner in which the child enters into the symbolic world. It does not wait for the encounter with those little black marks on paper involved in reading.

Developments in the Social Realm

It is not by chance that a change in social behavior accompanies the growing ability to operate and to symbolize. While the child is building symbol-forming intelligence he is continually accommodating to socially devised representational systems, i.e., language and numbers. In the move away from centered perceptions and transductive thought the child finally arrives at coordinated perceptions with reversibility, which allow for operativity in conservation, classification, seriation, number, and other logico-mathematical areas of thought. The rigid, static, irreversible structures typical of early preoperational thought begin "to 'thaw out' and become more flexible, mobile, and above all decentered and reversible in their operations."[49] This gradually developed flexibility of thought enables the child to drop his earlier position of considering his own as the only point of view, to a changed view of recognizing the possibility of many points of view. The move is toward an "other" orientation and socialized communication. Not surprisingly interest in games with rules supercedes symbolic play.

In the moral realm Piaget projected a transition of great magnitude in the early years that follows approximately the same development as other lines of thought. For Piaget the essential aspect of morality was the tendency to accept and follow a system of rules that regulate interpersonal behavior. The child in the stage of preoperational thought — centered about himself, failing to take into account the point of view of others, having a meager grasp of rules or of their origins — tends to follow rules sporadically. Since his is a relationship of constraint and unilateral respect for those older than he is, rules are quite external to him. These states of thought imbue the child's actions with what Piaget and Inhelder termed "'moral realism' in which obligations and values are determined by the law or the order itself, independent of intentions and relationships."[50] Thus under the influence of egocentric patterns of thought the focus is on external aspects rather than intentional or subjective aspects.

New moral relationships develop based upon a mutuality of respect, or of reciprocity that comes with advances in social cooperation and operative thinking. Then a sense of reciprocity, of mutuality among equals, involving as it does an attempt to put oneself in another's place, tends toward a morality of subjective understanding and forgiveness. But this is an advance not achieved by the preoperational child. For Piaget these developments did not take place independently; clearly he considered social and moral transformations to parallel the growth of intellectual operations.

Viewed in this manner the teacher working with children between the ages of two to seven or eight years gains a tremendous appreciation of the growth taking place. Some psychologists even narrow the span of years to include the five to seven range in which to delineate a significant transformation. Named by Sheldon White, the five-to-seven shift he designates a fundamental reorganization in all facets of the child's life.[51] Acknowledging these apparent developmental changes, Howard Gardner seeks to probe explanations for the shift and the controversies surrounding differing points of view.[52] The influence of social and cultural factors is fully recognized, but Piaget's contributions rank high: he has depicted the emergence of certain logical operations, the ability to take the role of another person, an ability to deal symbolically, among other developing attributes.

MECHANISMS OF TRANSITION

Clearly defining distinct stages supported by an underlying continuity of growth, Piaget also addressed the mechanisms that promote transitions from stage to stage: experience, maturation, social transmission, and equilibration. Already mentioned as four in number, these mechanisms need to be understood within the context of Piaget's conviction about the constructivist nature of learning. Interactionism is considered reciprocal. The environment is not something that determines the child's responses, rather, a response is always that of a living organism and thus constructed in part by the determinants of intrinsic structure already developed. This point is expressively stated by Gruber and Vonèche: "'To change as a mere reaction to environmental pressure would be to violate the organized integrity of the individual in his given state of development. Change is a serious matter; to accomplish it the individual must reconstruct himself."[53] So significant did Piaget consider the active role of the individual in mental growth that he frequently used the word "invent" to designate the learner's arrival at an adult mode of thought.

Small wonder, then, that Piaget considered equilibration a fundamental mechanism of growth. In applying equilibration to education he wrote:

> In the realm of education, this equilibration through self-regulation means that school children and students should be allowed a *maximum* of activity on their own, directed by means of materials which permit their activities to be cognitively useful. In the area of logico-mathematical structures, children have real understanding only of that which they invent themselves, and each time we try to teach them something too quickly, we keep them from reinventing it themselves.[54]

Experience, another significant factor in development, includes physical and logico-mathematical experience. It is always the child's action on objects, which Piaget underscores. Physical properties are abstracted through manipulation, and use. Gaining logico-mathematical knowledge is even more complex, for although it is grounded upon experience and action, it is the result of the coordination of actions (as in seriation, for example). Logical operations — the ability to deal with logico-mathematical questions — are "not read directly off the environment: they are the product of reflection and abstraction by the subject upon his own actions and their coordination into a meaningful system."[55] Furthermore, logical operations when achieved "cannot be performed on anything like raw or immediate experience, but only on highly refined mental products, that is, the signs that stand for such experiences."[56] Cognitive operations and symbolic representation, two strands of development that seem to quicken in tandem, reinforce each other in the slow, complex construction of reality.

While Piaget ascribed to maturation a role in mental growth, he viewed it as only one factor among many. In the unvarying order of successive stages the role of maturation is indispensable largely in opening up new possibilities. It forms "a necessary but not in itself sufficient condition for the appearance of certain behavior patterns."[57] In Piaget's opinion, the influence of the physical and social milieu tends to increase in importance with age.

The final factor used by Piaget to explain mental development is social transmission. Although necessary and essential, the impact of social transmission is limited by the child's ability to assimilate the material. To understand transmitted knowledge the active nature of the child comes into play; understanding depends upon the restructuring of the situation or transforming a given problem in terms of the subject's internal equilibrated structures. In simpler words, there must be a match between what is transmitted socially and the learner's ability to respond in terms of interiorized structures. The individual contributes as well as receives.

Piaget extended these four factors influencing cognitive development to the affective realm. In the following excerpt he explained this relationship:

> It may appear that these four major factors explain only the intellectual and cognitive evolution of the child and that the development of affectivity and motivation must be considered separately. It may even seem that affective, dynamic factors provide the key to all mental development and that in the last analysis it is the need to grow, to assert oneself, to love, and to be admired that constitutes the motive force of intelligence, as well as of behavior in its totality and in its increasing complexity.
>
> As we have seen repeatedly, affectivity constitutes the energetics of behavior patterns whose cognitive aspect refers to the structure alone. There is no behavior pattern, however intellectual, which does not involve affective factors as motives; but, reciprocally, there can be no affective states without the intervention of perceptions, or comprehensions which constitute their cognitive structure. Behavior is therefore a piece, even if the structures do not explain its energetics and if, vice versa, its energetics do not account for its structures. The two aspects, affective and cognitive, are at the same time inseparable and irreducible.
>
> It is precisely this unity of behavior which makes the factors in development common to both the cognitive and the affective aspects; and their irreducibility in no way rules out a functional parallelism which is rather striking even in details . . . it is impossible to interpret the development

of affective life and of motivations without stressing the all-important role of self-regulations, . . .

This interpretation can claim to give a fairly good account of the known facts, first of all because an equilibration is necessary to reconcile the role of maturation, experience with objects, and social experience.[58]

PIAGET'S INFLUENCE ON EARLY CHILDHOOD EDUCATION

The direct utilization of Piaget's theory has been too recent to provide a basis for the full assessment of its impact upon early childhood education, yet a growing emphasis is evident. Its influence in propelling a recognition of the importance of infancy for cognitive growth has already been noted. This has no doubt been instrumental in forwarding the wave of interest in helping parents become more effective, an influence designated under the questionable rubric of "parenting."

Beside the deluge of publications explaining or interpreting Piaget's ideas directly, major conceptions are being incorporated into child development literature. For example, threads of Piagetian theory are woven into Ira Gordon's *Human Development*.[59] In a simple understandable publication for the neophyte in child development, David Elkind has included salient material from the works of Jean Piaget.[60] Large segments of Howard Gardner's *Developmental Psychology*, intended as an introduction to the field, endeavor to put Piaget's contributions into perspective.[61] Efforts to probe the implications of Piaget's theory for education include articles by early childhood specialists.[62] Constance Kamii has worked to develop a curriculum for young children supported by a Piagetian framework and over the years has moved from a conception highly cognitive to one incorporating other areas of growth and placing cognition within the broader context of personal development.[63]

After experimenting in a classroom with some of Piaget's tasks, one teacher writes: "Never again will I look at children in the same way— and the change is for the better."[64] Other writers recommend using "Piaget as our guide for a new way to look at children and their intellectual development."[65] And Millie Almy suggests, "To put Piagetian concepts into action requires, above all else, a thinking teacher. He or she looks beyond the child's verbalization and manipulation and tries to understand what they mean for the child. This way of looking at and thinking about children is far from easy. It adds, however, a new and satisfying dimension to teaching."[66] All these writers, directing their articles to early childhood educators, highlight the revolutionary nature of Piaget's theory.

11 The Emergence of a Developmental-Interaction Point of View

Finally, the strong allegiance of early childhood educators to the two psychological constructs of maturation and fixed intelligence has been stripped away. An exclusive concern for a maturational theory of growth is no longer tenable. In a masterful analysis of dissonant evidence J. McVicker Hunt has undermined faith in genetically predetermined development as well as the general acceptance of intelligence as fixed at birth.[1] False assumptions had spawned a great deal of corroborative research. It was only when Hunt began to investigate Piaget's interactionist theory, which presents "a picture of behavioral development as a process of changes in the structure of behavior and of thought that come from the infant's or the child's interacting with his circumstances,"[2] that he undertook the analysis of data that revealed discrepancies. While data supported Hunt's new position, it was his questioning of basic assumptions and propositions that brought about new perceptions. He writes: "the depth of the dissonance between the outlooks and the conceptions of Piaget and Gesell has hardly yet been fully realized."[3] The same could be said about the great distance between faith in fixed intelligence and the belief that intellectual growth is a constructivist process.

These major transformations of thought derived from Piaget's work surfaced in the 1960s. The interactionist position, already familiar to followers of Dewey, supported the movement away from concern with normative data and the use of I.Q. tests. Biber writes about the elimination of "the dragon of fixed intelligence."[4] Bernard Spodek proposes that "an interactionist approach to early education, whereby education was seen as stimulating rather than supporting development, began to replace the maturationist view as the central thrust of early childhood education."[5] What a dramatic example of the way in which educational thought may

170

be seen paralleling changes in psychological perceptions! Let us examine changes in point of view regarding other aspects of child development.

STAGE THEORY

Developmental stage theory has been an aspect of most theories readily accepted by early childhood educators. Rousseau designated stages. Hall and Gesell's work, commonly referred to as "ages and stages," linked stages of growth to age norms. Freud pointed out psychosexual stages. Erikson delineated stages of ego development, formulating personality gains possible at each stage of growth. Piaget's is also a stage theory depicting qualitative changes in thinking at various periods of development, loosely tied to age.

That developmental psychologists have found the stage concept a particularly powerful and useful one is evident. They suggest very strongly that there is a definite order in the successive patterns of behavior and thought that in turn provides a framework for thinking about the education of children. One current manner of pinpointing a particular period of change is embodied in the five-to-seven shift, referred to earlier. Sheldon White has examined the diverse alterations in behavior that seem to take place during these years and concludes that a fundamental reorganization is taking place in all facets of the child's life.[6] White views these changes as occurring as the result of a confluence of causes, not the least being the emergence of certain logical operations designated by Piaget.

In its early use stage theory was accepted as revealing "facts" of growth. The whole new literature of descriptive data compiled by Gesell found its way into texts for early childhood educators, whose trust in child study was so strong that they included chapters depicting the physical growth, language ability, competence in routines, and similar traits easily measured by objective standards.[7] A picture of the "average" or "normal" child was presented as a guide to the teacher. Fallaciously, the norms derived from one segment of the population were generalized to all children.

Now even committed developmentalists recognize stage theory as providing only a metaphor, a way to think about human growth, with the user involved in the determination of how far to accept analogies. Certain basic assumptions are inherent: an acceptance of qualitative changes from stage to stage, and the tolerance of an implied end point. The issue of continuity resurfaces as psychologists probe Piaget's notion of qualitative changes in cognitive growth. The task of defining what development is continuous and what changes "seem most appropriately described as qualitative" is a formidable one.[8]

Even more widely in question today is the positing of a set of stages that eventuate in a mature end state, for such a position raises a moral question. Inherent in the concept of stages is growth toward maturity with each stage improving on the previous one. "We must define the domain of most developmental sequences in part by a statement of their end points," writes Kessen.[9] Because researchers reflect their own time with its fundamental beliefs, the end state of developmental research has been some definition of the educated adult in Western society. Thus the question of values reaches down into the very core of developmental psychology.

Furthermore, the maintenance of a focus upon the individual becomes almost impossible in developmental stage theory. For while psychological theory tends to be generated from close observation of individuals, "it is the nature of theory building to move from particularities of the individual to more general statements, from the concrete to the abstract. Theories are by definition nomothetic."[10] Generalizations or laws, thus derived from individuals, tend to move far away from the individual case. Not only do such principles become less usable by the teacher dealing with individuals but the whole view is antithetical to a child-centered, phenomenological point of view. Some aspects of stage theory make it "almost opaque with respect to the place of the individual," concludes Shapiro and Wallace.[11]

The assumptions and problems attached to accumulating data concerning stages can no longer be ignored by those who have found stage theory so congenial. Particularly for educators of the young child, whose developmental changes are often baffling, it has been helpful to impose segmentation on the intricate course of human development and to pinpoint the significant characteristics of development taking place. No longer, however, can principles of growth be honored as revealed fact but only as a metaphoric means of thinking about growth. Those who employ stage theory must assess their acceptance of associated assumptions.

DARWINIAN BASE

The word *development*, used to describe growth from stage to stage in the process of growing up, is itself an image borrowed from the biological research model. Optimism for gaining new understandings of children was high, when less than one hundred years ago, the methods of other disciplines were applied to the study of children, findings recorded, and a theoretical framework to account for observed changes in behavior sought. While the theoretical positions of researchers vary greatly in emphasis, both the nature of data collected and the conception of man employed have been a "proud adherent of the rational scientific tradition."[12] Developmental psychology, so valued by educators working with the child under the age of eight, was propelled by the urge to build a science of psychology that would ultimately supply enough information about the important domains of development to predict and control behavior.

Strikingly, all the theories from Hall to Piaget, including the quasi-psychological position of Dewey, are embedded in Darwin's biological and evolutionary ideas. In Piaget's system of thought, for example, knowledge, psychological structure, and physiological structures are all of a piece, "so that the conventional meaning of evolution — as it occurs in the evolution of biological forms — merges with Piaget's use of it for knowledge."[13] Take Piaget's own explanation of the growth of knowledge: "Logico-mathematical structures do, in fact, present us with an example, to be found no where else in creation, of a development which evolves without a break in such a way that no structuration brings about the elimination of those preceding it."[14]

The acceptance of Darwin's basic ideas influenced methodology, raised different questions, and produced a new manner of discussing child development; the scientific method in research became the only acceptable method for learning about human growth. The controlled experimental approach and even the more recently accepted clinical interview technique rest upon observations of behavior in a manner partaking of the Darwinian mode. They have in common a belief in the nature of growth as discernable through observational methodology and an acceptance of the phylogenetic scale as continuous and not discontinuous. Research on infrahuman species is given credence as having some relationship to human development. Schmidt finds the biological and evolutionary frame of reference evident "in the work of many psychologists who do not themselves experiment with animals but employ concepts borrowed from biology and use them sometimes as analogies or metaphors and sometimes as statements implying a fundamental identity between the functions of psychological processes from amoeba to mollusk to man."[15] These are evidences of the monumental shift in thinking brought about by Darwin, whose work outmoded earlier psychological study and influenced all that was to follow.

DIVERGENT POSITIONS

Ironically, psychologists with radically divergent views of the nature of man have relied upon Darwin's methodology and evolutionary ideas. Of course, opposing points of view came into being long before Darwin, indeed they can be traced back as far as Locke and Rousseau. Locke's beliefs of early nature as essentially a "blank slate" produced an extreme environmental position of which Thorndike and Skinner are direct descendents. They hold a deep skepticism regarding man's ability to understand "consciousness" or any of the inner workings of an individual. Inner states exist, are recognized, but are considered essentially irrelevant. They do not speak of intellect but of behavior as more or less adaptive to some environmental stimuli or reinforcement. Their rejection of predispositions, except for a few reflexes, leads to a view of the human organism as plastic, as a response mechanism subservient to the control of operant or respondent conditioning.

The emphasis in this view is on behavior, not persons. This mechanistic view, which fails to respect the subjective life of others, places awesome power in the hands of the educator. The curriculum designer has the power to select the goals and develop the means to these ends. In terms of Kessen's dimensions pointed out in the first chapter of this book, the child, in behaviorism, is considered a creature of nurture, a passive receiver of knowledge with behavior conceived as an additive bundle of elements.[16] The educational implications include impersonal handling, shaping, and reinforcement.

Rousseau may be said to have set in motion the view that partakes of the opposite designations given by Kessen: the child as a creature of nature, an active explorer generating knowledge and creating an integrated structure of thought.[17] Variations within this position are greater, yet all share an adherence to the three fundamentals. Within this strand of thought, tremendous respect for the inner forces of development has been constant. There has been, however, a growing recognition that maturational aspects of growth are mediated by environmental circumstances. The neo-Freudian's environmental emphasis, significant from the earliest years, was clear. Piaget's interactionist position gives the learner an active role in learning in every sense, including self-direction and self-regulation (equilibration), yet extensive interactions with the environment are considered essential for the child to proceed to the development of logical thought. Piaget would replace the stimulus-response paradigm with a circular one in which the learner takes from the situation and contributes to the response (see figure 1). Piaget does not start with an empty organism and considers no knowing to be merely a passive registration or reading of data in the external environment. Rather, knowledge is constructed progressively from equilibrated interactions with the environment. Both Dewey and Piaget have maintained the position that knowledge to be useful to the individual must become integrated into previous experience and the resulting generalized structures.

The tensions that persist between the two psychological schools of thought, so divergent in basic premises, have been augmented by Piaget's challenge to behaviorist theory. Yet until the past decade both schools

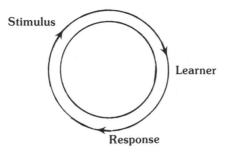

FIGURE 1.   An Interactive Design

of thought have held, even in the realm of intellectual development, to "the philosophical dictum that only that which is directly observable, and therefore measurable, can be dealt with meaningfully."[18] A great deal of research now focuses upon intellectual growth, the realm in which Zimiles has found research practically stymied by the stimulus-response paradigm. His analysis of current research and practice on intellectual functioning reveals how meager have been the results of the psychometric view and how important it is to move to an holistic perspective that can deal with more of the complexity of conceptual systems.[19] Harold Stevenson's overview of the voluminous research literature reveals how ill-equipped the basic framework of behaviorism is to deal with any but the simplest and explicit instances of behavior.[20] Urie Bronfenbrenner, in an article that he calls "presumptuous," argues "that the scientific model typically employed for research on human development is critically impoverished — both theoretically and empirically."[21]

ECOLOGICALLY VALID RESEARCH

The narrow perspective of scientific psychology is what Bronfenbrenner deplores, for he finds the model *ecologically invalid*. It has been "unidirectional," failing to include interactions characteristic of systems in which children develop. "And we continue to employ this model," he writes, "in the mistaken belief that it constitutes our only hope for scientific legitimacy."[22] He recommends that social situations be recognized in research as in life, with the model a two-way system. No longer, according to Bronfenbrenner, can the child be referred to as the "subject," but he must also be considered a part of the stimulus of events. The importance of reciprocality as a defining property in enhancing understanding of human development is what Bronfenbrenner underscores.

The uniformities of psychological development have been overestimated, writes Kenneth Keniston, because research in human development has been done essentially in America and Western Europe, where the patterns, timetables, and sequences prevalent among middle-class children have been taken as universal norms. Arguing for the relativity of human development Keniston states, "What we do know consistently supports the hypothesis that human development, from infancy onward, is contingent upon the characteristics of the environmental matrix."[23] Since the chart of human development is far from complete, Keniston envisions decades before the impacts of different environmental matrices upon distinct sectors of development can be understood.

The need for a methodology in child development that could take account of the complex interactional nature of a child's behavior within various environments was a recurring recognition in a Minnesota round table on early childhood education with noted child psychologists among the participants.[24] The importance of contexts that have an impact upon development, such as the family, the educational setting, and the cultural background, was a continuous theme. Corroborating this importance is a study incorporating the real-life environments in which behavior occurred; when extensive records of children's behaviors in varied settings were made, "some attributes of behavior varied less across children within settings than across settings within the days of children."[25] In other words knowledge of the settings helped predict behavior more adequately than knowledge of the behavior tendencies of a particular child. Clearly the lack of ecological data limits the understanding of behavior.

This removal of blinders existing in many earlier studies has spawned research, some of it reviewed by Bronfenbrenner.[26] An example from an even more recent study may be cited here. An ecological approach to infant behavior was used by Escalona and Corman in order to sharpen understanding of mother-child interactions and their role in shaping cognitive and personality development.[27] It was shown that the mother's close proximity or her disappearance had a marked impact on an infant. However, the direction of the effect varied; one child decreased responsiveness in the mother's absence, another child increased responsiveness and activity as if to fill a void.

Some earlier studies have by their very nature included ecological elements. One notable longitudinal piece of research in this category is the investigation of children's coping carried on at the Menninger Foundation under the direction of Lois Barclay Murphy. This extensive study, which investigated the situational components of children's coping with life experiences, illustrated the child's integrity as an autonomous growing person, who appraised his environment and developed whatever coping strategies he could devise to get along in the situation in which he found himself. So individual were the coping demands upon each child that Lois Murphy wrote: "Our children are choking in a stranglehold of norms. What do I mean by stranglehold? I am talking about the stifling, asphyxiating, smothering effect that comes from pigeonholing children in terms of test scores, of normative categories of pathology and nonconformity to social demands."[28] Rather than asking how a child fits into statistically based norms or unrealistic social expectations, Murphy would have us ask how a child is coping with the complex life situation in which he finds himself.

BROADENED PERSPECTIVES

The sober reanalysis of deficiencies in current knowledge of human development seems to make it a "time of disillusionment."[29] It certainly serves to temper the optimism and to point up the limitations of earlier eras; a renewed appreciation of the complexity of each child's behavior is surfacing. Is it not time to devise alternative ways of dealing with such complexity? Certainly it is a healthful sign that theories are beginning to recognize their own myths. As Ulich points out, "The evolutionary theory, however useful, is still an incomplete explanation of the course of nature."[30] Taking a much stronger position, Gould characterizes Darwin's as an empty and poorly developed world view.[31] With his depth of understanding Kessen proposes that an era of doubt, of openness, and of variation is rare in any science and that psychologists should make the most of it even if they "must invent new conceptual developments and try untested methods of study."[32]

In considering the behavioral sciences, it seems that "a paradox threatens when we begin to contemplate the idea of mankind. . . . The more we try to comprehend the human person, the more mysterious it becomes."[33] Broadened perspective is certainly essential to probe the paradox. A developmental psychologist himself, Sheldon White proposes that "all problems in human development involve biological, psychological and philosophical issues."[34] Ulich would push the perspectives into even greater realms in his statement: "In order to look at the whole problem from another perspective, we might ask if one is necessarily a philistine if he believes that the useful may also have some value for the individual and for the soul of mankind. Unless the vital, the intellectual, and the spiritual are seen as parts of the whole, the human being will never be fully understood."[35]

INTEGRATION OF THEORIES

Over the decades the various strands of psychology relating to growth and learning have continued amassing facts and concepts in singular isolation. As this insularity poses difficult problems for professionals endeavoring to apply theoretical ideas to practical problems, a number of efforts have been made to integrate theories. Gardner believes the radical shift opening up new dimensions will be the emergence of a new synthesizing model; of this he writes, "How satisfying it would be if increased understanding of the child's own changing models [of thought] were to culminate in a convincing model that could reconcile the competing theoretical strands in contemporary developmental psychology."[36]

Efforts to find relationships among various theories are inconclusive at best and differ in their assessment of the possibilities for synthesis. One psychologist, Alfred Baldwin, after an extensive examination of six different theoretical viewpoints of child psychologists, concluded "that they are not so much contradictory as unrelated."[37] He found theories of child development much like a patchwork quilt with little overlapping; few were the issues on which any two theories confront each other. From this Baldwin hazards a broad speculation: "The fact that these theories do not overlap also implies that they do not conflict. It may be possible, therefore, to write an eclectic yet integrated theory of the development of the child that capitalizes on the wisdom of each of the theories."[38]

At issue is the possibility of integrating stimulus-response theory into a metatheory of child development. Baldwin believes that while the principles of behaviorism have been poorly used by other theoretical positions, it is wise "to capitalize on the large body of data stemming from S→R theory and explicated in the principles of conditioning."[39] Children, in Baldwin's view, undeniably learn certain aspects of behavior through reinforcement. J. McVicker Hunt also wrestles with the problem of the role of S→R theory in relation to others, particularly Piaget's, and proposes a helpful distinction: Hunt distinguishes S→R methodology from S→R theory. "In emphasizing the observables of situation (or stimulus: S) and overt behavior (or response: R), the method is utterly sound," writes Hunt.[40] Yet he modifies this by stating that the empty organism between S and R is being refilled by tying intervening variables to roots in past experience and to manifestations of overt behavior.[41] Stimulus-response methodology cannot be denied; it is evident in many aspects of life where practice makes perfect, i.e., driving a car or playing the piano. The acceptance of the methodology is much more limited, however, than embracing S→R as a complete theory. One psychologist finds extreme behavioristic empiricism lessening in the mainstream of psychological theory today, for all have found it necessary to confront the inner functioning of the organism.[42]

PHILOSOPHICAL POSITIONS ESSENTIAL

Efforts at synthesis compel other searchers to probe not only the psychological but also the philosophical orientation undergirding each position to ascertain where theories support each other and where they collide. Robert Nye, for example, links psychological strands to philosophical views of man. In confronting the work of Freud, Skinner, and Rogers, Nye reasons that "Rogers' 'growth-motivated man' is quite different from Freud's 'tension-reducing man' or Skinner's 'programmable man.'"[43] The underlying views of human nature, according to Nye, differ dramatically among the three theorists: Freud is pessimistic and skeptical about man's future; Rogers is optimistic and emphasizes man as naturally growth-oriented and forward moving; Skinner simply moves out to consider how the environment can shape man. Can these opposing, fundamental beliefs relate to the same man? Nye believes they are but facets of the same man, for he writes, "it is my opinion that the ideas of Freud, Skinner and Rogers occupy critical niches in the progression of our thoughts about ourselves as human beings."[44]

Others are not so sanguine about the possibility of the integration of theories. In assessing the implications of the differing viewpoints of Skinner and Rogers, two workers at the Institute of Child Psychology at the University of Maryland concede that there appears to be truth in both views of man.[45] But the choice of either the behaviorist model or the phenomenological model they believe to greatly influence a number of human activities in both education and parenthood. It is precisely the basically divergent views of man that influence differing actions. These authors reinforce the cleavage presented concisely by Hitt in his conception of "Two Models of Man."[46]

To continue the critique of eclecticism Reese and Overton argue for internal consistency between an ideational superstructure and the nature of analysis of psychological functioning.[47] In an analysis of the mechanistic (reactive organism) and organismic (active organism) model, they find "the crucial difference . . . so fundamental and broad in its implications that syncretism is impossible, and the only rapprochement possible is like the parallel play of pre-schoolers in that the protagonists are separate, but equal and mutually tolerant."[48] On a metatheoretical level these two writers find the two models reflecting different and incompatible views of the world and of man.

A theorist's basic view of human nature either limits or extends psychological study. Including only personality theories in their study, two other writers terminate their discussion by stating "that basic assumptions about the nature of the human organism constitute the bedrock from which theories of personality are formulated and ultimately tested."[49] Furthermore, they find that "a theorist's basic assumptions about human nature simultaneously broaden and narrow his perspective on personality." Dimensions that influence the theorist's perspective include:

> freedom vs. determinism
> rationality vs. irrationality
> holism vs. elementism
> constitutionalism vs. environmentalism
> subjectivity vs. objectivity
> knowability vs. unknowability[50]

Ira Gordon relates the metaphoric concept of models to children and also delineates a dichotomous view.[51] The "linear causation model" child is depicted as a mechanistic, fixed, closed system characterized by an orderly unfolding, genetic determination and inaction until stimuli are presented; this view is heavily based in behaviorism and draws on Gesell's maturational theory. In contrast to this Gordon presents a "transactional model" child in which development has a genetic-experiential base and the child is viewed as an open-energy, self-organizing system; this view relies essentially on Piaget's theory. The end point of Gordon's transactional model man is uniqueness — an emphasis on unique growth continuously evolving from differing patterns of ecological experiencing as the child interacts with his environment.

Clearly, values based upon philosophical beliefs direct psychological research and application. Maslow recognized this relationship as his work progressed. "One aspect of Maslow's later thought deserves attention," wrote a coworker. "The older he got, the more 'philosophical' he became. It was impossible, he found, to isolate the pursuit of psychological truth from philosophical questions."[52]

SYNTHESIS OF THEORIES FOR EARLY CHILDHOOD EDUCATION

While any of the foregoing integrations of theories could have meaning in programs for young children, two distinct statements of position appearing early in the 1970s related synthesis directly to early childhood education. These new statements appeared almost simultaneously to counteract old developmental views and supplant them with revised psychological conceptions: "The Education of Young Children: A Developmental-Interaction Approach" by Edna Shapiro and Barbara Biber of Bank Street College of Education was published in *Teachers College Record* in September 1972; "Development as the Aim of Education" by Lawrence Kohlberg and Rochelle Mayer of Harvard University followed in the *Harvard Educational Review* in November 1972. Both articles not only incorporated current insights from psychological theory, they attempt to integrate compatible aspects of these theories.

A broadened perspective that was lacking in the earlier developmental approach enters each of these statements of position: a recognition that psychological theory alone cannot provide a full basis for curriculum building. Philosophical views and value definitions are requisite and need to be made explicit. It is not surprising that early childhood educators relied heavily upon psychological theory to build an appropriate curriculum for the young child; both were rapidly growing fields from the 1890s onward. The fundamental developmental changes taking place in the child between birth and the end of the primary years compelled leaders in early childhood education to turn to child study for understanding. The initial studies of young children undertaken at Clark University before the turn of the century immediately attracted those dealing with early childhood, as we have seen. The alliance between the two fields has not slackened since that time. The arresting aspect about these new statements of points of view, however, is the recognition, at least to a degree, of the infringement of philosophical premises undergirding both psychology and education.

Let us turn now to these statements of the 1970s to analyze their psychological and philosophical foundations. Both rest upon an integration of available theory and both make clear a value position.

Education as "Development"

When psychological theory is used to engage in curriculum construction it becomes an ideology, according to Lawrence Kohlberg and Rochelle Mayer; in their view "educational practice cannot be derived from psychological theory or science alone."[53] In a wide-ranging analysis of psychological theories, particularly as they relate to the education of the young, they point out the value-laden objectives of each rationale and the fallacy of believing any theory to be value-free: values are there whether explicit or implicit.

Organizing theoretical positions somewhat differently than we have viewed them in the preceding chapters, Kohlberg and Mayer describe and analyze three main streams of educational ideology that have influenced education in Western cultures: the romantic or child-centered approach, the cultural transmission or society-centered position, and a third still accurately called "progressive" in their view. Each is linked to a particular psychological base and to specific value commitments that, they believe, make it a distinct and separate strand within psychology and education today.

A romantic stream, initiated by Rousseau and made current by the work of Freud and Gesell, Kohlberg and Mayer designate as resting upon the biological metaphors of "health" and "growth." "To label this ideology 'romantic,'" write the authors, "is not to accuse it of being unscientific; rather it is to recognize that the nineteenth century discovery of the natural development of the child was part of a larger romantic philosophy, an ethic and epistemology involving a discovery of the natural and inner self."[54] Thus the philosophical base is presented here as an existential epistemology, defining reality as immediate, inner experience and self-awareness or self-insight as a form of truth with emotional as well as intellectual components. The educational objectives of romantics Kohlberg and Mayer define as a "bag of virtues" — a set of traits characterizing an ideal healthy or fully functioning person.

In contrast, the cultural-transmission ideology, grounded in the work of Thorndike and Skinner, is society-centered and tends toward the metaphor of the machine. Based upon associationist learning theory, this position sets fixed knowledge and skills as educational goals. Furthermore, "cultural transmission ideologies of education tend to involve epistemologies which stress knowledge as that which is repetitive and 'objective,' that which can be pointed to in sense-experience and measurement and which can be culturally shared and tested."[55] The strategy for defining goals becomes one of "industrial psychology" or the prediction of success; long-term objectives are selected that will eventuate in power and status in the social system.

The point is that each of these schools of thought has a distinctive psychological theory of development that tends to relate it to a definable philosophical position. The dichotomous conceptions of man and learning undergirding the two major streams seem to be accepted by Kohlberg and Mayer as irreconcilable; neither view do they believe to be adequate for education today. What is now progressive they consider to be a cognitive-developmental or interactionist theory of development, thus using the term *development* quite differently than it was formerly applied to curriculum.

The work of Dewey and Piaget forms the support for the cognitive-developmental view in which the metaphor is dialectical, not material. "In the dialectical metaphor," write Kohlberg and Mayer, "a core of universal ideas are redefined and reorganized as their implications are played out in experience and as they are confronted by their opposites in argument and discourse. These organizations define qualitative levels of thought, levels of increased epistemic adequacy. The child is not a plant or a machine; he is a philosopher or a scientist-poet."[56] The educational goal, then, is development — the eventual attainment of higher levels of mental functioning. Implied in the term *development* is a value position "that a more developed psychological state is more valuable or adequate than a less developed state."[57] All behavioral change does not contribute to this advanced state but only change toward greater differentiation and integration of thought and more adequate adaptation to the environment.

In uniting the theories of Dewey and Piaget in their point of view, Kohlberg and Mayer have selected strikingly compatible theories as we have seen in discussing them separately. Both view the key to the educative process as interaction between the learner and the environment. Meaning is derived as the learner integrates new understandings into those already established. Dewey spoke of this integration as the reconstruction of experience; Piaget redefined the process as assimilation and accommodation mediated through equilibration. The child is considered active at all levels, a purposer and a constructor of his own knowledge. Such interaction eventuates in more effective levels of dealing with the environment and solving problems with increased judgment and at higher levels of reasoning. Dewey's theory, as we have seen, was linked to the principles of democracy that provide the basis of ethical relationships. The outcome of development in Piaget's theory is the attainment of formal operations at which time the individual is capable of purely abstract, propositional thinking.

The "progressivism" outlined by Kohlberg and Mayer they consider to be a relationship between the developmental (or natural growth) and the "ethical ought." Certainly not considered a value-free approach, the cognitive-developmental position is considered to rest upon the value universals of ethical liberalism. Both Dewey and Piaget combined epistemological and logical criteria with psychological inquiry from the start of their work. Their functional or pragmatic epistemology equates knowledge with "an equilibrated or resolved relationship between an inquiring human actor and a problematic situation."[58] Thus only in interaction with the environment does the individual gain meaning and "truth," for "truth" is determined through interaction. The assumption here is that all individuals are intent upon organizing their interactions with the world into universal patterns of meaning. Education is conceived as facilitating movement from one level of adequacy to the next step, from an idiosyncratic to a more universal pattern of understanding including greater differentiation, integration, and adaptation.

In their intricately reasoned analysis in which they sort out basic premises, Kohlberg and Mayer clearly confront the issue of the relationship between philosophical and psychological positions. They believe the cognitive-developmental approach integrates the dichotomies of inner experience versus outer sense-reality, the empirical search for continuities between inner states and outer behavior focuses more heavily upon the cognitive than the affective. To broaden the conception of cognitive-logical development as an educational aim, these two authors turn to the inclusion of moral development or the consideration of "invariant stages of moral reasoning" as worked out by Kohlberg and other associates. However, it is clearly stated: "Particularly in the earlier childhood years, it is difficult to distinguish moral development from ego-development."[59] Ego-development, related clearly to cognitive development in a Piagetian sense, is here considered a parallel developmental aspect of growth. Developmental aims of education will, then, include ego development as well as the cognitive.

Labeling their plan for education a developmental-philosophical strategy, Kohlberg and Mayer suggest that any philosophically desirable end must be coordinated with "the facts of development." Their recommendations clearly stand on the proposition that "philosophical principles cannot be stated as ends of education until they can be stated psychologically. This means translating them into statements about a more adequate stage of development."[60] Stages to be considered more adequate require the method of philosophy or ethics for their determination.

The notion of education as development can be applied to all developmental levels, of course, but references to early childhood education appear throughout the Kohlberg and Mayer proposals. The Bereiter-Englemann early childhood program, a very behavioristic conception, is analyzed to describe the cultural transmission ideology; the Kamii curriculum for four- and five-year-olds based upon Piagetian constructs is discussed in terms of a cognitive-developmental model. Explicitly, Kohlberg himself linked the cognitive-developmental view to early childhood education in an article in which he proposed that Piaget's contributions clarified "the child-centered approach to education expressed in its broadest form by John Dewey."[61] At that point in time Kohlberg was willing to accept a broad range of programs "from Moore to Montessori" as compatible with cognitive-developmental theory so long as they "define their cognitive goals developmentally and center on relatively active and self-selective forms of cognitive stimulation for the child."[62] Thus no attempt was made to specify elements of an appropriate program for the early childhood educator.

Education as a Developmental-Interaction Approach

A different blending of theories attends the approach to education labeled "developmental-interaction" by Edna Shapiro and Barbara Biber, both of whom have been very involved in programs for young children on many levels. Noting the Kohlberg and Mayer designation of cognition and affect as parallel developments, Shapiro and Biber present an approach in which cognitive and affective elements are considered interactive. While developmental aspects of growth are respected, interaction is viewed in more than one way. The authors define developmental and interactive emphases in this manner:

> Developmental refers to the emphasis on identifiable patterns of growth and modes of perceiving and responding which are characterized by increasing differentiation and progressive integration as a function of chronological age. Interaction refers, first, to the emphasis on the child's interaction with the environment — adults, other children, and the material world, and second, to the interaction between cognitive and affective spheres of development. The developmental-interaction formulation stresses the nature of the environment as much as it does the patterns of the responding child.[63]

Three main theoretical positions support this approach according to the authors: the work of Freudian and neo-Freudian psychoanalysts, the gestalt and developmental psychologists concerned primarily with cognitive development, and educational theorists allied to functional learning. Many theorists are viewed as contributing insights. Erikson and Anna Freud are mentioned as those dealing with autonomous ego processes, but so are Hartman, Sullivan, and Rapaport, who have focused less on early childhood. Werner and Wertheimer are cognitive psychologists listed along with Piaget. John Dewey heads the list of advocates promoting functional learning, along with such practitioners as Harriet Johnson and Lucy Sprague Mitchell. While many theoretical and practical questions remain in attempting to integrate theories, Shapiro and Biber point to the use of stage theory by Freud, Erikson, Werner, and Piaget as a unifying factor. They write: "All hold that development is characterized by qualitative shifts in modes of experiencing and reacting, that such patterns, or stages, occur in invariant sequence, the earlier being necessary precursors for the later."[64]

The goals or aims of education derive not from the integration of psychological theory, but from the humanistic values "generally acceptable across the broad sweeps of Western culture."[65] The aims or goals are a definition of the human qualities valued by the educational system, thus no set of goals can be considered universally applicable. Elsewhere, Biber has allied her discussions of early childhood programs to democratic values, particularly the valuing of the intrinsic worth of the individual.[66] As a basic code of human functioning, Biber views the worth of the individual as a cornerstone, only when the fulfillment of each individual is combined with a widespread concern for the individuality of all other persons. Achievements at any stage are relative to developing abilities and conceptions. Such development must not be viewed as a simple progression of less to more, but as characterized by qualitative changes in the individual's means of interaction with the environment. Competence and autonomy are two goals of the developmental-interaction point of view to be fostered by the school. The specifics of a sense of autonomy — the concept of the self as unique; the ability to initiate, to make choices, to risk failure, to contradict — are to be cultivated from their earliest to later stages.

Furthermore, Shapiro and Biber reinforce a conception of education to promote the integration of functioning.

> It is a basic tenet of the developmental-interaction approach that the growth of cognitive functions — acquiring and ordering information, judging, reasoning, problem solving, using systems of symbols — cannot be separated from the growth of personal and interpersonal processes — the development of self-esteem and a sense of identity, internalization of impulse control, capacity for autonomous response, relatedness to other people. The interdependence of these developmental processes is the *sine qua non* of the developmental-interaction approach.[67]

In an earlier article Biber had directly related this integrated formulation to goals of the Bank Street curriculum designed to work with "disadvantaged" children. Two primary goals were designated:

(1)   to advance the child's ability to use language functionally and to be able to systematize experience through mastery of conceptual-cognitive processes; and

(2)   simultaneously to help him to develop a solid sense of self and an internalized code of behavior, to build ego-strength in terms of becoming an effective, nonpredatory person, capable of acting autonomously — making choices, taking initiative, setting his own course for problem-solving.[68]

The fullness that such an integrative view can give to the educational process together with the complexity of the teacher's role are evident in the dual mandate Biber describes as stemming from the goals: "To choose methods for fulfilling the first goal that support and never violate the second goal; and to choose methods for fulfilling the second goal that make the first goal more potentially realizable."[69] The school is responsible for translating concepts of integrated functioning into concrete classroom processes and practices.

While Kohlberg, in his statement, revealed an acceptance of diverse types of early education programs as compatible with the cognitive-developmental view, Shapiro and Biber take no such stance. Such a broad spectrum of educational environments is not considered equivalently appropriate for the developmental-interaction approach to early education. A precise curriculum content is not presented; rather, governing principles, making explicit assumptions of the point of view, have been outlined as well as means for facilitating learning. In summing up basic principles the authors write:

> The educational programs associated with the developmental-interaction approach are focused on process, on providing the experiences that make it possible for children to try out, shift backward as well as forward, to create where necessary the opportunities for the kind of interaction that is essential for the assimilation of experience, the achievement of new integrations, and the resolution of conflict — in both the cognitive and emotional realms.[70]

The enactment of this point of view Shapiro and Biber find most clearly in the Bank Street College of Education Children's School. While experiences would vary greatly from classroom to classroom, basic principles would hold. To make more explicit the operation of fundamental principles Shapiro and Biber delineated the role of the teacher, concepts of work and play, the school, and the environment. While the details of the teacher's role are expected to vary, the overriding principle states "that the teacher should respond and relate to the children as individuals."[71] Work and play are interwoven in such a curriculum, for a respect for the importance of workmanlike attitudes is matched with a conviction that a child's play is "purposeful and can be a medium for learning about the physical and social environment through symbolic recreation."[72] Continuity of learning demands an integration between the child's in-school and out-of-school experiences, which in turn rests upon valued interchange between home and school.

The teacher's decision-making function is magnified in this point of view. Goals are one source of guidance in decision-making and the cognitive goals are viewed from a developmental-interaction point of view and described in a separate study in which goals are amplified and illustrated.[73] Broad goals are translated into classroom processes and practices.

Extending the Point of View

The complexity of the conception of education as both developmental and interactive led a group of psychologists and educators to meet for the purpose of pursuing basic propositions, for such an encompassing conceptualization requires continual elucidation.[74] At this meeting, Frances Minor elevated the meaning children give to phenomena they have experienced as the heart of the developmental-interaction point of view, for it is in derived meaning that cognitive and affective aspects are merged. At this point it becomes not an interaction between the two, but an integration. The teacher necessarily deals with the real life integration taking place in each individual learner. Piaget's theory of cognition provides for an understanding of new levels of integration in human functioning.

The question of values threaded throughout the entire discussion, for as soon as the development of an individual or his interactions with the environment are related to curriculum decision making, an overlay of values is operating. Louise Berman elaborated the point that a classroom entails a set of images of persons that constitute underlying values. For example, the position is not ordinarily taken that any kind of individuality can emerge, as only some parameters of individuality are allowed in a specific classroom. A selection of values requires a next step, the determination of the nature of the educational settings leading to the inculcation of these values. Bernard Spodek linked the values of the developmental-interaction position to the liberal tradition gradually evolving in the first half of the century and including an ideal of freedom or of individual fulfillment. This means the learner is necessarily involved in the decisions regarding the means and ends of education; he has control over some variables in the educative process.

Further elaboration of the values inherent in the developmental-interaction approach as enacted at the Bank Street Children's School is incorporated into Barbara Biber's chapter in the publication that followed the conference. She views the value base as remaining relatively constant even as changing understandings of the developmental process have required new psychological perspectives. Biber finds three psychological domains embraced in a system of values projected developmentally: "the nature of individuality, the quality of relations between persons, and the relation between the individual and society."[75] Extending this idea further Biber writes:

> The educational experience is designed to provide gradually a reciprocal relation between individual fulfillment and socialized experience so that the moral implications of the school community are built not on principles of sacrifice, compromise, and denial, but rather on the psychological interchange of sources of gratification expressed through balancing the experience of satisfying the self with yielding it — rather exchanging it — for the pleasures of social mergence. Only a certain kind of curriculum, where there is opportunity for more collective than competitive enterprise, supports that process.[76]

Clearly, a number of curriculum practices are ruled out by this value position: education toward conformism within the context of an authoritarian system, the verbalization of moral maxims, methods that attempt to treat value education as a separate curriculum area, and reliance upon just conceptual insights to influence behavioral decisions. Rather, the basic assumption rests upon a gradual internalization of values as they are embedded in the school's goals and experienced through modes of learning and interchange. This calls for continual rethinking of the learning experience and renewed adventure into curriculum design.

Comparison of Points of View

When Jersild sought a formulation of the relationships between child psychology and curriculum construction he presented a vision of child development data contributing directly to programs for young children. His vision embodied the developmental approach of his day as well as an attitude of respect for children at all stages of growth. No diminution of that attitude of respect is in order; indeed, much current research serves as a bulwark to expand respect to the utter uniqueness of individuals. This is further reinforced by the value dimensions recognized as inherent in both emerging approaches to education. Whether derived from democratic values or ethical universals, the uniqueness of the individual is central.

A number of commonalities are embedded in the two designated positions. Both have historical underpinnings and selected theoretical statements, but neither Shapiro and Biber nor Kohlberg and Mayer include behaviorism in their position. The active organism framework of learning is too strong to permit an acceptance of stimulus-response theory. Both hold to psychologically derived stages of growth, yet ally these to the understanding of learning requiring environmental interaction. Thus, in their integration of available theory, both positions utilize maturational and interactive elements of growth. This brings a recognition of the values of the play mode of learning so readily operating in the young child. One of the greatest departures from the earlier developmental position is the incorporation by these theorists of a value dimension as an essential in curriculum building. Philosophical premises accompany the psychological in program construction.

A much more radical stance has been taken by Kieran Egan concerning the place of psychology in education. He makes a frontal attack upon the use of psychological theory in developing a theory for curriculum building. He argues that "no psychological theory has, or can have, legitimate implications for educational practice."[77] Egan's disagreement rests not so much on a probing of the hidden values inherent in psychological theory as on the fact that such theory does not offer what education needs. Indeed, Egan believes that the dominance psychological theory holds over educational practice has produced vacuousness and ineffectiveness. Education, according to Egan, should be supported by *educational* theories. In stating this belief he puts educational planners in a difficult impasse for he clearly recognizes that education "is characterized by its theoretical poverty."[78] Egan went back to Plato to find a curriculum clearly based upon an educational theory. Some curriculum theorists might deny the theoretical poverty in education, but no curriculum theorist has had much impact on early childhood education.

In one dimension, however, Egan agrees with the position of Shapiro and Biber and that of Kohlberg and Mayer. While Egan would not accept the particular synthesis of psychological premises put forward by either pair, he does recognize the primacy of values in curriculum building. "Designing a curriculum," he writes, "is a value-saturated and culture-bound task."[79] The curriculum designer must prescribe how people can best be enabled to reach a specific, carefully considered end-state of educated maturity.

CONCLUSIONS

What conclusions loom large from this analysis of extant theoretical positions, whether directed at early childhood education or presented at large? What clues can we gain that will enable us to assess programs for young children preparing them for life near the end of the twentieth century and beyond? Surely the balance swings away from norms, fixity, and mechanistic considerations to conceptions of individuality and uniqueness. Active learning in an ecological provision for richness and complexity are requisites. The child must be viewed as active at all levels — as a purposer, an investigator, a constructor of his own knowledge. Individuality and uniqueness may well be the established goal of an educational program. The concern for active learning, however, is allied to a learning theory evolving over decades, one supported by Rousseau, Dewey, and Piaget. It is a learning theory conceived to promote individuality and uniqueness.

Education cannot wait for an *educational* theory to be developed, however essential work in that direction must be. Education goes on inexorably — day by day, minute by minute. However, an examination of values can proceed immediately as a necessary first step for theory building.

Primarily each educational program calls for a reexamination of inherent value dimensions, for we have seen how values undergirding psychological theory have largely gone unrecognized. Can we afford to allow outmoded theories to continue to dominate educational practice? What end points of the educational program can encompass the respect for children, worth of each individual, and expanding uniqueness so essential in the points of view just discussed and, indeed, for society today? In the next chapter we will consider new thoughts concerning values in the schools and turn to emerging historical perspectives that will take us into new domains of thought.

12 The Curriculum for Early Childhood

"All history is written from a perspective that is invariably shaped out by one's existential present," writes Clarence J. Karier.[1] In the opinion of one historian, history by its very nature includes interpretation[2] and a new generation of historians arising in the 1960s have undertaken a revision of educational history that reflects radical social and political views. Their interpretations, rooted in present social concerns, delineate the growth of public schools in America in starkly negative terms.

REVISIONIST HISTORY

Three major trends of thought have been identified as significant in the writing of educational history in the United States over the years. The three interpretive schools have been labeled pietist, cultural, and radical.[3] The work of Ellwood Cubberly illustrates the first emphasis on the development of the common school with a positive attitude toward its role in American society. Cubberly and Paul Monroe, who restricted their account to the formal institutions of schooling, are considered to have "lost the capacity to see education in the full context."[4] The cultural revisionists, illustrated by Lawrence Cremin, broadened the scope of their study to include institutions other than schools — the family, community, and church — and to place their theory in the context of earlier periods and of political developments. Butts considers a recurrent theme of the cultural revisionists to be "a stress upon education as paideia, the deliberate pursuit of an ideal."[5] This group basically believed in America and the potential of the school to contribute to the perfectibility of society. Taking the opposite position, the radical revisionists engage in trenchant criticism of schools as racist, bureaucratic, and biased in favor of certain classes who used power to impose their values on others. Optimism about schools and society is replaced by a quest for the source of present educational and social dilemmas in past educational failures.

Katz has written: "Aside from the people who live off the education system, and I do not mean the teachers, it has served no one very well."[6] Karier contends that American public education was designed "to help fit people into a social system" so structured as to "foster a dehumanizing quest for status, power and wealth."[7] Such strong statements have drawn equally vigorous rebuttal and provided lively and controversial discussions among educational historians over the past two decades. Cohen, who finds the radical revisionists overly hostile toward American schools, writes: "There is a finality and rationality in their work that terribly oversimplifies the ambiguity, the incompleteness of the complexity of historical events."[8] Maxine Greene views these writers of radical history as "largely preoccupied with images of monoliths and patternings, nevertheless, the revisionists see all-pervasive victimization; they see us all submerged in a system we never chose."[9] Some writers now call for a balanced view, a new synthesis "that will account for the school as the focal point of idealism as well as self-interest," that will take into consideration exaggerated expectations of schools and will "adjure the premise that the American school has been an unequivocal failure, for such a premise — like the earlier presumption of success — precludes the explanation of change over time."[10] While some writers decry the pessimism and presentism of radical revisionists, they recognize that the efforts to strip away false assumptions have led us to more heterodox thoughts about education. Screens that clouded our perceptions are being reduced.

SCHOOLS AND BUREAUCRACY

Since this book concentrates on early childhood education one may well ask why it is important to include this contemporary thought about the past. There are two propelling reasons for a more in-depth analysis: first, an examination of the growing bureaucratization of public schools will enable us to assess the ability of schools to change in the light of new insights; second, the purposes of education rest upon values so essential in curriculum design. How free are teachers to incorporate new understandings of how children learn? Can they structure a classroom to allow children to construct their own knowledge? What values prevail today? Some responses to these questions should emerge through the following analysis.

Michael Katz, the leading discloser of the growth of a basic and enduring bureaucratic structure, has written: "Between the early and late nineteenth century North American school promoters established bureaucratic systems of public education and reorganized teaching into an occupation complete with a hierarchy, source of training, entrance requirements and active national organization."[11] Katz proposes that bureaucracy "developed quickly and thoroughly within large cities and has remained entrenched there ever since."[12] These contentions are illustrated in detail by Katz in his study of the organizational model as it developed in Boston between 1800 and 1885, in which the school system became a full-scale bureaucracy. In addition, David Tyack has found a parallel movement centralizing rural schools as an outcome of state departments of education that grew in size and influence and led in "the enforcement of uniform educational standards."[13] According to Tyack, it was a corporate model of governance the proponents of centralization urged school systems to adopt. A hierarchical system resulted in which superintendents added numbers of specialists and administrators so that the work of the tiers of officials became segmented into functional divisions. Carl Kaestle finds the ever-expanding system of public education "basically but not totally supportive of the majoritarian ethic and the evolving economic system."[14] Katz frankly designates the factory to be the metaphor used "to centralize and standardize education in a way reminiscent of the process of production."[15] Efficient, effective basic education was to be the product as literacy became a minimum requirement for life in the larger economy.

One outgrowth of the demand for efficiency was the institutionalizing of the graded system in schools. An expanding population with an increasing number of children of school age contributed to "the conviction that the most efficient way to educate them was in large graded schools."[16] With one-room schools replaced by graded classrooms, hopes were raised for a more carefully planned curriculum. In actuality grading contributed to a more rigid organization of subject matter, resulting in the false assumption that there existed a specific first- or second-grade curriculum suitable for all children. Instead of allowing teachers to individualize instruction more for a narrower age range, grading worked in just the opposite manner. In a one-room school there was an opportunity for children to progress at their own rate; in a graded classroom the rate of learning became dictated by a curriculum guide.[17] Grade isolation increased the problems of children who were not promoted.

Fundamentally, Katz's central point is that school bureaucracies assert values. The characteristics he finds prominent in American education, a century ago as well as today, he lists as universal, tax-supported, free, compulsory, bureaucratic, racist, and class-biased.[18] It is racist because society in North America has been racist. It is class-biased because the bureaucracy that developed reflected a crystallization of bourgeois social attitudes serving powerful interests. For Katz, the main purpose of schools as thus characterized is to make "children orderly, industrious, law-abiding and respectful of authority."[19] In this manner schools served the economic system. Schools, thus, do not equalize opportunity; they are not

democratic engines for identifying talent and matching it with opportunity. The children of the affluent are given the best marks and gain the best
jobs. Karier agrees with this assessment and asserts: "In a mass-produc-
tion-oriented society the schools were used to standardize the future citizen as interchangeable parts for an intricate production and consumption
system. Testing, guidance and curriculum reform movements all helped
to objectify and rationalize the child for his place within the system."[20]
If inequities of education were questioned, real inequities "were usually
met with a call for more schooling which would increase the achievement
level for more and more children."[21] This only substantiates Katz's contention that the staunchly embedded bureaucratic structure, reflecting
patterns ensconced in American society, has made schools enormously
resistant to change.

   Thus revisionist historians strip away the long-held belief that schools
were a major force in promoting democracy. An extensive study of schools
in four communities in the United States at the turn of the century led
Patricia Graham to the same conclusion: the belief that schools served
as a democratizing agent was largely a myth.[22] The assumption that one
school would serve children of diverse social, economic, and ethnic backgrounds was never realized in practice. In actuality most schools were
based on residential patterns and served children of mostly homogeneous
communities. In Marquette, Michigan poor children attended school in
South Marquette while children of the rich went to school in another area
of town. New York City, with its ethnic ghettos, set up education for
Italian children in Little Italy while children from Jewish families had
their own schools on the lower east side. In Johnson City, Indiana whites
went to school with whites, and blacks with blacks, until high school.
Schools in Butler County, Alabama were rigidly separated by race. Furthermore, the bureaucratic structure of schools already determined by
the turn of the century set a pattern of authority that left little room for
democratic patterns to emerge within classrooms. Schools may have aided
in the formation of attitudes essential to an industrial society; they did
not instill democratic values in a Deweyan or any other sense. The key
to learning to act democratically for Dewey was in action, a mode of be-
having that balanced individual judgment and the consideration of the
well-being of the group. Schooling under the aegis of bureaucracy tended toward the inculcation of conformist behavior.

RELEVANCE TO EARLY CHILDHOOD

   In the light of these claims let us investigate the impact of bureaucratization upon early childhood education. One great impetus to concern for
the lives of young children came through the kindergarten movement.

Kindergartens were initiated and expanded in the United States through private philanthropy; thus they developed for a number of decades outside the public school system. This allowed them to be enormously responsive to new forces in psychology and education. When first introduced in this country, the kindergarten program expressed a pure form of Froebelian ideas. We have seen the manner in which the fallacies of this program were gradually recognized by leaders in the field and how it was replaced through trial and error by new conceptions gained from Hall, Dewey, and eventually Thorndike. The curriculum, as reconstructed in an entirely new form in the decades between 1890 and 1930, retained Froebel's recognition of the value of play and of the child's self-activity, but redirected these to conform to new psychological and philosophical revelations. Experimental at first, it became the basic kindergarten curriculum, a monumental change that leaders of the movement could effect because they were free from administrative fiat. This curriculum transformation is a dramatic example of what a deeply committed group of educators could evolve through the application of the preferred ideas of their period. With a child development base, it was not too difficult to incorporate some new ideas stemming from the work of Gesell and, later, of neo-Freudians.

Unaware of the freedom to devise new curricula accorded them by their independent status, supporters of the kindergarten desired a connection with public schools. The swelling population in urban centers which increased school attendance meant many more children who could profit from the kindergarten experience. In 1929 the incorporation of kindergarten in public schools was described in this way: "Philanthropy turned to the public schools asking them to include the kindergarten as a part of their organization. The opening wedge was made by giving permission to use vacant rooms in public schools. The salaries of teachers and other running expenses were still defrayed by philanthropic agencies that were convinced of the educational as well as the philanthropic value of the kindergarten. The next step was to persuade boards of education to accept full responsibility. Thus in time the kindergarten became a part of many school systems."[23]

Philanthropic support for kindergartens, so widespread in the early years of the movement, was based upon a conviction about its moral benefits both for the individual and for society. Early exponents of the kindergarten had done their work convincingly as they attributed to it the power to start the child toward effective social living. During the years when philosophical idealism prevailed, philanthropic support accounted for a growth of kindergartens from less than a dozen in 1870 to not less than four hundred in 1880 scattered over thirty states; by 1890 organizations had been established in many cities to work for the expansion of kindergarten education.[24]

The Purpose of Early Childhood Education

This increase of kindergarten centers coincided with a major reform movement in the United States. Settlement houses were established in major cities in the 1880s and 1890s to alleviate the distress of people caught in the squalor of urban slums, an outgrowth of industrialization and vast population growth as immigrants poured into the country. The kindergarten was incorporated into many settlements as a way to directly support young children. But, above all, in starting children on the correct path in life, the kindergarten was believed to provide hope for an improved future generation. Kindergartens swept across the country as part of the vision of fostering the perfectibility of man and society. The purpose, then, of kindergarten was character building. Moral goals prevailed; industry, neatness, reverence, self-respect, and cooperation were expected to result from a properly directed kindergarten education. The ideals of good behavior were to be continually presented to the child in story, song, games, and by direct example.

Later, a new conception of moral growth replaced the one so appealing to early philanthropic supporters; in the reconstructed kindergarten it was the Deweyan conception of growth grounded in democratic participation. As already pointed out, this conception included a dual process of value formation gained through participation in problem solving that entailed working together in democratic social relationships and that increased the ability to understand and reconstruct daily experiences in the environment. In this active form of education interest, energy, initiative, cooperation, and problem solving abilities were the positive virtues to be attained. The process was greatly modified: the goal of character building was retained.

As Katz clearly summarizes, "the primary purpose of early education was the formation of attitudes rather than the development of skills."[25] What happened to this major purpose as kindergartens were amalgamated into public schools? Even in 1929 it was recognized that kindergarten teachers were confronted with the problem of maintaining their own aims and purposes while at the same time adjusting to existing conditions in the school. For a time there existed a gap between the work of the kindergarten and that of the remainder of the school. In an effort to bridge the gap many teachers "laid undue emphasis on the formal preparation of the children for first grade."[26] As new generations of teachers directed kindergarten activities, goals of the past became less clear and they were drawn more and more into the structure of the total school system, until they, too, became caught up in the one dominant goal of literacy. Reading readiness exercises and other skill development activities became a major part of the curriculum. In the 1980s we learn about a transitional "pre-first grade year" designed to give children a head start in skill learning. School days have been lengthened for kindergartens in New York City to pursue these more modest aims; over 50,000 children attend a full-day session of kindergarten in 1983–84, up from 18,000 the year before.

"Ours is the first society that has narrowed the scope of education in this way," asserts John Sommerville.[27] In his opinion this stems from a widespread doubt about values now, toward the end of the twentieth century. "Children," he contends, "are going to school for an ever-longer period, but we seem less and less sure about what they should be getting from it."[28] He finds the belief that schools should build character to be generally denied or even ridiculed. A crisis of confidence and moral direction finds society in the 1980s lacking the affirmation of ultimate values that could guide education in arranging values in a scale useful for curriculum building. "And so the schools concentrate on intellectual skills, ignoring the fact that they cannot help but teach values so long as there are adult models in the classroom," concludes Sommerville.[29] The constriction of educational goals to such a limited conception ignores the fact that literacy and the building of skills are only preconditions to effective education.

What has happened to the ability of the kindergarten curriculum to respond to ever-changing concepts of how children learn, of redefined social goals, and of recurrent concern for individuality of growth? This process of change so apparent in earlier years now seems denied by its joining the bureaucracy of the school systems and becoming, as did other levels, impermeable to reformist thrusts. How often do teachers of young children decry their inability to test out some Piagetian constructs because bureaucratic demands obliterate any possible opportunity for change!

Unification of Kindergarten and Primary Grades

Early specialists of kindergarten education worked not just for more kindergartens, but also for the extension into the primary grades of the principles and the philosophy of the education they espoused so heartily. Those staunch reformers believed their "new" educational design to ensure a more child-centered curriculum employing different methods and procedures for early learning. They also believed that the nature of children of five, six, and seven years of age was similar; in social, emotional, and intellectual characteristics they were much alike. So adult leaders strove toward the unification of kindergarten-primary education. As we have seen, they did produce curricula in written form that embraced both levels. Teacher training at colleges and universities by the 1930s very generally combined kindergarten and primary instruction.[30] Historians have also suggested that the kindergarten had some leavening influence, crediting it with affording greater freedom of movement, more cooperative social attitudes, a less rigid discipline, and increased deference to individual needs.[31]

The main force in narrowing the gap between kindergarten and the primary grades probably came from the progressive education movement. Kindergarten specialists, as we have seen, relied heavily on Deweyan progressive theory to reconstruct the curriculum. Progressive thought influenced the program of the primary grades in many private and some public classrooms. This author taught a first and then a second grade in a public system in the heartland of Wisconsin, where the superintendent sought teachers who could put progressive theory into practice. It was less accepted in upper elementary grades for it seemed to become more difficult to put into operation as children grew older. The age-grade standards and testing procedures of public schools put increasing limits on teachers and children, for progressive education could really not work within this structure. Progressivism did not alter that bureaucratic structure. The same situation exists in regard to the current reform movement misnamed "open education." The goals and procedures are at odds with the public system of education.

Were there never any classrooms that worked as a democratizing agent as their developers truly believed? In the sense that Graham analyzed schools, the urge to include in a given situation children from many social and ethnic backgrounds waited until the 1970s and 1980s and is still under fire. But the classroom as a miniature society in which children had some part in both the means and the ends of their educational enterprises was a vision many early childhood educators worked very hard to achieve. They stressed the relationship between the child's out of school experiences and in-school activities as well as the active participation of the learner. They always expected the teacher to be the guide in learning experiences, and this, Katz suggests, is the element that led to control. He writes:

> That role became largely the creation of an environment, a carefully planned group context that would provide children with a sequence of experiences, which, despite their apparent spontaneity, were in fact meticulously elicited. Those experiences would lead the children to develop habitual ways of responding, to internalize the norms of democratic living. . . . Education, by implication, served to instill conformist behavior, a set of inner controls that would make external social controls unnecessary.[32]

Revisionist historians have come to view progressive education as a part of a driving social-reformist commitment. Particularly Karier and Paul Violas contend that "the emphasis on community in Jane Addams and the definitions of democracy and experience in Dewey provide particularly subtle and sophisticated instances of the widespread attempt in their time to foster modes of social control appropriate to the complex urban environment."[33] While the kindergarten leaders were convinced they were contributing to social betterment, it is doubtful that they viewed their curriculum reconstruction within this broad a context of social reform. They endeavored to devise a program with greater freedom and individualization than Froebel provided; this they achieved and Deweyan thought assisted them.

All the efforts to bring about the unification of kindergarten-primary education in their own terms seem lost. Curricula are now seldom written to span the levels, nor does teacher training encompass both as formerly developed. Strong support, however, for the conviction that children age five to seven are psychologically one is given by Piagetian theory, which includes those ages in the preoperational period, and also upholds the active learning the new curriculum sustained. If, however, discontinuities between the kindergarten and primary grades are no longer apparent, it is because the kindergarten curriculum has been allied to the standards and norms of the public school system in which it now resides. The direction of unification is quite the reverse of that which early optimism foresaw.

Child care for those under kindergarten age has never been part of organized institutions. Even sporadic talk about the inclusion of nursery schools in public school systems raises concern that this would modify day-to-day work with children. The curriculum of nursery schools, which increased rapidly in number in the 1920s and 1930s, was similar in form to the reconstructed curriculum for five-year-olds, although the nursery school was influenced more by neo-Freudian thought. Because of the freedom from imposition of ideas from an administrative hierarchy, nursery schools have had more opportunity to maintain experiences appropriate to the child's interests and needs as defined by the adults in charge. They have not, however, existed untouched by the American fetish for early literacy; here it takes the form of parents' anxiety and zeal for their children to have a head start in reading. Day care, a more recent addition in early childhood education, has probably been modified most by time arrangements and parent needs. A whole new set of problems and demands is added in the day care setting with the increased amount of time children spend under this care.

In conclusion it must be conceded that the history of kindergarten education substantiates the analysis of revisionist historians that uncovers the strength and influence of bureaucratization. True, in searching for trends and patterns, revisionists have glossed over differences among schools. There are schools that have never narrowed their focus to cognitive skills, that have maintained a curriculum exemplifying the best known about the child's development, but most of these exist outside the public school establishment. Revisionists may also be prone to an oversimplification of social control, which leads in Greene's view "to a setting aside of the problem of socialization."[34] There will always be tension between the individual and civilization, according to Greene, for on the next page she defines education as taking "place at the intersection where the demands for social order and the demands for autonomy conflict." This is exactly one of the problems with which the progressives were dealing. But the revisionists have opened our eyes to some inherent shortcomings and to the inflexibility that characterizes many schools today.

EARLY CHILDHOOD AND SOCIAL REFORM

Those revisionist historians, who are purported to see the function of the history of education as serving the cause of social reform, may well reflect on the continual viewing of the education of the young as a means for the betterment of society. In strong language Steven Schlossman proposes that: "At different times common schools, high schools, junior high schools, vocational training, guidance, kindergartens, administrative efficiency, and testing have been touted as educational panaceas. . . . From Mann to Dewey to Conant, educational reform has symbolized our egalitarian aspirations and has been heralded as a secular savior of our industrial democracy."[35] Not only kindergartens in the past, but early childhood in the late 1960s and early 1970s became a part of the efforts to establish a "great society." The 1960s saw a widespread adoption of Head Start programs aimed at counteracting the effects of proverty and bringing these children into the mainstream of social progress. Schlossman also views the current stress on parent education as a popular tool for social reform.[36] Turning to instruction in "parenting" as a means of improving childhood and society in general, as many institutions began to do in the 1970s, is no new phenomenon. The dissemination of a scientific knowledge base on children in the 1920s through support of the Child Study Association of America and the establishment of *Parent's Magazine* has been linked to the Laura Spelman Rockefeller Memorial under the direction of Lawrence Frank.[37] This was social reformism in the 1920s, where Rockefeller money was enlisted to create a better social order by revitalizing the family's role as educator. Not surprisingly each enthusiastic effort at reform has tended to take place in isolation and to be forgotten by the future prophets of reform.

The reasons for early childhood education being caught up in the great efforts for social reform are easy to identify. Because it is the first exposure of the child to a group outside his home, it seems the best opportunity to establish desired behavior and ideals. Yet, there is a long time lapse between the young child's early education and his becoming an adult citizen. The effects of Head Start programs, for example, were found to be greatly diminished unless there was a follow through program to continue the gains already made. In the larger perspective we may well ask whether the contributions of education to social reform can substitute for more overt and deliberate reforms in society at large.

Yet the role of education in influencing the formation of values, forming codes of behavior, and establishing common frames of knowledge and belief cannot be avoided. We return to the need in the American system of education for a redefinition of public purpose and public values. This is a monolithic task since we are torn between conflicts that seem to gainsay resolution. The following statement captures some of the current dimensions: "In attempting to socialize the younger generation to the political culture and recruit persons to perform the tasks required for the orderly and effective conduct of the political system, education is caught up in the contests between the goals of social cohesion versus cultural pluralism, assimilation versus ethnicity, religious values versus secular morality, equality of opportunity versus economic individualism, egalitarianism versus intellectual hierarchy, complex bureaucracy versus creative professionalism, social justice versus racial or class separatism, civil liberty versus national security and national interests versus international comity."[38] To resolve these dilemmas Butts, writing in 1974, calls for a *re-vision* of the historic public purposes of American education.

Instead, however, of searching for a vision of what education could become as we move nearer to the twenty-first century, the response to the growing concern about education in the 1980s has been a turn toward a stricter regimen in the schools: more stringent adherence to age-grade standards, more use of tests, more conformity, and a longer school day. This is a reinforcement of old methods that never worked very well. Instead of incorporating new insights into the learning process, drill and practice become ensconced methodology. But drill and practice without understanding never produced effective learning. The danger in turning back to old strategies is that the concern for human dignity and social relationships will be sacrificed without any corresponding gain in cognitive skills.

If only the outpouring of anxiety about education, reaching its peak and illustrated by numerous national education studies in the 1980s, could be turned away from reliance on standardized tests of students' achievement, and sometimes that of teachers, as a proof of progress. Progress needs to be in terms of each person reaching his fullest potential. The climate of education must be revised so that "educators may begin concerning themselves with making schools not only 'satisfying places to be' but places where individuals may discover their originality, *create* their own autonomy. They may cease treating schools like factories and students like products if they recognize that schools, under present circumstances, cannot — and probably never will — successfuly meet what is called 'market demand.'"[39] Katz believes that such a radical reformulation of educational objectives "requires a radical restructuring of educational forms."[40] It certainly demands a retreat from attempts to standardize where we know that unique individuality prevails. The outcomes of education could be multiplied if curricula were built in accord with the nature of children and the ways in which they learn with ease. Education could then build on their uniqueness, strength, and power.

EARLY CHILDHOOD PROGRAMS TODAY

The cumulative perspectives developed in preceding chapters make it possible to assess early childhood programs as they now exist. Let us turn back to the excerpts used in the first chapter and evaluate them theoretically. They illustrate strong dichotomous positions and represent theories from Thorndike to Piaget.

Three programs reflect a firm behavioristic base with some aspects closer to Thorndike's connectionism than Skinner's reinforcement theory. All of these originated as government-funded programs outside of public school systems, so there was no pressure for them to adhere to bureaucratic values. Yet, the goals of each program are narrowly limited to skills derived from the learning of specific subject matter. The program directors pay homage to the child's need to build a positive self-image, which they believe is attained through success in mastering skills broken down into easy incremental steps. The Englemann-Becker program is clearly founded on a traditional stimulus-response position with the aim of all children gaining specific skills in reading, arithmetic, and language through drill procedures. The Intensive Learning Model also relies upon a sequential presentation of content but adds behavior analysis techniques and the use of reinforcement to attain goals. In the third, the Behavior Analysis curriculum, Sidney Bijou recognized in his statement that this program rests upon Skinnerian theory. Methodology includes the programming of materials and the effective use of reinforcers. Bijou recommends that the teacher "distribute reinforcement on a schedule that will keep the behavior vigorous, starting with frequent reinforcement and gradually reducing the frequency."[41]

In viewing these theories we have found that they embrace a concept of the learner as passively following the dictates of the program planner, in a process of gaining knowledge bit by bit in an additive manner based on the assumption that the individual will integrate these bits of knowledge together and into his life whether or not they have meaning for him. It seems an unflattering portrait of man to believe all learning is pretty much a result of reward and punishment conditioning.

These programs are illustrations of how vigorously behaviorism reached down into the preschool in the 1960s and 1970s. We have seen how Patty Smith Hill was influenced by Thorndike in developing a revised kindergarten program, yet behavioristic premises were loosely applied; there was still consideration given to the active nature of the child. At a later period reading readiness workbooks were inserted into preschool curricula; these were very close to programmed learning. These recent programs, however, are tightly grounded in the metaphor of the machine. They are based upon a prediction of success as in industrial psychology, with the emphasis given to culturally shared knowledge that is testable. Measurement techniques tend to dominate curriculum planning with the tail wagging the dog; the tests determine the direction of the curriculum.

The determination of what is to be mastered is all outside the learner. The malleability of the person is so highly regarded that little recognition has been given in behaviorism to stage theory or any other aspect of psychological study that points to the unique inner forces in man. The qualitative differences between children and adults which have taken literally centuries to be revealed are ignored. Rather, efforts are made to bring children into the mainstream of human thought as fast and as young as possible. Conformity is an obvious result of this molding of behavior.

Such a program misses the opportunity of education to strengthen the child as a unique person and an independent thinker. Freedom to build personal and interpersonal strengths are limited, for initiative and the making of choices are minimal in this educational plan. The creative play of the young child is superceded by prescribed cognitive tasks and programmed learning. Creativity is not a goal of high priority. Yet this approach pays little heed to and cannot control what the child is learning around the periphery of designated tasks.

The remaining three excerpts represent curricula grounded upon the opposite concept of man as active and purposeful with learning conceived to be correspondingly active, frequently self-initiated, and experiential. The EDC program and the Tucson Early Education Model were also government funded in their initial stages, and the educators who created them incorporated broad goals relating to a spectrum of human behavior, learning, and values. A key element of the EDC approach, drawing inspiration from the revised English infant schools, is the freedom of children to explore an interest deeply, to plan their own activities so that a classroom has a variety of activities going on simultaneously. Action, both physical and intellectual, is central to the program promoted by Kamii and De Vries. These curriculum designers take as a fundamental premise the planful, inventive, constructive, and hopeful nature of man. The learning that ensues is conceived, in the Tucson Early Education Model, as integrated for it is functionally acquired. No skill is gained in isolation, but in the pursuit of a goal larger than itself; it is developed to contribute to a broader purpose. Therefore, the skill has meaning to the child, is integrated into a more generalized conception, and probably has a relationship to life outside the classroom. The manner in which language, intellectual, motivational, and social learnings evolve from a single context was defined by the Tucson Early Education Model as "orchestration."

The uniqueness accorded learners brings great variability to specific programs so that it is difficult to describe a curriculum. The theoretical position these programs hold in common, drawn largely from the work of Dewey and Piaget, provides underlying principles and procedures. For example, there is a concern for the commerce between the inner and the outer phases of the child's growth and a sensitivity to the periphery of learning in which attitudes and values are formed. Drawing from the postulates of ego-psychologists, educators plan for a psychological climate that promotes effective interactions among people. Social settings, which are both challenging and functional, encourage learners to participate fully. A challenge is more than a stimulus; it is an interest, concern, and motivation that brings deep involvement on the part of the child. In this conception of learning the educator recognizes that stimuli have meaning only to the degree that the child can assimilate them or accommodate to them by means of existing structures. The educator can resonate more clearly with the qualitative shifts in children's thinking as new structures evolve.

Freedom is an essential for programs so conceived: freedom to explore, initiate, solve problems, and build rational thought. But the variables of openness are not without control. The impetus for the limitations put upon quixotic personal freedom stems from a sense of responsibility to others. Since the young child's egocentrism may place limitations upon his concern for others, the nature of the teacher's guidance in this realm becomes crucial. The necessity for modifying certain egocentric behavior is balanced with the need to preserve the child's sense of autonomy and to promote reciprocity in social relationships.

With the emphasis upon interaction, it is conceivable that these curricula have more possibility of adjusting to new revelations of ecological research as they occur. This would provide an integral way of incorporating sociological understandings into curriculum planning — an integral means of incorporating the background elements of the lives of children who have lived in either economically or psychologically disadvantaged environments.

The two sets of curriculum models just discussed reflect two diverse and incompatible views of man. The irreducible differences between the two points of view are formed upon different value-laden images of man and these basic assumptions about the nature of human functioning constitute the bedrock upon which curricula rest. The behavioristic position put forward by Thorndike has been modified by Skinner's emphasis on operant conditioning and behavior modification. All is dealt with, however, from the point of view that man's behavior needs outside stimuli to produce growth and to control it.

The opposite, transactional view of man has been consistently changed and modified as new understandings have influenced persons engaged in unifying theoretical elements to form a sound curriculum base. It has already been pointed out that the new notions of ecological psychology can probably be readily integrated. Actually it is perfectly possible for behavioristic methodology to also be a part of program development when it fits into a larger whole. Note, this refers to behavioristic methodology as distinct from behavioristic theory.

The latter three programs illustrate the devotion of groups of educators to a set of values not narrowed to the single dimension of literacy, so accepted by public schools and the public at large. They represent many elements of a developmental-interaction point of view.

WHAT EDUCATION COULD BECOME

Some curriculum designers are even moving away from either a developmental-interaction or a cognitive-developmental position to a more phenomenological position. This is characterized by a vigorous philosophical stance with strong existential leanings and by less emphasis upon accumulated psychological knowledge. The keystone of this approach is a commitment to a person-oriented program that allows choice and freedom in the struggle for personal meaning. The existential moment-by-moment environmental interaction of the learner supercedes an interest in — even a recognition of — developmental factors. The departure from stage theory is due in part to discomfiture with a designated end point for all children. The sheer uniqueness of persons may never really be realized unless curriculum designers make a stronger break from the Darwinian developmental emphasis.

The term *individual* tends to be used as a psychological metaphor. These new curriculum specialists would not turn their back on the individual as in behaviorism, but they would enhance the faith in the importance of the individual by planning for each as a distinct *person*. "Inherent in our view of the person," write Louise Berman and Jessie Roderick, "is the concept that man is a dynamic organism capable of deciding, becoming involved, and interrelating with his fellows in humane ways."[42] James Macdonald puts it this way: "If there is no article of faith in the worth, dignity, integrity and uniqueness of each person there is no need for open schools."[43]

Not much early childhood literature has expropriated the latter manner of discussing curriculum. Indeed one of the main discontinuities of our time is that the school and home still operate to a great extent on a mechanistic image of the child, while the data supporting an interactive, unique view accumulate rapidly. How important it is for each educator to recognize the assumptions undergirding the curriculum so that they do not violate their own basic beliefs. This writer concludes that persons are open learners constantly acting upon and changing their environment, continually interacting with the world. They can never be closed systems; action producing reaction is not an adequate explanation for developing understanding. The active nature of learning helps children to derive meaning from their inner experience and the outer world that confronts them. Meaning is enhanced when children's dynamic interactions with the people and the objects in their world call upon all their powers of understanding — cognitive, social, and affective — in an integrated manner. This is the antithesis of building verbal facades; instead, meaning expands through the confrontation of genuine life problems eliciting the child's total involvement.

Moving into Reading and Writing

Meaning is enhanced in the play of the young child. Gradually the theoretical recognition of the value of play has embraced the cognitive. We have seen how Froebel elevated play, how Dewey recognized the reconstruction of experience inherent in it, and how the neo-Freudians valued the opportunities for autonomous action. Piaget's theory credits play as a means by which the child "freely assimilates reality to the ego." Play is a child's way of making sense out of the world. The child's active manipulation of objects, his repeated activity with people and things, leads to a growing awareness that objects have properties, and that they can be viewed along different dimensions. Through continual use of materials — lifting, sorting, arranging, building — the child comes to note similarities and differences, to work out his own imagery. In Piaget's words, "Play constitutes the extreme pole of assimilation of reality to the ego, while at the same time it has something of the creative imagination which will be the motor of all future thought and even of reason."[44]

One dominant characteristic of play is its symbolic nature as we have seen. In play a child lets an object stand for something else: a few blocks may be a garage, a hat and a pair of gloves may transform an individual into a mother. The child's entry into the symbolic world is through such different activities as images, play, imitation, and language. The child gives evidence of mental images when he has attained object permanence in the sensorimotor period. Play and imitation dominate the life of the child in the preoperational period and this proclivity for play engages him in creating his own idiosyncratic symbols. The greatest growth in language, in which the person acquires the relatively autonomous system of symbols of his particular culture, occurs simultaneously. In all these ways the learner is constructing and using symbol-forming intelligence; he is deeply and meaningfully involved in the symbolic (or semiotic) function. This ability to represent and to understand representation widens the knowing life to an unprecedented degree while at the same time it supplies the "readiness" sought by those who devised reading readiness exercises in the 1940s and 1950s. Workbooks, as developed earlier, imposed the mechanics of reading upon a child, while in the newer conception he constructs information about the use of symbols in his own meaningful context. When the individal eventually confronts those little black marks on paper to read them, it is to derive meaning, not to be overwhelmed by the mechanics of the process. All this is reiterated to show how vastly different is the conception of the role of symbols in the life of the child today and how his symbol-forming intelligence is constructed in a world filled with symbols.

A symbol has no actual existence as part of the physical world; it has meaning. Symbols are objects that stand for meanings. "The possibility of symbolization," writes Phenix, "is dependent on the unique human power of self-transcendence, for the dual quality of reflective awareness is required to understand a symbol."[45] This dual quality of reflective awareness permits an individual to be both identified with a symbolic referent and yet distinguished from it; the word *doll* is not a doll, yet by the power of thought it stands for a doll. Cassirer calls it "reflection" or "reflective thought" that allows man to single out "from the whole undiscriminate mass of the stream of floating sensuous phenomena" certain elements in order to concentrate on them symbolically.[46] Self-transcendence or reflective thought as integral to the understanding and use of symbols is derived from those symbols constructed in the real or phantasy life of the child where they imbue them with meaning. As "an animal symbolicum" the child mediates his world and through the potential for making the act of reference can denote objects, feelings, and concepts. Development at this level results only when meaning is maximized, when the symbolic is an extension of inner meaning.

Some of the most stimulating educational research of this era is probing the manner in which children go beyond these early stages of symbolism and through their own constructive processes acquire knowledge of the patterns and structure of reading and writing.[47] This research has revealed that given an appropriate environment children learn to read without being instructed in the traditional sense; they are abstractors of information, constructors of knowledge, formulators of rules. "'Readiness' for reading has no meaning in such a view," writes Schickedanz. "Children are ready, and do learn to read in a constant progression from the moment they are born, if supplied with a print-rich environment."[48] The emergence of phonetic strategies to create words, developed independently by some children, seems to be related to the print-rich environment to which Schickendanz refers. The ingredients for this environment are defined as "printed materials of various kinds; materials for creating print of one's own; adult mediation of print in the environment such as naming letters, the child's name, and modeling reading and writing; reading to children; answering the child's questions; and allowing the child wide latitude in exploring how words are created."[49]

Whereas the usual reading instruction leads to increasingly teacher-directed and dependent behavior, this construction of their own emergent reading abilities promotes a complex range of metalinguistic awareness. Children, according to David Doake, proceed from a state of relative globality and lack of differentiation to a state of increased differentiation and hierarchical integration.[50] He found that as children move from a global use of context in retrieving a story to concentrating on the graphphonic information on a page, not only is there a gain in skills but there is complete involvement in the task. They learn to self-correct; they gain the ability to predict what is coming next; their reading is characterized by fluency; and the competence they feel gives them confidence in their own ability. The building of literacy is enhanced as children maintain enthusiasm for the process as they gain meaning from it. Apparently the main requisites are time, an appropriately prepared environment, and an empathetic adult who understands children's gradual gains. Children's hearty, personal involvement in the process augurs well that we will have not only older children who can read but *do* read. The literacy, then, so valued by society, becomes not just an educational goal, but a precursor for subsequent educational growth.

Continuity in Learning

Continual interaction with materials in the classroom supports the construction of knowledge and meaning for the learner. No cutoff age of six exists for such interaction. Throughout the period of concrete operations — even to the age of eleven or twelve — classrooms need to be workshops where freedom for use of materials prevails. There is no theoretical support to substantiate diverse classroom organization for four- and five-year-olds as opposed to six- to eight-year-olds. During all the early childhood years the search for meaning is facilitated or impeded by the nature of the environment; opportunities for exploration, discovery, and the integration of learnings are essential. Interaction is not limited to the physical alone. Some misapplications of Dewey's position arose from a limited conception of what interaction entails. For Dewey learning was always a process of reconstructing experience through dynamic interaction of person and environment. Out of experience a genuine problem will arise from which thinking begins as the learner applies information and makes new observations. The method of reflective thinking, based upon firsthand experience, underlies the educative process. Today's frequently stated goal of "learning how to learn" is probably a direct descendent of Dewey's emphasis on the process of reflective thinking.

Similar misconceptions could stem from Piaget's theory. Frequently overemphasis is given to the stages articulated in his theory. While they serve as a descriptive tool, Gruber and Vonèche suggest that "Piaget's interactionism, his ideas of assimilation and accommodation, his recent equilibration model, the idea of progressive decentering, and his elaboration of the idea of intellectual operations — all these might stand without the stage concept."[51] In another vein Kamii and De Vries have argued that certain applications of Piaget's position have merely read into it their own empiricist biases.[52] They suggest we must look beyond manipulation to *what* and *how* learning is taking place. From a Piagetian point of view the child constructs knowledge from his own activity, but what is "read off" from reality is always something constructed in part according to the determinants of his own intellectual structure. What the child has already assimilated determines his interaction with a stimulus; therefore, responses vary from child to child and also are different for a given child at subsequent ages. Furthermore, much knowledge, particularly logico-mathematical knowledge, goes far beyond sensory experience itself. Classification, for example, is not in the materials, but in the ability to reason about them, or, to use a more Piagetian term, the learner's ability to reflectively abstract from the given data. How can these more intricate beliefs about the nature of interactive learning be incorporated into programs for young children?

Finally the continuity in learning throughout the early childhood years so long sought by leaders concerned with young children can be achieved. Strong new support not only opens possibilities but offers new insights to facilitate a continuous process of learning throughout all the learning years.

FOCUS ON CHILDREN

When meaning is divorced from the learning process for individuals, they become alienated from learning, alienated from what the school tries to offer. The efficiency schools attempted to achieve through age-grade standards and testing procedures proved to be ultimately inefficient for many children. Drill and practice on skills may have enabled them to perform well on a test, but unless the exercises contained meaning for the learner what seemed to be gained was soon lost. This is not to imply that no drill and practice should be a part of the learning process; it does suggest the necessity for practice to be allied to a genuine purpose.

We cannot be satisfied with mere literacy as the major purpose of learning in early childhood. For one thing it is a purpose that fails to recognize the wholeness of growth. The concomitant learning of attitudes and values proceeds whether recognized or not. Our society cannot afford the rigid regimen that spawns a child's negative concept of his own abilities, or that cultivates feelings of resentment and rebellion. Only those schools that foster a respect for children and a concern for individual worth contribute positively to society by promoting persons who will reach out for solutions. Faith in the constructive, planful, inventive, hopeful nature of man forms the bedrock of educational planning. The active participation of the learner is thus engaged, a matter of great significance for he alone can put into operation *his* ability for reflective abstraction, *his* developing symbolic sense. Only thus is lasting learning established.

Amid the accent on social reformism and the political debates on U.S. educational policy, it is imperative that the most important person of all not be overlooked: the learner. A whole view of learning and growth stands out as an educational necessity. Our view of persons must reflect a holistic integration of all facets of his character in order to help him become more effective in his world. "To be fully human," states Rich, "will equip man with all the ability and creativity to live meaningfully and fruitfully at a high level in today's complex world."[53] "To be fully human" is a value statement based on philosophical as well as psychological premises. A redefinition of educational values by schools includes a confrontation of the source of values. The final judgment about an educational program rests upon decisions concerning the nature of persons conceived as outcomes. The needs of society and the needs of the individual converge in that curriculum that enables each child to develop unique capacities to the fullest. Millie Almy opens up this possibility: "Guiding today's young children for tomorrow's world, lighting the lamps of their own intelligence is, of course, a matter of providing a physical and social environment in which they can act, interact, do, think, and become. But it is also a matter of providing time, space, and atmosphere in which they can experience and be — a matter of lighting the spirit as well as the mind."[54] More than ever before, we know this must begin in early childhood.

NOTES
ABOUT THE AUTHOR
INDEX

Notes

CHAPTER 1. IDEOLOGIES IN PERSPECTIVE

1. Ellis D. Evans, Contemporary Influences in Early Childhood Education, 2nd ed. (New York: Holt, Rinehart and Winston, 1975).

2. Mary Carol Day and Ronald K. Parker, The Preschool in Action: Exploring Early Childhood Programs, 2nd ed. (Boston: Allyn and Bacon, 1977), p. x.

3. All examples are from material written by the director(s) of the program and sent out by the Head Start Office during the late 1960s.

4. The Tucson Early Education Model, Marie M. Hughes, director, University of Arizona, Tucson, Arizona.

5. The Intensive Learning Model, Research and Development Center in Educational Stimulation, University of Georgia, Athens, Georgia.

6. University of Illinois Program, Wesley Becker and Siegfried Engelmann, directors, University of Illinois, Champaign, Illinois.

7. The EDC Head Start Approach, David E. Armington, director, Education Development Center, Newton, Massachusetts.

8. Sidney W. Bijou, "Behavior Analysis Applied to Early Childhood Education," in Early Childhood Education: Issues and Insights, ed. Bernard Spodek and Herbert J. Walberg (Berkeley: McCutcheon, 1977), pp. 146-47.

9. Constance Kamii and Rheta DeVries, "Piaget for Early Education," in The Preschool in Action, ed. Mary Carol Day and Ronald K. Parker (Boston: Allyn and Bacon, 1977), pp. 368-69.

10. William E. Martin, "Rediscovering the Mind of the Child: A Significant Trend in Research in Child Development," Merrill-Palmer Quarterly 6 (Jan. 1960): 67-76.

11. Charles Darwin, The Origin of Species (New York: Modern Library, 1936).

12. William Kessen, The Child (New York: Wiley, 1965), p. 116.

13. William James, Principles of Psychology (New York: Dorer Publications, 1918).

14. Patricia A. Graham, Progressive Education: From Arcady to Academe (New York: Teachers College Press, 1967), p. 6.

15. William Heard Kilpatrick, "Dewey's Influence on Education," in The Philosophy of John Dewey, ed. P. A. Schlipp (New York: Tuder Publishing, 1939), p. 456.

16. John Dewey, The Influence of Darwin on Philosophy (Bloomington: Indiana University Press, 1910), p. 19.

17. Graham, Progressive Education, p. 146.

18. Lawrence Cremin, The Transformation of the School (New York: Knopf, 1962), p. 239.

19. Calvin S. Hall and Gardner Lindzey, Theories of Personality, 2nd ed. (New York: Wiley, 1970), p. 117.

20. Ibid., p. 118.

21. J. McVicker Hunt, Intelligence and Experience (New York: Ronald Press, 1961).

22. Ira Gordon, "New Conceptions of Children's Learning and Development," in Learning and Mental Health in the Schools, ed. Walter B. Waltjen (Washington, D.C.: Association for Supervision and Curriculum Development, 1966), pp. 49-73.

23. Millie Almy, "Guiding Children for Life in Tomorrow's World," in Education in Anticipation of Tomorrow, ed. Robert H. Anderson (Worthington, Ohio: Charles A. Jones, 1973), pp. 42-49.

24. Kessen, The Child, pp. 1, 6.

25. Ibid, p. 4.

CHAPTER 2. THE ROOTS OF EARLY CHILDHOOD EDUCATION

1. Plato, The Republic, book 2, 377, trans. B. Jowett (New York: Random House, 1941), p. 72.

2. R. Freeman Butts, A Cultural History of Western Education (New York: McGraw-Hill, 1955), p. 46.

3. Robert Ulich, History of Educational Thought (New York: American Book Co., 1945), p. 5.

4. A. E. Taylor, Plato--The Man and His Work (New York: Dial Press, 1936), p. 280.

5. Werner Jaeger, Paideia: The Ideals of Greek Culture, vol. 2 (New York: Oxford University Press, 1943), p. 213.

6. Ibid., p. 277.

7. Butts, A Cultural History of Western Education, p. 31.

8. Naomi Noisworth, "Infant Education," in A Encyclopedia of Education, vol. 3, ed. Paul Monroe (New York: Macmillan, 1912), p. 446.

9. Quintilian, "Institutes of Oratory," in Three Thousand Years of Educational Wisdom, book 1, ed. Robert Ulich (Cambridge, Mass: Harvard University Press, 1945), p. 104.

10. Butts, A Cultural History of Western Education, p. 140.

11. Frederick B. Artz, The Mind of the Middle Ages (New York: Knopf, 1958), p. 82.

12. Butts, A Cultural History of Western Education, p. 155.

13. Philippe Ariès, Centuries of Childhood (New York: Knopf, 1962), p. 128.

14. Ibid., p. 130.

15. Ibid., pp. 132-33.

16. John Amos Comenius, The Great Didactic, trans. M. W. Keatings (New York: Russell and Russell, 1910), p. 59.

17. Johann Amos Comenius, School of Infancy, ed. Will S. Monroe (Boston: D. C. Heath, 1896), p. 45.

18. Butts, A Cultural History of Western Education, p. 239.

19. Ibid., p. 288.

20. John Locke, Some Thoughts Concerning Education (Cambridge: Cambridge University Press, 1913), p. 1.

21. Paul Nash, Models of Man (New York: John Wiley, 1968), p. 235.

22. Elmer H. Wilds and Kenneth V. Lottick, The Foundations of Modern Education, 4th ed. (New York: Holt, Rinehart and Winston, 1970), pp. 292-93.

23. Butts, A Cultural History of Western Education, pp. 207-08.

24. Nash, Models of Man, p. 263.

25. Will and Ariel Durant, Rousseau and Revolution (New York: Simon and Schuster, 1967), p. 1.

26. Ibid.

27. Irving Babbitt, Rousseau and Romanticism (Boston: Houghton Mifflin, 1919), p. 44.

28. John S. Brubacher, A History of the Problems of Education (New York: McGraw-Hill, 1966), p. 589.

29. Jean Jacques Rousseau, Émile, trans. Barbara Foxby (London: J. M. Dent, 1911), p. 168.

30. Ibid., p. 5.

31. Ibid., p. 120.

32. Ibid., pp. 42-43.

33. Ibid., p. 1.

34. Butts, A Cultural History of Western Education, pp. 290-91.

35. Rousseau, Émile, p. 90.

36. Ibid., p. 126.

37. Ibid., p. 1.

38. Ibid., p. 71.

39. Johann Heinrich Pestalozzi, The Evening Hour of a Hermit, trans. Robert Ulich, in Ulich, ed., Three Thousand Years of Educational Wisdom, p. 480.

40. Johann Heinrich Pestalozzi, How Gertrude Teaches Her Children, trans. Lucy Holland and Frances Turner (London: George Allen and Unwin Ltd., 1894), p. 6.

41. Ibid., p. 26.

42. Ulich, History of Educational Thought, p. 287.

43. Pestalozzi, How Gertrude Teaches Her Children, p. 85.

44. Ibid., pp. 182-89.

CHAPTER 3. A DISTINCTIVE PROGRAM FOR THE YOUNG CHILD

1. T. Raymont, A History of Education of Young Children (New York: Longmans, Green, 1937), p. 45.
2. Edward H. Reisner, The Evolution of the Common School (New York: Macmillan, 1930), p. 257.
3. H. Courthope Bowen, Froebel and Education Through Self-Activity (New York: Scribner's, 1903), pp. 6-7.
4. R. Freeman Butts, A Cultural History of Western Education (New York: McGraw-Hill, 1955), p. 383.
5. Friedrich Froebel, Autobiography, trans. Emilie Michaelis and H. Keatley Moore (Syracuse, N.Y.: C. W. Bardeen, 1889), p. 40.
6. Bowen, Froebel and Education Through Self-Activity, pp. 15-16.
7. Froebel, Autobiography, p. 83.
8. Ibid., pp. 87-88.
9. Friedrich Froebel, The Education of Man, trans. William N. Hailmann (New York: D. Appleton, 1887), pp. 1-2.
10. Ibid., p. 7.
11. John S. Brubacher, A History of the Problems of Education (New York: McGraw-Hill, 1966), p. 124.
12. Froebel, The Education of Man, pp. 54-55.
13. Ibid., p. 21.
14. Friedrich Froebel, Education by Development, trans. Josephine Jarvis (New York: D. Appleton, 1899), p. 178.
15. Ibid., p. 180.
16. Froebel, The Education of Man, p. 287.
17. Froebel, Education by Development, p. 309.
18. Ibid., p. 293.
19. Friedrich Froebel, Pedagogics of the Kindergarten, trans. Josephine Jarvis (New York: D. Appleton, 1895), pp. 204-05.
20. Froebel, The Education of Man, p. 283.
21. Robert Ulich, History of Educational Thought (New York: American Book Co., 1945), p. 179.
22. Froebel, Pedagogics of the Kindergarten, pp. 222-24.
23. Friedrich Froebel, Mutter-und Kose-Lieder (Liepzig: A. Pichler's Witwe und Sohn, 1911).
24. Froebel, Pedagogics of the Kindergarten, p. 270.
25. Brubacher, A History of the Problems of Education, p. 622.
26. Evelyn Weber, The Kindergarten: Its Encounter with Educational Thought in America (New York: Teachers College Press, 1969), pp. 18-44.
27. Richard Emmons Thursfield, Henry Barnard's American Journal on Education (Baltimore: Johns Hopkins University Press, 1945), p. 233.
28. Henry Barnard, ed., Kindergarten and Child Culture Papers (Hartford, Conn.: Office of Barnard's American Journal of Education, 1890), unpaged.
29. Elizabeth P. Peabody and Mary Mann, Guide to the Kindergarten and Moral Culture in Infancy (New York: E. Steiger, 1877), p. iii.

30. William T. Harris, "Kindergarten in the Public School System," in Barnard, ed., Kindergarten and Child Culture Papers, pp. 629-30.

31. See, for example: J. W. Dickenson, "What Froebel's System of Kindergarten Is and How It Can Be Introduced Into Our Public Schools," (1873);

Mrs. John Kraus-Boelte, "Characteristics of Froebel's Method, Kindergarten Training with Illustrations" (1876); and

William N. Hailmann, "From Pestalozzi to Froebel" (1880),

all in Addresses and Proceedings of the National Education Association.

32. William N. Hailmann, "Schoolishness in the Kindergarten," Addresses and Proceedings of the National Education Association (1890): 566.

CHAPTER 4. A SCIENTIFIC APPROACH TO CHILD STUDY

1. Louise Alder, "The Effect of the Scientific Spirit upon the Kindergarten in Relation to Materials," Addresses and Proceedings of the National Education Association (1913): 439.

2. In the early 1890s an International Kindergarten Union was formed as a means of disseminating knowledge of kindergarten expansion and change. The Proceedings of the annual meetings of this organization reveal the intense debates and gradual acceptance of new ideas.

3. Henry Steele Commager, The American Mind (New Haven: Yale University Press, 1950), p. 44.

4. Merle Curti, The Growth of American Thought, 2nd ed. (New York: Harper, 1951), p. 548.

5. Ibid.

6. Perry Miller, ed., "Introduction," American Thought: Civil War to World War I (New York: Rinehart and Co., 1954), p. xv.

7. G. Stanley Hall, "Child Study," Addresses and Proceedings of the National Education Association (1893): 173.

8. Charles E. Strickland and Charles Burgess, Health, Growth, and Heredity (New York: Teachers College Press, 1965), p. 14.

9. G. Stanley Hall, "The Pedagogy of the Kindergarten," Educational Problems, vol. 1 (New York: D. Appleton, 1911), p. 20.

10. Ibid., p. 18.

11. G. Stanley Hall, "The Contents of Children's Minds," The Princeton Review 11 (May 1883): 249-53.

12. Sara E. Wiltse, "The History of Child Study," The Pedagogical Seminary 4 (Oct. 1896): 112.

13. Hall, Educational Problems, p. 16.

14. Strickland and Burgess, Health, Growth, and Heredity, p. 5.

15. Edwin G. Boring, "The Influence of Evolutionary Theory upon American Psychological Thought," in Evolutionary Thought in America, ed. Stow Persons (New Haven: Yale University Press, 1950), p. 269.

16. Lawrence A. Cremin, "Preface," in Strickland and Burgess, Health, Growth, and Heredity, p. viii.

17. A. C. Ellis and G. S. Hall, "A Study of Dolls," Pedagogical Seminary 4 (1896): 129-75.

18. G. Stanley Hall, "Address of Dr. Hall to the N.E.A." Kindergarten Review 12 (Sept. 1901): 45.

19. G. Stanley Hall, "The Ideal School as Based on Child Study," Addresses and Proceedings of the National Education Association (1901): 475.

20. Ibid., pp. 476-77.

21. Merle Curti, The Social Ideas of American Educators (Paterson, N.J.: Littlefield, Adams, 1959), pp. 400-02.

22. E. H. Russell, "Observation and Experiment Essential in Pedagogical Inquiry," Addresses and Proceedings of the National Educational Association (1899): 276.

23. G. Stanley Hall, "From Fundamental to Accessory in Education," The Kindergarten Magazine 11 (May 1899): 559-60.

24. G. Stanley Hall, Educational Problems, vol. 1 (New York: D. Appleton, 1911), p. 1.

25. Strickland and Burgess, Health, Growth, and Heredity, p. 18.

26. Milton J. Senn, Insights on the Child Development Movement in the United States, monograph of the Society for Research in Child Development, vol. 40, nos. 3-4 (Aug. 1975), p. 32.

27. Arnold Gesell and Frances Ilg, The Child from Five to Ten (New York: Harper, 1946), p. 6.

28. Arnold Gesell, "Maturation and the Patterning of Behavior," in A Handbook of Child Psychology, ed. C. Murchison (Worcester, Mass: Clark University Press, 1931), p. 209.

29. Ibid., p. 210.

30. Ibid., pp. 211, 212.

31. Gesell and Ilg, The Child from Five to Ten, p. 20.

32. Murchison, ed., A Handbook of Child Psychology, p. 223.

33. Gesell and Ilg, The Child from Five to Ten, p. 23.

34. Arnold Gesell and Frances L. Ilg, Infant and Child in the Culture of Today (New York: Harper, 1943), p. 10.

35. Gesell and Ilg, The Child from Five to Ten, p. 6.

36. Ibid., p. 23.

37. Ibid., p. 26.

38. Ibid., p. 20.

39. William Kessen, The Child (New York: Wiley, 1965), p. 211. Jerome Kagan is also quoted as expressing the same opinion in Senn, Insights on the Child Development Movement in the United States, p. 30.

40. Arnold Gesell, "The Changing Status of the Preschool Child," Progressive Education 2 (Jan.-Mar. 1925): 8.

41. Mary Dabney Davis, "Nursery Schools: Their Development and Current Practices in the United States," U.S. Office of Education bulletin, no. 9 (Washington, D.C.: Government Printing Office, 1932), p. 1.

42. Arnold Gesell, "The Downward Extension of Kindergarten," Childhood Education 2 (Oct. 1926): 55.

43. See, for example: Arnold Gesell, "Significance of the Nursery School," Childhood Education 1 (Sept. 1925): 11-20; and Arnold Gesell, "The Yale Clinic of Child Development," Childhood Education 8 (May 1932): 468-69.

44. Josephine C. Foster and Neith E. Headley, Education in the Kindergarten (New York: American Book Co., 1936), p. 1.

45. Ilse Forest, "The Responsibility of the Kindergarten in the Schools' Readiness Program," Education in Transition, 47th Annual Schoolmen's Week Proceedings (Philadelphia: University of Pennsylvania Press, 1960), p. 125.

46. Ibid., p. 135.

47. Lois Barclay Murphy, "Child Development: Then and Now," Childhood Education 44 (Jan. 1968): 302.

48. J. McVicker Hunt, Intelligence and Experience (New York: Ronald Press, 1961), p. 43.

49. Ibid., p. v.

CHAPTER 5. THE SEARCH FOR A SCIENCE OF EDUCATION

1. Patty Smith Hill, "Introduction," in A Conduct Curriculum for Kindergarten and First Grade, Agnes Burke et al. (New York: Scribners, 1923), p. xii.

2. Ibid., p. xiv.

3. Edward L. Thorndike, "What is 'Scientific' Method in the Study of Education?," in On the Teaching of English in Elementary and High Schools, ed. Manfred J. Holmes, 5th yearbook, National Society for the Study of Education, part 1 (Chicago: University of Chicago Press, 1906), p. 82.

4. J. McKeen Cattell, "Thorndike as Colleague and Friend," Teachers College Record 27 (Feb. 1926): 461.

5. William T. Harris, "Psychological Inquiry," Addresses and Proceedings of the National Education Association (1885): 95.

6. Merle Curti, The Growth of American Thought (New York: Harper, 1951), p. 556.

7. William James, Talks to Teachers on Psychology: And to Students on Some of Life's Ideals (New York: Henry Holt, 1899), p. 29.

8. This statement was written in James's own handwriting at the head of the chapter on habit in his Psychology: A Briefer Course, published in 1892. Ralph Barton Perry, The Thought and Character of William James (Cambridge, Mass: Harvard University Press, 1948), p. 196.

9. Merle Curti, The Social Ideas of American Educators (Paterson, N.J.: Littlefield, Adams, 1959), p. 470.

10. Edward L. Thorndike, "The Foundations of Educational Achievement," Journal of Proceedings and Addresses of the National Education Association, 1914, p. 199.

11. For a description of the use of the term reflex arc see Morris L. Bigge and Maurice P. Hunt, Psychological Foundations of Education (New York: Harper and Row, 1968), pp. 35-36.

12. Lawrence Cremin, The Transformation of the School (New York: Knopf, 1962), p. 111.

13. Ernest R. Hilgard, Theories of Learning, 2nd ed. (New York: Appleton-Century-Crofts, 1956), p. 18.

14. Ibid., p. 19.

15. Edward L. Thorndike, The Principles of Teaching (New York: A. G. Seiler, 1906), p. 110.

16. Curti, The Social Ideas of American Educators, pp. 470-71.

17. Edward L. Thorndike, "Notes on Psychology for Kindergartners," Teachers College Record 4 (Nov. 1903): 377-408. The term Kindergartner at this period of time was used to refer to the teacher or leader in kindergarten education.

18. Ibid., p. 380.

19. Ibid., pp. 386-87.

20. Ibid., pp. 389-90.

21. Ibid., p. 400.

22. Ibid., p. 393.

23. Ibid., p. 395.

24. Burke et al., A Conduct Curriculum for Kindergarten and First Grade, pp. 22-25.

25. Richard Hofstadter, Social Darwinism in American Thought (Boston: Beacon Press, 1955), p. 165.

26. R. Freeman Butts and Lawrence A. Cremin, A History of Education in American Culture (New York: Henry Holt, 1953), p. 338.

27. Curti, The Social Ideas of American Educators, p. 483.

28. Ibid., p. 481.

29. J. McVicker Hunt, Intelligence and Experience (New York: Ronald Press, 1961), p. 10.

30. Charles Hubbard Judd, Introduction to the Scientific Study of Education (Boston: Ginn and Co., 1918), p. 228.

31. Edward L. Thorndike, "The Nature, Purposes, and General Methods of Measurement of Educational Products," in The Measurement of Educational Products, ed. Guy W. Whipple, 17th yearbook of the National Society for the Study of Education, part II (Bloomington, Ill.: Public School Publishing Co., 1918), p. 16.

32. Walter S. Monroe, "Existing Tests and Standards," in Whipple, ed., The Measurement of Educational Products, pp. 71-104.

33. Thorndike, "Notes on Psychology for Kindergartners," pp. 396-97.

34. Thorndike, "The Nature, Purposes, and General Methods of Measurement of Educational Products," p. 16.

35. Henry J. Baker, "The Detroit Kindergarten Test," Proceedings of the Twenty-Eighth Annual Meeting of the International Kindergarten Union, 1921, pp. 188-95. Bess V. Cunningham, "A New Series of Group Tests for Use

in the Kindergarten and Primary Grades," Proceedings of the Twenty-Ninth Annual Meeting of the International Kindergarten Union, 1922, pp. 164-88.

36. Edward L. Thorndike, Educational Psychology: Briefer Course (New York: Teachers College, Columbia University, 1917), p. 268.

37. Edward L. Thorndike, Animal Intelligence: Experimental Studies (New York: Macmillan, 1911), p. 150. These experimental studies were first published in 1898. In the preface to the 1911 volume Thorndike wrote that they were reprinted "since they represent the first deliberate and extended application of the experimental method in animal psychology" (p. v).

38. Thorndike, "Notes on Psychology for Kindergartners," p. 388.

39. Ibid.

40. Edward L. Thorndike, "Education as Cause and Symptom," a 1939 Kappa Delta Pi lecture reprinted in Geraldine M. Joncich, Psychology and the Science of Education: Selected Writings of Edward L. Thorndike (New York: Teachers College, Columbia University, Bureau of Publications, 1962), p. 133.

41. Edward L. Thorndike, Individuality (Boston: Houghton-Mifflin, 1911), p. 51

42. Samuel J. Braun and Esther P. Edwards, History and Theory of Early Childhood Education (Worthington, Ohio: Charles A. Jones, 1972), p. 265.

43. Charlotte Jammer, "Patty Smith Hill and Reform of the American Kindergarten" (Ph.D. dissertation, Teachers College, Columbia University, 1960), p. 160.

44. Cremin, The Transformation of the School, p. 369.

45. Bigge and Hunt, Psychological Foundations of Education, p. 354.

46. M. C. Wittrock and Arthur A. Lumsdaine, "Instructional Psychology," in vol. 28, Annual Review of Psychology, ed. Mark R. Rosenzweig and Lyman W. Porter (Palo Alto, Calif.: Annual Reviews Inc., 1977), pp. 417-18.

47. B. F. Skinner, Science and Human Behavior (New York: Macmillan, 1953), p. 23.

48. John B. Watson, Behaviorism, rev. ed. (New York: Norton, 1930), p. 104.

49. Bigge and Hunt, Psychological Foundations of Education, p. 363.

50. Skinner, Science and Human Behavior, p. 68.

51. Ibid., p. 91.

52. Skinner in dialogue with Evans. Richard I. Evans, B.F. Skinner: The Man and His Ideas (New York: Dutton, 1968), pp. 33-34.

53. Skinner, Science and Human Behavior, p. 171.

54. B. F. Skinner, Beyond Freedom and Dignity (New York: Knopf, 1971), p. 28.

55. Skinner, Science and Human Behavior, p. 72.

56. Ibid., p. 386.

57. B. F. Skinner, "Teaching Machines," Science 128 (Oct. 1958): 970.

58. Ibid., p. 971.

59. B. F. Skinner, "The Free and Happy Student," Phi Delta Kappan 55 (Sept. 1973): 15.

60. B. F. Skinner, "The Science of Learning and the Art of Teaching," Harvard Educational Review 24 (Spring 1954): 94.

61. Evans, B. F. Skinner: The Man and His Ideas, pp. 67-68.

62. B. F. Skinner, Walden Two (New York: Macmillan, 1948).

63. Skinner, Beyond Freedom and Dignity, pp. 200, 205.

64. Ibid., p. 215.

65. Skinner, "The Science of Learning and the Art of Teaching," p. 97.

66. Patrick Suppes, "Plug-In Instruction," Saturday Review (July 23, 1966): 25ff. See also "Those Computers in Palo Alto," The Reading Newsreport 2 (Oct. 1967): 14-23.

67. Wayne K. Howell, "Technology and the Human Need," Theory into Practice 7 (Oct. 1968): 155.

68. Teressa M. Pratt, "A Positive Approach to Disruptive Behavior," Today's Education 62 (Jan. 1973): 18-19.

69. Charles K. Madsen and Charles H. Madsen, Jr., "Behavior Modification," Instructor 81 (Oct. 1971): 56.

70. Journal of Applied Behavior Modification, vol. 3 (1970): L. Keith Miller and Richard Schneider, "The Use of a Token System in Project Head Start," pp. 213-220; Frank D. Kirby and Hayward C. Toler, Jr., "Modification of Preschool Isolate Behavior," pp. 308-14; R. C. Schutte and B. J. Hopkins, "The Effects of Teacher Attention on Following Instructions in a Kindergarten Class," pp. 117-22.

71. Arthur W. Combs, "Intelligence from a Perceptual Point of View," Journal of Abnormal and Social Psychology 47 (July 1952): 663.

72. Benjamin Bloom, Stability and Change in Human Characteristics (New York: Wiley, 1964), p. 88.

73. Hunt, Intelligence and Experience, p. 362. For evidence dissonant with the idea of fixed intelligence see pp. 10-34.

74. Arthur B. Jensen, "Social Class and Genetics: Implications for Education," American Educational Research Journal 5 (Nov. 1968): 1-42.

75. Ira J. Gordon, "New Conceptions of Children's Learning and Development," in Learning and Mental Health in the School, ed. Walter B. Waetjen and Robert R. Leeper, yearbook of the Association for Supervision and Curriculum Development (Washington, D.C.: ASCD, 1966), pp. 56-57.

76. Curti, The Social Ideas of American Educators, pp. 451-52, 490-91.

77. Skinner, Science and Human Behavior, pp. 46-47.

78. Donald Snygg, "A Cognitive Field Theory of Learning," in Waetjen and Leeper, eds., Learning and Mental Health in the Schools, p. 83.

79. Ibid., p. 82.

80. John Martin Rich, Humanistic Foundations of Education (Worthington, Ohio: Charles A. Jones, 1971), p. 20.
81. Hunt, Intelligence and Experience, pp. 351-52.
82. Wittrock and Lumsdaine, "Instructional Psychology," p. 418.

CHAPTER 6. THE RECONSTRUCTION OF EXPERIENCE

1. Alice Temple, "Extending the Child's Social Understanding," Childhood Education 5 (April 1929): 420.
2. Ibid., pp. 421-23.
3. "Alice Temple," Leaders in Education (New York: Science Press, 1932), p. 916.
4. Ermine Cross, "The Work of the Chicago Free Kindergarten," Kindergarten Magazine 10 (April 1898): 509-15.
5. Alice Temple, "Subject Matter in the Curriculum," Addresses and Proceedings of the National Education Association (1919): 175-78.
6. May Hill, "Alice Temple," Childhood Education 8 (June 1932): 539.
7. Minnie E. Glidden, "Conference on Gifts and Occupations," Proceedings of the Seventh Annual Convention of the International Kindergarten Union (1900), p. 36.
8. Mary Boomer Page, Ibid., p. 44.
9. Alice Temple, Ibid., pp. 92, 89.
10. Alice H. Putnam, Ibid, p. 76.
11. Patty Smith Hill, Ibid., p. 83.
12. Bertha Hofer-Hegner, Ibid., p. 98.
13. John Dewey, "Froebel's Educational Principles," Elementary School Record 1 (June 1900): 143-51.
14. Ibid., p. 144.
15. Ibid., p. 145.
16. Ibid., p. 147.
17. Ibid., p. 149.
18. Ibid.
19. Ibid., p. 150.
20. Ibid., p. 151.
21. Ibid., p. 143.
22. Richard J. Bernstein, "Introduction," in On Experience, Nature and Freedom, ed. Richard J. Bernstein (Indianapolis: Bobbs-Merrill, 1960), p. xxiv.
23. Martin S. Dworkin, "John Dewey: A Centennial Review," in Dewey on Education, ed. Martin S. Dworkin (New York: Teachers College, Columbia University, Bureau of Publications, 1959), p. 6.
24. John Dewey, The Influence of Darwin on Philosophy and Other Essays in Contemporary Thought (New York: Henry Holt, 1910), p. 15.
25. John Dewey, "An Added Note as to the Practical," Essays in Experimental Logic (Chicago: University of Chicago Press, 1916), p. 330.
26. John Dewey, Experience and Education (New York: Macmillan, 1938), pp. 16-17.
27. Ibid., pp. 38-39.
28. Ibid., pp. 41-42.
29. Ibid., p. 41.

30. Ibid., p. 27.

31. Ibid., pp. 31-32.

32. Ibid., p. 47.

33. Ernest E. Bayles and Bruce L. Hood, Growth of American Educational Thought and Practice (New York: Harper and Row, 1966), p. 261. See also pp. 257-58.

34. Edwin G. Boring, A History of Experimental Psychology (New York: Appleton-Century-Crofts, 1950), p. 554.

35. John Dewey, The Child and the Curriculum (Chicago: University of Chicago Press, 1902), p. 9.

36. Dewey, Experience and Education, p. 43.

37. John Dewey and A. F. Bentley, "Interaction and Transaction," Knowing and the Known (Boston: Beacon Press, 1949), pp. 103-18.

38. Bernstein, ed., On Experience, Nature and Freedom, p. xl.

39. John Dewey, "The Reflex Arc Concept in Psychology," Psychological Reviews 3 (1896): 357-70. This paper is reprinted in Wayne Dennis, ed., Readings in the History of Psychology (New York: Appleton-Century-Crofts, 1948), pp. 355-65. (For criticism, see p. 355.)

40. Frederick J. McDonald, "The Influence of Learning Theories on Education," in Theories of Learning and Instruction, ed., Ernest R. Hilgard, 63rd yearbook of the National Society for the Study of Education (Chicago: University of Chicago Press, 1964), p. 11.

41. Patty Smith Hill, "Conference on Training," Proceedings of the Seventh Annual Convention of the International Kindergarten Union (1900), p. 108.

42. Liberal Report, "Report of the Committee of Nineteen," Proceedings of the Sixteenth Annual Convention of the International Kindergarten Union (1909), p. 131.

43. Geneva Clippinger, "A Visit to the Sub-Primary Class of Dr. Dewey's School," Kindergarten Review 11 (March 1901): 424-26.

44. Georgia P. Scates, "The Sub-Primary," The Elementary School Record 1 (June 1900): 129-42.

45. Louise Alder, presentation at roundtable meeting on "Present Day Problems Attending the Making of a Course of Study," Proceedings of the Twenty-Third Annual Convention of the International Kindergarten Union (1916), pp. 136-37.

46. John Dewey, "My Pedagogic Creed," The School Journal 54 (1897): 77-80.

47. John Dewey, School and Society (Chicago: University of Chicago Press, 1900), pp. 3-4.

48. Ibid., p. 3.

49. John Dewey, Democracy and Education (New York: Macmillan, 1916).

50. Herbert Spencer, The Study of Sociology (New York: D. Appleton, 1874).

51. John Dewey, The Ethics of Democracy (Ann Arbor: University of Michigan, 1888).

52. Dewey, Democracy and Education, pp. 101, 102.

53. Dewey, The Child and the Curriculum, p. 17.

54. John Dewey, "How Much Freedom for New Schools?" The New Republic 63 (July 9, 1930): 205.

55. Richard Hofstadter, Social Darwinism in American Thought (Boston: Beacon Press, 1955), pp. 135-36.

56. Dewey, "My Pedagogic Creed," p. 79.

57. See, for example, Paul Nash, Models of Man (New York: John Wiley, 1968), p. 358.

58. John Dewey and Evelyn Dewey, Schools for Tomorrow (New York: E.P. Dutton, 1915), pp. 296, 298, 167.

59. Round Table Conference on Programs, Proceedings of the Eighth Annual Convention of the International Kindergarten Union (1901), pp. 50-52.

60. Merle Curti, The Social Ideas of American Educators (Paterson, N.J.: Littlefield, Adams, 1959), p. 523.

61. Liberal Report, "Report of the Committee of Nineteen," p. 132.

62. Samuel Chester Parker and Alice Temple, Unified Kindergarten and First Grade Teaching (Boston: Ginn, 1925), p. 310.

63. Ibid., pp. 19-25.

64. Oscar Handlin, John Dewey's Challenge to Education (New York: Harper, 1959), p. 41.

65. Richard S. Peters, "John Dewey's Philosophy of Education," in John Dewey Reconsidered, ed. R. S. Peters (London: Routledge and Kegan Paul, 1977), p. 103.

66. Curti, The Social Ideas of American Educators, p. 538.

67. Francis T. Villemain, "Dewey and the Critical Faculty," Saturday Review 42 (Nov. 21, 1959): 26.

68. Peters, "John Dewey's Philosophy of Education," p. 112.

69. Handlin, John Dewey's Challenge to Education, p. 45.

70. See, for example: Lawrence A. Cremin, The Genius of American Education (Pittsburgh: University of Pittsburgh Press, 1965), p. 43; and Villemain, "Dewey and the Critical Faculty," p. 52.

71. John Dewey, "Progressive Education and the Science of Education," Progressive Education 5 (1928): 199.

72. Barbara Biber, "The 'Whole Child,' Individuality, and Values in Education," in A New Look at Progressive Education, ed. James R. Squire (Washington, D.C.: Association for Supervision and Curriculum Development, 1972), p. 53.

73. Ibid., pp. 52-53.

74. Ibid., p. 53.

CHAPTER 7. THE PSYCHOANALYTIC VIEW OF MAN

1. Mary Dabney Davis and Rowna Hansen, Nursery Schools: Their Development and Current Practices in the U.S., Office of Education Bulletin no. 9 (Washington, D.C., 1932).

2. Helen T. Woolley, "Pre-School and Parent Education at the Merrill-Palmer School," Progressive Education 2 (Jan.-Mar. 1925): 36.

3. Margaret Pollitzer, "Foundations of the Walden School," Progressive Education 2 (Jan.-Mar. 1925): 17.

4. Harriet M. Johnson, Children in the Nursery School (New York: John Day, 1928), p. 12.

5. Grace Owen, "Nursery School Education," in Nursery School Education, ed. Grace Owen (New York: Dutton, 1923), p. 24.

6. Olive A. Wheeler, "The Mind of the Child," in Owen, ed., Nursery School Education, p. 52.

7. Arnold Gesell, "The Significance of the Nursery School," Childhood Education 1 (Sept. 1925): 13.

8. Rose H. Alschuler, "What Has the Nursery School to Offer?" Child Study (Jan. 1939): 132.

9. Josephine C. Foster and Marion L. Mattson, Nursery School Procedure (New York: D. Appleton, 1929), p. 1.

10. Ilse Forest, Preschool Education: A Historical and Critical Study (New York: Macmillan, 1927), p. 223.

11. Jerome S. Bruner, "Freud and the Image of Man," in Freud and the 20th Century, ed. Benjamin Nelson (Cleveland: World Publishing Co., 1957), p. 279.

12. Gardner Murphy, "The Current Impact of Freud on American Psychology," in Nelson, ed., Freud and the 20th Century, p. 104.

13. William Kessen, The Child (New York: John Wiley, 1965), p. 247.

14. David Shakow and David Rapaport, The Influence of Freud on American Psychology (New York: International Universities Press, 1964), p. 20.

15. Lionel Trilling, "Introduction," in Ernest Jones, The Life and Work of Sigmund Freud, ed. and abridged Lionel Trilling and Steven Marcus (New York: Basic Books, 1961), p. ix.

16. Jones, The Life and Works of Sigmund Freud, p. 373.

17. Ibid., p. 66.

18. Ibid., p. 159.

19. Ibid., p. 210-11.

20. Ibid., p. 29.

21. Shakow and Rapaport, The Influence of Freud on American Psychology, p. 53.

22. Calvin S. Hall and Gardner Lindzey, "Psychoanalytic Theory and Its Applications in the Social Sciences," in Handbook of Social Psychology, ed. Gardner Lindzey (Cambridge, Mass.: Addison-Wesley, 1954), p. 148.

23. Jones, The Life and Works of Sigmund Freud, p. 310.

24. Murphy, "The Current Impact of Freud on American Psychology," p. 103.

25. David Rapaport, "The Structure of Psychoanalytic Theory," in Psychology: A Study of a Science, ed. Sigmund Koch, vol. 3 (New York: McGraw-Hill, 1959), p. 90.

26. Sigmund Freud, "Infantile Sexuality," in The Basic Writings of Sigmund Freud, trans. and ed. A. A. Brill (New York: Random House, 1938), pp. 587-88.

27. Calvin S. Hall and Gardner Lindzey, Theories of Personality (New York: John Wiley, 1970), p. 33.

28. Sigmund Freud, An Outline of Psychoanalysis, trans. James Strachey (New York: Norton, 1949), p. 15.

29. Ibid., p. 17.

30. Ibid., p. 19.

31. David Stafford Clark, What Freud Really Said (New York: Schocken, 1965), p. 129.

32. Alfred Kazin, "The Freudian Revolution Analyzed," in Nelson, ed., Freud and the 20th Century, p. 17.

33. Kessen, The Child, p. 269.

34. Ibid., p. 270.

35. Sigmund Freud, A General Introduction to Psycho-Analysis, trans. Joan Riviere (New York: Liveright, 1920), p. 327.

36. Jones, The Life and Works of Sigmund Freud, p. 267.

37. Sigmund Freud, Five Lectures on Psycho-Analysis (1910 [1909]), vol. 11 of The Standard Edition of the Complete Psychological Works of Sigmund Freud, trans. and ed. James Strachey (London: Hogarth Press, 1953).

38. Ibid., p. 30.

39. Ibid., p. 32.

40. Ibid., pp. 30-31.

41. Ibid., p. 33.

42. Ibid., p. 36.

43. Ibid., p. 43.

44. Ibid., p. 46.

45. Ibid., p. 41.

46. Ibid., p. 48.

47. Ronald W. Clark, Freud: The Man and the Cause (New York: Random House, 1980), p. 284.

48. Howard Gardner, The Arts and Human Development (New York: John Wiley, 1973), p. 3.

49. John Martin Rich, Humanistic Foundations of Education (Worthington, Ohio: Charles A. Jones, 1971), p. 16.

50. Kessen, The Child, p. 269.

51. Harriet M. Johnson, Children in the Nursery School (New York: John Day, 1928), p. 84.

52. Harriet M. Johnson, School Begins at Two (New York: New Republic, 1936), p. 30.

53. Ilse Forest, The School for the Child From Two to Eight (Boston: Ginn, 1935), p. 240.

54. Mary Dabney Davis, Nursery-Kindergarten-Primary Education in 1924-1926, Bureau of Education Bulletin no. 28 (Washington, D.C.: U.S. Printing Office, 1927).

55. Johnson, School Begins at Two, p. 10.

56. Harold Rugg, "The Reconstruction of the American School Curriculum," The New Era 10 (April 1929): 83.

57. Harold Rugg and Ann Shumaker, The Child-Centered School (Yonkers-on-Hudson, N.Y.: World Book, 1928).

58. Lawrence A. Cremin, The Transformation of the School (New York: Knopf, 1961), p. 183.

59. Hughes Mearns, Creative Power: The Education of Youth in the Creative Arts (New York: Dover, 1929), p. 235.

60. Hughes Mearns, "The Curriculum and the Creative Spirit," The New Era 10 (April 1929): 114.

61. Cremin, The Transformation of the School, p. 214.

62. Shakow and Rapaport, The Influence of Freud on American Psychology, p. 117.

63. Kazin, "The Freudian Revolution Analyzed," p. 21.

64. Ibid.

CHAPTER 8. FOCUS ON AFFECTIVE GROWTH

1. Urie Bronfenbrenner, "Developmental Theory in Transition," in Child Psychology, ed. Harold W. Stevenson, 62nd yearbook of the National Society for the Study of Education (Chicago: University of Chicago Press, 1963), p. 531.

2. William Kessen, The Child (New York: John Wiley, 1965), p. 269.

3. Recounted in Milton J. E. Senn, Insights on the Child Development Movement in the United States, monographs of the Society for Research in Child Development, vol. 40, nos. 3-4 (August 1975), p. 15.

4. Ibid., p. 18.

5. Ibid., p. 22 (a statement by Helen Lynd).

6. Lawrence K. Frank, "The Fundamental Needs of the Child," Mental Hygiene 22 (July 1938): 353-79.

7. Ibid., p. 354.

8. Ibid., p. 353.

9. Ibid., p. 356.

10. Ibid., pp. 356-57.

11. Ibid., p. 359.

12. Ibid., p. 361.

13. Ibid., pp. 368-69.

14. Ibid., p. 378.

15. Ruth E. Hartley, Lawrence K. Frank, and Robert M. Goldenson, Understanding Children's Play (New York: Columbia University Press, 1952), p. viii.

16. Ibid., p. 4.

17. Ibid., p. 17.

18. Ibid., p. 32.

19. Ibid., p. 112.

20. Ibid., pp. 190-91.

21. Lawrence K. Frank, "Play in Personality Development," American Journal of Orthopsychiatry 25 (July 1955): 585.

22. American Council on Education, Helping Teachers Understand Children (Washington, D.C.: American Council on Education, 1945).

23. Ibid., p. 1.

24. Ibid., pp. 8-9.

25. Ibid., p. 11.

26. Ibid., p. 12.

27. Ibid., p. 380.

28. Daniel A. Prescott, The Child in the Educative Process (New York: McGraw-Hill, 1957), pp. 433-36.

29. Ibid., pp. xii-xiii.

30. Ibid., p. 27.

31. Ibid., p. 31.

32. Erik H. Erikson, "The First Psychoanalyst," in Freud and the 20th Century, ed. Benjamin Nelson (New York: World Publishing Co., 1957), pp. 100-01.

33. Erik H. Erikson in dialogue with Richard I. Evans. Richard I. Evans, Dialogue with Erik Erikson (New York: E.P. Dutton, 1969), p. 81.

34. Ibid., p. 62.

35. Ibid., p. 17.

36. Ibid.

37. Erik H. Erikson, Childhood and Society (New York: W.W. Norton, 1950).

38. See, for example: Erik H. Erikson, "Growth and Crises of the 'Healthy Personality,'" in Personality in Nature, Society and Culture, ed. Clyde Kluchkhohn and Henry A. Murray (New York: Knopf, 1961), pp. 185-225; Erik H. Erikson, "Growth and Crises in 'Healthy Personality,'" in Symposium on the Healthy Personality, ed. Milton J. Senn, supplement II (New York: Josiah Macy, Jr. Foundation, 1950), pp. 91-146.

39. Erikson, Childhood and Society, p. 32.

40. Ibid., p. 218.

41. Ibid., p. 219.

42. Erik H. Erikson, A Healthy Personality for Every Child: A Digest of The Fact-Finding Report to the Mid-century White House Conference on Children and Youth (Raleigh, N.C.: Health Publications Institute, Inc., 1951), p. 9.

43. Ibid., p. 11

44. Erikson, Childhood and Society, p. 223.

45. Ibid., p. 224.

46. Erikson, A Healthy Personality for Every Child, p. 16.

47. Ibid., p. 17.

48. Erikson, Childhood and Society, p. 272 (2nd edition, 1963).

49. Ibid., p. 182 (1st edition, 1950).

50. Ibid., p. 195.

51. Erik H. Erikson, "Studies in the Interpretation of Play," Genetic Psychological Monographs 22 (1940): 557-71.

52. Henry W. Maier, Three Theories of Child Development (New York: Harper and Row, 1965), p. 16.

53. Erikson, Childhood and Society, p. 12.

54. Erikson, in Evans, Dialogue with Erik Erikson, p. 13.

55. Howard Gardner, Developmental Psychology (Boston: Little, Brown, 1978). See, for example, pp. 50-54, 235-36, 528-32.

56. Robert F. Biehler, Child Development: An Introduction (Boston: Houghton Mifflin, 1976).

57. Ibid., p. 388.

58. Roma Gans, Celia Stendler, and Millie Almy, Teaching Young Children (Yonkers-on-Hudson, N.Y.: World Book, 1952), p. 315.

59. Emma Sheehy, The Fives and Sixes Go to School (New York: Henry Holt, 1954), p. 87.

60. Gans, Stendler, and Almy, Teaching Young Children, p. 29.

61. Sadie D. Ginsberg, "Changing Attitudes About Children," Forty-fifth Annual Schoolmen's Week Proceedings (Philadelphia: University of Pennsylvania Press, 1958), p. 338.

62. John E. Anderson, "The Theory of Early Childhood Education," in Early Childhood Education, ed. Nelson B. Henry, 46th yearbook of the National Society for the Study of Education, part 2 (Chicago: University of Chicago Press, 1947), p. 83.

63. Natalie R. Cole, The Arts in the Classroom (New York: John Day, 1940), p. 8.

64. Ibid., p. 43.

65. Viktor Lowenfeld, Creative and Mental Growth (New York: Macmillan, 1947), p. 7.

66. Viktor Lowenfeld, The Meaning of Creative Expression for the Child (New York: Bank Street Pub., n.d.), p. 13.

67. Daniel M. Mendelowitz, Children Are Artists (Stanford: Stanford University Press, 1953), p. 35.

68. Maria Bird, "Rhythmic Movement in School," The New Era 15 (May-June 1934): 141-43.

69. Emma D. Sheehy, Children Discover Music and Dance (New York: Henry Holt, 1959), p. 154.

70. John E. Anderson, "Child Development: An Historical Perspective," Child Development 27 (June 1956): 194.

71. D. Bruce Gardner, "The Influence of Theoretical Conceptions of Human Development on the Practice of Early Childhood Education," mimeographed (paper presented at the Annual Convention of the National Association for the Education of Young Children, Salt Lake City, November 14, 1969), p. 20.

72. Barbara Biber and Margery B. Franklin, "The Relevance of Developmental and Psychodynamic Concepts to the Education of the Preschool Child," Journal of the American Academy of Child Psychiatry 6 (Jan. 1967): 19.

CHAPTER 9. THE CHILD DEVELOPMENT POINT OF VIEW

1. John E. Anderson, "The Theory of Early Childhood Education," in Early Childhood Education, ed. Nelson B. Henry, 46th yearbook of the National Society for the Study of Education, part 2 (Chicago: University of Chicago Press, 1947), p. 74.

2. Arthur T. Jersild, Child Development and the Curriculum (New York: Bureau of Publications, Teachers College, Columbia University, 1946), p. 1.

3. Robert S. Sears, "Your Ancients Revisited: A History of Child Development," in Review of Child Development Research, ed. E. Mavis Hetherington, vol. 5 (Chicago: University of Chicago Press, 1975), p. 34.

4. Arthur T. Jersild, In Search of Self (New York: Bureau of Publications, Teachers College, Columbia University, 1952); Arthur T. Jersild, When Teachers Face Themselves (New York: Bureau of Publications, Teachers College, Columbia University, 1955).

5. Jersild, Child Development and the Curriculum, p. v.
6. Ibid., pp. 1-2.
7. Ibid., pp. 2-3.
8. Ibid., p. 9.
9. Ibid., pp. 27.
10. Ibid., p. 99.
11. Ibid., p. 65.
12. Ibid., pp. 83-84.
13. Carleton Washburn, "Introduction," in Child Development and the Curriculum, ed. Guy M. Whipple, 38th yearbook of the National Society for the Study of Education, part 1 (Bloomington, Ill.: Public School Publishing Co., 1939), p. 3.
14. John E. Anderson, "Problems of Method in Maturity and Curricular Studies," in Whipple, ed., Child Development and the Curriculum, p. 413.
15. John E. Anderson, "Methods in Child Psychology," in Manual of Child Psychology, ed. Leonard Carmichael (New York: Wiley, 1946), pp. 6, 3.
16. Myrtle McGraw, Growth: A Study of Johnny and Jimmy (New York: D. Appleton-Century, 1935).
17. Myrtle McGraw, "Maturation of Behavior," in Carmichael, ed., Manual of Child Psychology, 1946, pp. 363, 364.
18. Recounted in Milton J. E. Senn, Insights on the Child Development Movement in the United States, monograph of the Society for Research in Child Development, 161, vol. 40, nos. 3-4 (August 1975), p. 33.
19. Florence L. Goodenough, "The Measurement of Mental Growth in Childhood," in Carmichael, ed., Manual of Child Psychology, 1946, p. 454.
20. Harold Jones, "Environmental Influences on Mental Development," in Carmichael, ed., Manual of Child Psychology, 1946, ch. 11.
21. Kurt Lewin, "Behavior and Development as a Function of the Total Situation," in Carmichael, ed., Manual of Child Psychology, 1946, p. 839.
22. Urie Bronfenbrenner, "Developmental Theory in Transition," in Child Psychology, ed. Harold W. Stevenson, 62nd yearbook of the National Society for the Study of Education, part 1 (Chicago: University of Chicago Press, 1963), p. 526.
23. Arthur T. Jersild, "Emotional Development," in Carmichael, ed., Manual of Child Psychology, 1946, p. 752.
24. Jersild, "Emotional Development," in Carmichael, ed., Manual of Child Psychology (New York: Wiley, 1954), p. 834.
25. Harold H. Anderson and Gladys L. Anderson, "Trends in Psychological Thinking," in Carmichael, ed., Manual of Child Psychology, 1954, pp. 1163-64.
26. Kurt Lewin, "Behavior and Development as a Function of the Total Situation," in Carmichael, ed., Manual of Child Psychology, 1954, p. 921.
27. Sibylle Escalona, "The Influence of Topological and Vector Psychology upon Current Research in Child Development: An Addendum," in Carmichael, ed., Manual of Child Psychology, 1954, p. 982.
28. Anderson and Anderson, "Trends in Psychological Thinking," p. 1165.

29. James L. Hymes, Jr., A Child Development Point of View (Englewood Cliffs, N.J.: Prentice-Hall, 1955).

30. Ibid., pp. v-vi.

31. Senn, Insights on the Child Development Movement in the United States, p. 8.

32. Hymes, A Child Development Point of View, p. 6.

33. Ibid., pp. 140-41.

34. Lawrence Frank, "Forces Leading to the Child Development Viewpoint and Study," unpublished paper, quoted in Senn, Insights on the Child Development Movement in the United States, p. 89.

35. Willard C. Olson, "Developmental Theory in Education," in The Concept of Development, ed. Dale B. Harris (Minneapolis: University of Minnesota Press, 1957), p. 259.

36. John E. Anderson, "Dynamics of Development: System in Process," in Harris, ed., The Concept of Development, p. 27.

37. Dale B. Harris, "Problems in Formulating a Scientific Concept of Development," in Harris, ed., The Concept of Development, p. 10.

38. Heinz Werner, "The Concept of Development from a Comparative and Organismic Point of View," in Harris, ed., The Concept of Development, p. 146.

39. Ilse Forest, "The Responsibility of the Kindergarten in the Schools' Readiness Program," in Education in Transition, 47th Annual Schoolmen's Week Proceedings, 1959 (Philadelphia: University of Pennsylvania Press, 1960), p. 124.

40. Ibid., p. 135.

41. David H. Russell, Children Learn to Read (Boston: Ginn, 1961), p. 167.

42. Nila Banton Smith, "Readiness for Reading," Elementary English 27 (Jan. 1950): 31.

43. Nila Banton Smith, "Readiness for Reading," Elementary English 27 (Feb. 1950): 99.

44. Myrtle M. Imhoff, Early Elementary Education (New York: Appleton-Century-Crofts, 1959), pp. 48-60.

45. See, for example: Roma Gans, Celia Stendler, and Millie Almy, Teaching Young Children (Yonkers-on-Hudson, N.Y.: World Book, 1952), pp. 32-39; Helen Heffernan and Vivian Edmiston Todd, The Kindergarten Teacher (Boston: D.C. Heath, 1960), pp. 16-23.

46. Gans, Stendler, and Almy, Teaching Young Children pp. 29, 42; Heffernan and Todd, The Kindergarten Teacher, pp. 26-30.

CHAPTER 10. THE STUDY OF COGNITION

1. See, for example: J. McVicker Hunt, "The Impact and Limitations of the Giant of Developmental Psychology," in Studies in Cognitive Development, ed. David Elkind and John Flavell (New York: Oxford University Press, 1969), pp. 3-66; William Kessen and Clementina Kuhlman, "Comments and Conclusions," in Thought in the Young Child, ed. William Kessen and Clementina Kuhlman (Chicago: University of Chicago Press, 1970), p. 139; and Robert

Coles, "Reconsideration: Jean Piaget," The New Republic
(March 18, 1978): 36.
2. John H. Flavell, "Historical and Bibliographical
Note," in Kessen and Kuhlman, eds., Thought in the Young
Child, p. 3.
3. David Russell, Children's Thinking (Boston: Ginn,
1956), pp. 160-61.
4. Ibid., p. 160.
5. Kessen and Kuhlman, "Comments and Conclusions,"
p. 133.
6. Charles D. Smock, "Introductory Comments" to a
symposium on "Some Current Research and Thinking about
Cognitive Processes in Children," Merrill-Palmer Quarterly
6 (July 1960): 246.
7. Russell, Children's Thinking, p. 163.
8. Ibid., p. 279.
9. Ibid., p. 54. See also pp. 55, 59, 277.
10. See: Roma Gans, Celia Stendler, and Millie Almy,
Teaching Young Children (Yonkers-on-Hudson, N.Y.: World
Book, 1952), pp. 37-39; Helen Heffernon and Vivian Edmiston Todd, The Kindergarten Teacher (Boston: D.C. Heath,
1960), pp. 17-19.
11. The emergence of these programs are described in
Caroline Pratt, I Learn from Children (New York: Simon
and Schuster, 1948); Lucy Sprague Mitchell, Young Geog-
raphers (New York: John Day, 1934).
12. Lucile Lindberg, "Learning Through Searching,"
Childhood Education 38 (Oct. 1961): 59.
13. Tom Bower, "Competent Newborns," in Child Alive,
ed. Roger Lewin (Garden City, N.Y.: Anchor Press, 1975),
p. 123.
14. Programs included: A Parent Education Project,
directed by Ira Gordon, in Gainesville, Florida; The
Children's Center, directed by Bettye M. Caldwell, in
Syracuse, N.Y.; Frank Porter Graham Child Development
Center, directed by Halbert B. Robinson, in Chapel Hill,
N.C. For a brief report of these programs see Evelyn
Weber, Early Childhood Education: Perspectives on
Change (Worthington, Ohio: Charles A. Jones Publishing
Co., 1970), pp. 55-70.
15. John H. Flavell, The Developmental Psychology of
Jean Piaget (Princeton, N.J.: D. Van Nostrand, 1963),
p. 1.
16. Ibid., p. 2.
17. Jean Piaget, Autobiographie, in A History of
Psychology in Autobiography, vol. 4, ed. Carl Murchison
and E. G. Boring (Worcester, Mass.: Clark University
Press, 1952), pp. 237-38.
18. E. James Anthony, "How Children Cope in Families
with a Psychotic Parent," in Infant Psychiatry: A New
Synthesis, ed. Eveoleen N. Rexford, Louis W. Sander,
and Theodore Shapiro (New Haven: Yale University Press,
1968), pp. 241-42.
19. Ibid., p. 241.
20. Jean Piaget in dialogue with Richard I. Evans,
Jean Piaget: The Man and His Ideas (New York: E.P.
Dutton, 1973), pp. 4, 5.

21. Ibid., p. 7.

22. Barbel Inhelder and Jean Piaget, The Growth of Logical Thinking (New York: Basic Books, 1958), p. 349.

23. Ibid., pp. 348-49.

24. Ibid., p. 350.

25. Howard E. Gruber and J. Jaques Voneche, eds., "Introduction," The Essential Piaget (New York: Basic Books, 1977), p. xxxi.

26. Ibid., pp. xxxii-xxxiii.

27. Jean Piaget, Genetic Epistemology, trans. Eleanor Duckworth (New York: Columbia University Press, 1970), pp. 12-13.

28. Ibid., p. 77.

29. Jean Piaget and Barbel Inhelder, The Psychology of the Child (New York: Basic Books, 1969), p. 5.

30. Ibid., p. 6.

31. Jean Piaget, Six Psychological Studies (New York: Random House, 1967), p. 8.

32. Jean Piaget, "Problems of Equilibration," an address by Jean Piaget to the Jean Piaget Society, Philadelphia, 1975. In Equilibration: Theory, Research, and Application, ed. Marilyn H. Appel and Louis S. Goldberg (New York: Plenum Press, 1972), p. 12.

33. Jean Piaget, "Foreword," in Young Children's Thinking, Millie Almy, Edward Chittenden, and Paula Miller (New York: Teachers College Press, 1966), p. v.

34. Flavell, The Developmental Psychology of Jean Piaget, p. 411.

35. Piaget and Inhelder, The Psychology of the Child, p. 152.

36. Ibid., p. 153.

37. Flavell, The Developmental Psychology of Jean Piaget, p. 414.

38. Piaget and Inhelder, The Psychology of the Child, p. 128.

39. Piaget, Genetic Epistemology, p. 50.

40. Ibid., p. 18.

41. Ibid., p. 21.

42. Piaget, Six Psychological Studies, pp. 22, 23.

43. Jean Piaget, Play, Dreams and Imitation in Childhood (New York: Norton, 1962).

44. Barbara Biber, "Preschool Education," in Education and the Idea of Mankind, ed. Robert Ulich (New York: Harcourt, Brace and World, 1964), pp. 90-91.

45. Piaget and Inhelder, The Psychology of the Child, p. 91.

46. Ibid., pp. 58-59.

47. Ibid., p. 58.

48. Ibid., p. 57.

49. Flavell, The Developmental Psychology of Jean Piaget, p. 163.

50. Piaget and Inhelder, The Psychology of the Child, p. 125.

51. Sheldon H. White, "Some General Outlines of the Matrix of Developmental Changes between Five and Seven Years," Bulletin of the Orton Society 20 (1970): 41-57.

52. Howard Gardner, Developmental Psychology (Boston: Little, Brown, 1978), pp. 265-92.
53. Gruber and Vonèche, eds., The Essential Piaget, pp. xxviii-xxix.
54. Jean Piaget, "Foreword," in Young Children's Thinking, Millie Almy et al., p. vi.
55. Gruber and Vonèche, eds., The Essential Piaget, p. 481.
56. Ibid.
57. Piaget and Inhelder, The Psychology of the Child, p. 154.
58. Ibid., pp. 157-58, 159.
59. Ira Gordon, Human Development: From Birth Through Adolescence, 2nd ed. (New York: Harper and Row, 1969).
60. David Elkind, A Sympathetic Understanding of the Child: Birth to Sixteen (Boston: Allyn and Bacon, 1974).
61. Gardner, Developmental Psychology.
62. See, for example: Millie Almy, "New Views on Intellectual Development in Early Childhood Education," in Educational Implications of Piaget's Theory, ed. Irene J. Athey and Duane O. Rubadeau (Waltham, Mass.: Xerox College Publishing, 1970), pp. 61-75; Constance Kamii, "Piaget's Interactionism and the Process of Teaching Young Children," in Piaget in the Classroom, ed. Milton Schwebel and Jane Raph (London: Routledge and Kegan Paul, 1974), pp. 216-30.
63. Constance Kamii, "One Intelligence Indivisible," Young Children 30 (May 1975): 228-38.
64. Margaret Smart, "Piaget's Conservation Concept" (part of a symposium), Childhood Education 44 (Jan. 1968): 294.
65. Ann M. Bingham-Newman and Ruth A. Saunders, "Take a New Look at Your Classroom with Piaget as a Guide," Young Children 32 (May 1977): 62.
66. Millie Almy, "Piaget in Action," Young Children 31 (Jan. 1976): 96.

CHAPTER 11. THE EMERGENCE OF A
DEVELOPMENTAL-INTERACTION POINT OF VIEW

1. J. McVicker Hunt, Intelligence and Experience (New York: Ronald Press, 1961), pp. 3-64.
2. J. McVicker Hunt, "The Impact and Limitations of the Giant of Developmental Psychology," in Studies in Cognitive Development: Essays in Honor of Jean Piaget, ed. David Elkind and John H. Flavell (New York: Oxford University Press, 1969), p. 11.
3. Ibid., p. 6.
4. Barbara Biber, "Cognition in Early Childhood Education: An Historical Perspective," in Issues and Insights in Early Childhood Education, ed. Bernard Spodek and Herbert J. Walberg (Berekeley, Calif.: McCutcheon, 1977), p. 51.
5. Bernard Spodek, "Curriculum Construction in Early Childhood Education," in Spodek and Walberg, eds., Issues and Insights in Early Childhood Education, p. 126.

6. Sheldon White, "Some General Outlines of the Matrix of Developmental Changes Between Five to Seven Years," Bulletin of the Orton Society 20 (1970): 41-57.

7. See, for example: Josephine C. Foster and Neith E. Headley, Education in the Kindergarten (New York: American Book Co., 1936), ch. 1. Clarice D. Wills and William H. Stegeman, Living in the Kindergarten (Chicago: Follett, 1950).

8. Howard Gardner, Developmental Psychology (Boston: Little, Brown, 1978), pp. 258-59.

9. William Kessen, "Questions for a Theory of Cognitive Development," in Concept of Development, Monographs of the Society for Research on Child Development, serial no. 107, vol. 31, no. 5 (1966), p. 64.

10. Edna Shapiro and Doris Wallace, "Developmental Stage Theory and the Individual" (paper presented at a joint Bank Street-Wheelock College Conference on the Developmental-Interaction Point of View, Wheelock College, Boston, June 8-10, 1978), p. 13.

11. Ibid., p. 1.

12. Gardner, Developmental Psychology, p. 151.

13. Brian Rotman, Jean Piaget: Psychologist of the Real (Ithaca, N.Y.: Cornell University Press, 1977), p. 60.

14. Jean Piaget, Biology and Knowledge (Edinburgh, Scotland: Edinburgh University Press, 1971), p. 355.

15. W. H. O. Schmidt, Child Development (New York: Harper and Row, 1973), p. 5.

16. William Kessen, The Child (New York: Wiley, 1965), p. 4.

17. Ibid.

18. Herbert Zimiles, "Contrasting Views of Intellectual Functioning and Their Implications for Education," in Spodek and Walberg, eds., Issues and Insights, p. 25.

19. Ibid., pp. 25-40.

20. Harold W. Stevenson, "Learning in Children," in Carmichael's Manual of Child Psychology, vol. 1, ed. Paul H. Mussen (New York: Wiley, 1970), pp. 859-938.

21. Urie Bronfenbrenner, "A Theoretical Perspective for Research on Human Development," in Childhood and Socialization, Recent Sociology, no. 5, ed. Hans P. Dreitzel (New York: Macmillan, 1973), p. 337.

22. Ibid., p. 338.

23. Kenneth Keniston, "Psychological Development and Historical Change," The Journal of Interdisciplinary History 2 (Autumn 1971): 341.

24. Among the participants were Millie Almy, Willard Hartup, William Kessen, Harold Stevenson, and Herbert Zimiles. Reported in Sally Kilmer and Richard A. Weinberg, "The Nature of Young Children and the State of Early Education: Reflections from the Minnesota Round Table," Young Children 30 (Nov. 1974): 62.

25. Roger G. Barker, Ecological Psychology: Concepts and Methods for Studying the Environment for Human Behavior (Stanford: Stanford University Press, 1968), p. 3.

26. Bronfenbrenner, "A Theoretical Perspective for Research on Human Development," pp. 350-54.

27. Sybille Escalona and H. H. Corman, "The Impact of Mother's Presence Upon Behavior: The First Year," Human Development 14 (1971): 2-15.

28. Lois Barclay Murphy, "The Stranglehold of Norms on the Individual Child," Childhood Education 49 (April 1973): 343.

29. Irving Siegel, "Where is Preschool Education Going: Or Are We En Route Without a Road Map?" Assessment in a Pluralistic Society (Princeton, N.J.: Proceedings of 1972 Invitational Conference on Testing Problems, ETS, 1973), pp. 99-116.

30. Robert Ulich, "The Humanities," in Education and the Idea of Mankind, ed. Robert Ulich (New York: Harcourt, Brace and World, 1964), p. 275.

31. Stephen Gould, The Mismeasure of Man (New York: W.W. Norton, 1981), p. 332.

32. William Kessen, "Questions for a Theory of Cognitive Development," in Concept of Development, p. 70.

33. Anne Roe, "The Behavioral Sciences," in Ulich, ed., Education and the Idea of Mankind, p. 206.

34. Sheldon H. White, "Human Research in Human Affairs," paper presented at symposium, "The Developmental Sciences: State and Fate of Research Funding," American Association for the Advancement of Science, Chicago, December 1970, in Human Development in Today's World, ed. Sheldon H. White (Boston: Little, Brown, 1976), p. 8.

35. Ulich, ed., Education and the Idea of Mankind, p. 272.

36. Gardner, Developmental Psychology, p. 472.

37. Alfred L. Baldwin, Theories of Child Development (New York: Wiley, 1967), p. vii.

38. Ibid., p. 587.

39. Ibid., p. 596.

40. J. McVicker Hunt, Intelligence and Experience (New York: Ronald Press, 1961), p. 46 fn.

41. Ibid., p. 352.

42. Kenneth H. Wodtke, "Comments on ASCD Symposium Papers: Evaluation in Open Education," mimeo (paper presented at the Annual Meeting of the Association for Supervision and Curriculum Development, Miami, Florida, March 1976), p. 5.

43. Robert D. Nye, Three Views of Man: Perspectives from Sigmund Freud, B.F. Skinner and Carl Rogers (Monterey, Calif.: Brooks/Cole, 1975), p. 117.

44. Ibid.

45. Frank Milhollan and Bill E. Forisha, From Skinner to Rogers: Contrasting Approaches to Education (Lincoln, Neb.: Professional Educators Publications, 1972), p. 16.

46. William D. Hitt, "Two Models of Man," American Psychologist 24 (July 1969): 651-57.

47. Hayne W. Reese and Willis F. Overton, "Models of Development and Themes of Development," in Life-Span Development Psychology, ed. L. R. Goulet and Paul B. Bates (New York: Academic Press, 1970).

48. Ibid., p. 116.

49. Larry A. Hjelle and Daniel J. Ziegler, Personality Theories: Basic Assumptions, Research and Applications (New York: McGraw-Hill, 1976), p. 232.

50. Ibid., p. 10.

51. Ira J. Gordon, "New Conceptions of Children's Learning and Development," in Learning and Mental Health in the School, ed. Walter Waetjen (Washington, D.C.: Association for Supervision and Curriculum Development, 1966), pp. 49-50.

52. Henry Geiger, "Introduction," in Abraham H. Maslow, The Farthest Reaches of Human Nature (New York: Viking, 1971), p. xix.

53. Lawrence Kohlberg and Rochelle Mayer, "Development as the Aim of Education," Harvard Educational Review 42 (Nov. 1972): 463.

54. Ibid., p. 452.

55. Ibid., p. 460.

56. Ibid., p. 456.

57. Ibid., p. 477.

58. Ibid., p. 460.

59. Ibid., p. 491.

60. Ibid., p. 485.

61. Lawrence Kohlberg, "Early Education: A Cognitive Developmental View," Child Development 39 (Dec. 1968): 1056.

62. Ibid.

63. Edna Shapiro and Barbara Biber, "The Education of Young Children: A Developmental-Interaction Approach," Teachers College Record 74 (Sept. 1972): 59-60.

64. Ibid., p. 60.

65. Ibid., p. 61.

66. Barbara Biber, "Preschool Education," in Ulich, ed., Education and the Idea of Mankind, pp. 73-76.

67. Shapiro and Biber, "The Education of Young Children," p. 61.

68. Barbara Biber, "Goals and Methods in a Preschool Program for Disadvantaged Children," Children (Jan.-Feb. 1970): 16.

69. Ibid.

70. Shapiro and Biber, "The Education of Young Children," p. 68.

71. Ibid., p. 69.

72. Ibid., p. 70.

73. Barbara Biber, Edna Shapiro, and David Wickens, Promoting Cognitive Growth: A Developmental-Interaction Point of View (Washington, D.C.: National Association for the Education of Young Children, 1971).

74. Joint Bank Street-Wheelock College Conference on the Developmental-Interaction Point of View, Wheelock College, Boston, June 8-10, 1978.

75. Barbara Biber, "The Evolution of the Developmental-Interaction View," in Cognitive and Affective Growth: Developmental Interaction, ed. Edna K. Shapiro and Evelyn Weber (Hillsdale, N.J.: Erlbaum, 1981), p. 11.

76. Ibid., p. 12.
77. Kieran Egan, Education and Psychology: Plato, Piaget, and Scientific Psychology (New York: Teachers College Press, 1983), p. ix.
78. Ibid., p. 181.
79. Ibid., p. 9.

CHAPTER 12. THE CURRICULUM FOR EARLY CHILDHOOD

1. Clarence J. Karier, ed., Shaping the American Educational State: 1900 to the Present (New York: Free Press, 1975), p. xvi.
2. Edward Hallet Carr, What Is History? (New York: Vantage, 1967), p. 26.
3. Wayne J. Urban, "Historiography," in Encyclopedia of Educational Research, vol. 1, 5th ed., ed. Harold F. Mitzel (New York: Collier/Macmillan Publications, 1982), p. 792.
4. Sol Cohen, "The History of the History of American Education 1900-1976: The Uses of the Past," Harvard Educational Review 46 (Aug. 1976): 301.
5. R. Freeman Butts, "Public Education and Political Community," History of Education Quarterly 14 (Summer 1974): 168.
6. Michael B. Katz, Class, Bureaucracy, and Schools (New York: Praeger, 1975), p. 146.
7. Karier, Shaping the American Educational State, pp. xx, xvii.
8. Cohen, "The History of the History of American Education," p. 328.
9. Maxine Greene, "Identities and Contours: An Approach to Educational History," Educational Researcher 2 (April 1973): 6.
10. Carl F. Kaestle, "Social Reform and the Urban School," History of Education Quarterly 121 (Summer 1972): 217.
11. Michael B. Katz, "Reflections on the Purpose of Educational Reform," Educational Theory 30 (Spring 1980): 77.
12. Katz, Class, Bureaucracy, and Schools, p. 56.
13. David B. Tyack, "Ways of Seeing: An Essay on the History of Compulsory Schooling," Harvard Educational Review 46 (Aug. 1976): 373.
14. Carl F. Kaestle, "Conflict and Consensus Revisited: Notes Toward a Reinterpretation of American Educational History," Harvard Educational Review 46 (Aug. 1976): 396.
15. Katz, Class, Bureaucracy, and Schools, p. 155.
16. Patricia Albjerg Graham, Community and Class in American Education, 1865-1918 (New York: Wiley, 1974), p. 17.
17. Ibid., pp. 16-17.
18. Katz, Class, Bureaucracy, and Schools, p. xviii.
19. Ibid., p. xvi.
20. Karier, Shaping the American Educational State, p. 9.

21. Ibid., p. 3.

22. Graham, Community and Class in American Education, p. 9.

23. Guy M. Whipple, ed., Preschool and Parental Education, 28th yearbook of the National Society for the Study of Education (Bloomington, Ill.: Public School Publishing Co., 1929), p. 248.

24. Evelyn Weber, The Kindergarten: Its Encounter with Educational Thought in America (New York: Teachers College Press, 1969), p. 36.

25. Katz, Class, Bureaucracy, and Schools, pp. 121-22.

26. Whipple, ed., Preschool and Parental Education, p. 249.

27. C. John Sommerville, The Rise and Fall of Childhood (Beverly Hills: Sage, 1982), p. 17.

28. Ibid., p. 16.

29. Ibid., p. 17.

30. For a discussion of these developments see Weber, The Kindergarten, ch. 7.

31. R. Freeman Butts, A Cultural History of Western Education (New York: McGraw-Hill, 1955), p. 492.

32. Katz, Class, Bureaucracy, and Schools, pp. 118-19.

33. As reported by Katz, Ibid., p. 118.

34. Greene, "Identities and Contours," p. 8.

35. Steven L. Schlossman, "Before Home Start: Notes Toward a History of Parent Education in American 1892-1929," Harvard Educational Review 46 (Aug. 1976): 437.

36. Steven L. Schlossman, "The Parent Education Game: The Politics of Child Psychology in the 1970s," Teachers College Record 79 (May 1978): 788-808.

37. Steven L. Schlossman, "Philanthropy and the Gospel of Child Development," History of Education Quarterly 21 (Fall 1981): 281-99.

38. Butts, "Public Education and Political Community," p. 165.

39. Greene, "Identities and Contours," p. 9.

40. Katz, Class, Bureaucracy, and Schools, p. 144.

41. Sidney W. Bijou, "Behavior Analysis Applied to Early Childhood Education," in Early Childhood Education: Issues and Insights, ed. Bernard Spodek and Herbert J. Walberg (Berkeley, Calif.: McCutchan, 1977), p. 147.

42. Louise M. Berman and Jessie A. Roderick, Curriculum: The What, How and Why of Living (Columbus, Ohio: Merrill, 1977), p. 25.

43. James Macdonald, "The Open School: Curriculum Concepts," in Open Education, proceedings of a conference (Washington, D.C.: National Association for the Education of Young Children, 1970), p. 24.

44. Jean Piaget, Play, Dreams and Imitation in Children, trans. C. Gategno and F. M. Hodgson (New York: Norton, 1962), p. 166.

45. Philip H. Phenix, Realms of Meaning (New York: McGraw-Hill, 1964), p. 24.

46. Ernst Cassirer, An Essay on Man (New Haven, Conn.: Yale University Press, 1944).

47. One such project directed by Judith Schickedanz at the Boston University Pre-Elementary Reading Improvement Collaborative was funded by Grant No. G007-605-403 from the U.S. Office of Education.

48. Judith A. Schickedanz, "What Do Preschoolers Know About Reading?" (paper presented at the annual meeting of the International Reading Association, April 26, 1979, Atlanta, Georgia), p. 11.

49. Judith A. Schickedanz, "The Acquisition of Written Language in Young Children," in Handbook of Research in Early Childhood Education, ed. Bernard Spodek (New York: Free Press, 1982), pp. 249-50.

50. David Doake, "Book Experience and Emergent Reading Behavior," (paper presented at the annual meeting of the International Reading Association, April 1979, Atlanta, Georgia).

51. Howard E. Gruber and J. Jacques Vonèche, The Essential Piaget (New York: Basic Books, 1977), p. xxvi.

52. Constance Kamii and Rheta De Vries, "Piaget for Early Education," in The Preschool in Action, ed. Mary Carol Day and Ronald K. Parker (Boston: Allyn and Bacon, 1977), pp. 366-67.

53. John Martin Rich, Humanistic Foundations of Education (Worthington, Ohio: Charles Jones, 1971), p. 4.

54. Millie Almy, "Guiding Children for Life in Tomorrow's World," in Education in Anticipation of Tomorrow, ed. Robert H. Anderson (Worthington, Ohio: Charles A. Jones, 1973), p. 49.

About the Author

Evelyn Weber has worked in the field of early childhood education as a teacher of young children and as a professor teaching classes for teachers of the young. She has guided undergraduate and graduate students at Wheelock College in Boston and the University of Wisconsin–Milwaukee. Along with a consistent interest in effective practice in the classroom for young children, Dr. Weber has developed a concern for the theoretical underpinnings of that practice as they have grown over the decades.

The impetus for this book was a year of viewing early childhood education as it was practiced throughout the United States and in England. A study grant provided by Carnegie Corporation permitted a year devoted to this task. The great variety of classroom procedures observed led naturally to a probing of the basic ideas upon which each one rested. The great theorists of past and present eras were thus drawn into focus.

Two earlier books were written by Dr. Weber. *The Kindergarten: Its Encounter with Educational Thought in America*, published in 1969, was a historical study of kindergarten education. The second book, *Early Childhood Education: Perspectives on Change*, published in 1970, was a survey of educational practice as it existed in the late 1960s. Both books were included in the annual Pi Lambda Theta Book Lists as one of twenty outstanding educational books published during those years. The latter book was also listed in a recommended bibliography included in *Young Children*, the journal of the National Association for the Education of Young Children.

Index